John Keble

Sermons for Septuagesima to Ash-Wednesday

With sermons for confirmation and on the litany

John Keble

Sermons for Septuagesima to Ash-Wednesday
With sermons for confirmation and on the litany

ISBN/EAN: 9783337084257

Printed in Europe, USA, Canada, Australia, Japan

Cover: Foto ©Lupo / pixelio.de

More available books at **www.hansebooks.com**

SERMONS

FOR

SEPTUAGESIMA

TO

ASH-WEDNESDAY

WITH SERMONS FOR CONFIRMATION
AND ON THE LITANY

BY THE LATE
REV. JOHN KEBLE,
AUTHOR OF "THE CHRISTIAN YEAR."

SOLD BY
JAMES PARKER AND CO., OXFORD,
AND 377, STRAND, LONDON.
1880.

ADVERTISEMENT.

The Septuagesima Season being the vestibule of Lent, Sermons preached in it seemed to require a place for themselves. As however the season is so short, two other series have been added to them; 1) Sermons preached for candidates for Confirmation, or the newly confirmed; 2) Sermons on the Litany.

I. Confirmation, under his preparation, was often (as it ought to be) a turning-point in the life of the young committed to him, an increased Presence of God the Holy Ghost in the soul. "ᵃThe children whom he prepared, came to him either in classes or singly, every week before the Confirmation." The Sermons are a gathering up, as it were, of that assiduous private teaching.

II. The course of Sermons on the Litany is a good example of his way of explaining, and drawing instruction from the Church Services. He first catechized the children upon them, and then summed up the lessons given, in his Sermon. They exhibit in a very striking manner, the "plainness of speech" which it was his wont to use, in pastoral warnings and instructions, on subjects, where plainness is always a difficulty, and must have cost no small effort. Every word of John Keble if weighed, evinces, in its simplicity, the depth of his reality. But

ᵃ Letter in Coleridge's Life of John Keble. p. 510.

to see in mind the Sexagenarian (as he then was) finding his way with his lantern at 5.30 A. M. on Wednesdays and Fridays, sometimes in snow, on winter mornings, to say the Litany [b] for the Church in "her present distress," will bring home what the Litany was to him. Sometimes there was only one other worshipper. But a Third was there, Who said, "Where *two* or three are gathered together in My Name, there am I in the midst of them."

E. B. P.

CHRIST CHURCH,
    EPIPHANY, 1879.

[b] It was so said from May or June 1850, until the autumn of 1853. He used to remain for half an hour or an hour in the Church afterwards. He himself alludes to it below p. 358.

CONTENTS.

SERMON I.
MANY CALLED, FEW CHOSEN.
SEPTUAGESIMA.
S. Matt. xx. 16.

"*So the last shall be first, and the first last: for many be called, but few chosen.*" . . . . pp. 1—9.

SERMON II.
THE FIRST, LAST.
SEXAGESIMA.
S. Matt. xx. 16.

"*So the last shall be first, and the first last; for many be called, but few chosen.*" . . . pp. 10—20.

SERMON III.
THE LAST, FIRST.
QUINQUAGESIMA.
S. Matt. xx. 16.

"*So the last shall be first, and the first last: for many be called, but few chosen.*" . . pp. 21—30.

SERMON IV.

THE THIEF ON THE CROSS AN EXAMPLE OF FAITH.

SEPTUAGESIMA.

S. Luke xxiii. 41.

"*And we indeed justly; for we receive the due reward of our deeds: but this Man hath done nothing amiss.*"

pp. 31—42.

SERMON V.

CHRISTIAN HOPE.

SEXAGESIMA.

Rom. viii. 28.

"*We know that all things work together for good to them that love God.*" . . . . . pp. 43—53.

SERMON VI.

CHRISTIAN CHARITY.

QUINQUAGESIMA.

1 Tim. i. 5.

"*The end of the commandment is charity, out of a pure heart, and of a good conscience, and of faith unfeigned.*"

pp. 54—64.

SERMON VII.

ALMIGHTY GOD NOTES THE USE WHICH WE MAKE OF HIS GIFTS.

SEPTUAGESIMA.

Ps. xciv. 9.

"*He that planted the ear, shall He not hear? or He that made the eye, shall He not see?*" . pp. 65—74.

SERMON VIII.

FAITH THE FOUNDATION OF ALL RELIGION.

SEPTUAGESIMA.

HEB. xi. 6.

"*Without faith it is impossible to please Him: for he that cometh to God must believe that He is, and that He is a rewarder of them that diligently seek Him.*"   pp. 75—84.

SERMON IX.

WORK, THE LAW OF OUR LORD'S KINGDOM, BOTH NATURAL AND SPIRITUAL.

SEPTUAGESIMA.

S. MATT. xx. 6.

"*Why stand ye here all the day idle?*"   .   pp. 85—95.

SERMON X.

HOW TO PROFIT BY SAINTLY EXAMPLES.

SEPTUAGESIMA.

S. MATT. x. 41.

"*He that receiveth a righteous man in the name of a Righteous Man, receiveth a righteous man's Reward.*"   .
pp. 96—107.

SERMON XI.

THE FIRST AND SECOND CREATION OF MAN.

SEPTUAGESIMA.

GEN. ii. 7.

"*The Lord God formed man of the dust of the ground, and breathed into his nostrils the breath of life, and man became a living soul.*"   .   .   .   pp. 108—117.

SERMON XII.

NOT SIN ALONE BUT THE OCCASIONS OF SIN TO BE AVOIDED.

SEXAGESIMA.

GEN. iii. 3.

"Neither shall ye touch it, lest ye die."   pp. 118—128.

SERMON XIII.

GOD'S MERCIFUL CALLS, AND HOW TO ANSWER THEM.

SEXAGESIMA.

GEN iii. 9.

"The Lord God called unto Adam, and said unto him, Where art thou?" . . . . . pp. 129—138.

SERMON XIV.

NECESSITY OF CONFESSION.

SEXAGESIMA.

GEN. iii. 8, 9.

"And they heard the voice of the Lord God walking in the garden in the cool of the day: and Adam and his wife hid themselves from the presence of the Lord God amongst the trees of the garden. And the Lord God called unto Adam, and said unto him, Where art thou?"   pp. 139—150.

SERMON XV.

THE SOWER AND THE SEED.

SEXAGESIMA.

S. MARK iv. 3.

"Hearken: Behold, a sower went forth to sow."
pp. 151—160.

SERMON XVI.

THE PERIL OF WEARING OUT THE LONG SUFFERING OF GOD THE HOLY GHOST.

SEXAGESIMA.
Gen. vi. 3.

"And God said, My Spirit shall not always strive with man, for that he also is flesh; yet his days shall be a hundred and twenty years." . . . pp. 161—170.

SERMON XVII.

AS IT WAS IN THE DAYS OF NOAH.

QUINQUAGESIMA.
Gen. vii. 1.

"And the Lord said unto Noah, Come thou and all thy house into the ark, for thee have I seen righteous before Me in this generation." . . . . . pp. 171—180.

SERMON XVIII.

THE TENDERNESS OF ALMIGHTY GOD TO HIS FALLEN CREATURES.

QUINQUAGESIMA.
Gen. iii. 21.

"Unto Adam also and to his wife did the Lord God make coats of skins, and clothed them." . pp. 181—190.

SERMON XIX.

OUR NEED OF SPIRITUAL SIGHT.

QUINQUAGESIMA.
S. Luke xviii. 42.

"And Jesus said unto him, Receive thy sight, thy faith hath saved thee." . . . . . pp. 191—199.

SERMON XX.

HOW TO LEARN THE LOVE OF GOD.

QUINQUAGESIMA.

1 S. JOHN v. 3.

"This is the love of God, that we keep His commandments: and His commandments are not grievous." pp. 200—208.

SERMON XXI.

PREPARATION FOR HOLY COMMUNION, PREPARATION FOR DEATH AND FOR JUDGEMENT.

QUINQUAGESIMA.

AMOS iv. 12.

"Prepare to meet thy God, O Israel." pp. 209—220.

SERMON XXII.

THE VENTURES OF LOVE APPROVED OF BY OUR LORD.

BEFORE A CONFIRMATION.

S. MATT. xiv. 28, 29.

"And Peter answered Him and said, Lord, if it be Thou, bid me come unto Thee on the water. And He said, Come." pp. 221—229.

SERMON XXIII.

THE WORLD'S THREE TEMPTATIONS.

BEFORE A CONFIRMATION.

1 S. JOHN ii. 16.

"All that is in the world, the lust of the flesh, and the lust of the eyes, and the pride of life, is not of the Father, but is of the world." . . . . pp. 230—239

SERMON XXIV.

GOD OR THE WORLD.

BEFORE A CONFIRMATION.

S. MATT. vi. 24.

"*Ye cannot serve God and mammon.*" pp. 240—248.

SERMON XXV.

THERE IS NO DISAPPOINTMENT AT LAST IN THE SERVICE OF GOD.

BEFORE A CONFIRMATION.

JOEL ii. 26.

"*My people shall never be ashamed.*" pp. 249—258.

SERMON XXVI.

THE BREAD OF LIFE.

BEFORE A CONFIRMATION.

S. JOHN vi. 32.

"*My Father giveth you the true Bread from Heaven.*"
pp. 259—269.

SERMON XXVII.

OUR LORD'S PROVIDENTIAL DEALINGS ARE AS WARNING LOOKS, TO REMIND US OF HIS WORD.

BEFORE A CONFIRMATION.

S. LUKE xxii. 61.

"*The Lord turned and looked upon Peter, and Peter remembered the word of the Lord.*" . . pp. 270—280.

SERMON XXVIII.

A CONFIRMATION A SPECIAL REMINDER OF THE WORD OF CHRIST.

BEFORE A CONFIRMATION.

S. LUKE xxii. 61.

"*The Lord turned, and looked upon Peter, and Peter remembered the word of the Lord.*" . . pp. 281—292.

SERMON XXIX.

OUR LORD'S SPECIAL LOVE FOR THE YOUNG AND EAGER.

BEFORE A CONFIRMATION.

S. MARK x. 21.

"*Then Jesus beholding him, loved him.*" pp. 293—302.

SERMON XXX.

HARD TRIALS, OUR LORD'S LOVE TOKENS.

AFTER CONFIRMATION.

S. MARK x. 21.

"*Then Jesus, beholding him, loved him, and said unto him, One thing thou lackest: Go thy way, sell all that thou hast and give to the poor, and thou shalt have treasure in heaven; and come, take up the Cross, and follow Me.*"
pp. 303—312.

SERMON XXXI.

HOW WE SHOULD DEAL WITH RELIGIOUS DISAPPOINTMENTS.

AFTER CONFIRMATION.

JER. xiv. 8.

"*O the Hope of Israel, the Saviour thereof in time of trouble, why shouldest Thou be as a stranger in the land, and as a wayfaring man that turneth aside to tarry but a night?*"
pp. 313—322.

SERMON XXXII.

THE NEED OF STIRRING UP THE GIFT OF GOD.

AFTER CONFIRMATION.

2 TIM. i. 6.

"*Wherefore I put thee in remembrance, that thou stir up the Gift of God which is in thee by the putting on of my hands.*"
pp. 323—332.

SERMON XXXIII.

THE MYSTERIOUS WORKING OF GOD THE HOLY GHOST.

AFTER CONFIRMATION.

S. JOHN iii. 8.

"*The wind bloweth where it listeth, and thou hearest the sound thereof, but canst not tell whence it cometh nor whither it goeth : so is every one that is born of the Spirit.*"
pp. 333—34.

SERMON XXXIV.

THE HIDDEN PRESENCE OF CHRIST OUR LORD.

AFTER CONFIRMATION.

S. JOHN viii. 59.

"*Jesus hid Himself.*"   pp. 343—351.

SERMON XXXV.

ON THE LITANY. I.

INTRODUCTORY AND ON THE INVOCATION OF THE HOLY TRINITY.

JOEL ii. 17.

"*Let the Priests, the ministers of the Lord, weep between the Porch and the Altar, and let them say, Spare Thy people, O Lord.*"   pp. 352—361.

SERMON XXXVI.

ON THE LITANY. II.

ON THE SPECIAL INVOCATION OF OUR LORD IN THE "REMEMBER NOT &c."

JOEL ii. 17.

"Let the Priests, the ministers of the Lord, weep between the Porch and the Altar, and let them say, Spare Thy people, O Lord, and give not Thine heritage to reproach, that the heathen should rule over them."   pp. 362—371.

SERMON XXXVII.

ON THE LITANY. III.

THE DEPRECATIONS.

2 CHRON. vi. 28, 30.

"Whatsoever sore or whatsoever sickness there be: what prayer or what supplication soever shall be made of any man, or of all Thy people Israel, when every one shall know his own sore and his own grief, and shall spread forth his hands in this house; then hear Thou from heaven, Thy dwelling place, and forgive:"   pp. 372—380.

SERMON XXXVIII.

ON THE LITANY. IV.

THE DEPRECATIONS.

2 THESS. iii. 3.

"The Lord is faithful, Who shall stablish you, and keep you from evil."   pp. 381—390.

SERMON XXXIX.

ON THE LITANY. V.

THE DEPRECATIONS.

HEB. ii. 14, 15.

"*Forasmuch then as the children are partakers of flesh and blood, He also likewise took part of the same; that through death He might destroy him that had the power of death, that is the devil; and deliver them who through fear of death were all their lifetime subject to bondage.*" pp. 391—401.

SERMON XL.

ON THE LITANY. VI.

THE INTERCESSIONS.

1 TIM. ii. 1, 2.

"*I exhort therefore, that, first of all, supplications, prayers, intercessions, and giving of thanks, be made for all men: for kings and all that are in authority, that we may lead a quiet and peaceable life in all godliness and honesty.*"
pp. 402—410.

SERMON XLI.

ON THE LITANY. VII.

THE INTERCESSIONS.

HEB. xiii. 18.

"*Pray for us: for we trust we have a good conscience, in all things willing to live honestly.*"   pp. 411—420.

SERMON XLII.

ON THE LITANY. VIII.

THE PRIVATE INTERCESSIONS.

HEB. vii. 25.

"He is able to save them to the uttermost that come unto God by Him, seeing He ever liveth to make intercession for them."
pp. 421—431.

SERMON XLIII.

ON THE LITANY. IX.

CONCLUSION.

Ps. xxxiii. 22.

"Let Thy merciful kindness, O Lord, be upon us, like as we do put our trust in Thee." pp. 432—443.

SERMON I.

MANY CALLED, FEW CHOSEN.

SEPTUAGESIMA.

S. Matt. xx. 16.

"So the last shall be first, and the first last: for many be called, but few chosen."

Whatever else may be contained in the meaning of that mysterious parable of the labourers in the vineyard, which we hear in to-day's Gospel; one thing it surely teaches us: that the judgement of God in the Last Day will be in some sense far unlike what men expect: far different from the judgements which we pass one upon another, here in this present world. This we are taught in other places of Holy Scripture, and most expressly in that aweful place where our Lord describes Himself as separating the sheep from the goats: He will set the sheep on the right hand, and the goats on the left: but neither will understand at first why they are placed where they are. The elect will say, "When saw we Thee an hungred and fed Thee?" And the castaways will say, "When saw we Thee an hungred and did not minister unto Thee?" The one will not know why they are saved, until He has declared it to them: nor will the others know why they are lost. The deep, and true humility of the first will hide from them their own blessing: and the blinding power of sin, long indulged, will hide from the other their own condemnation. Both ways, there will be a great surprise. Both salvation and condemnation will come upon men strange and unexpected. It is well we should know this beforehand, to keep us both from depending on ourselves, and from rashly judging others. Therefore the Scripture gives us many notices of it. All the many warnings which our Lord gave to the Jews and other Pharisees, that they were in danger of being cast out, to make room for the Gentiles and Publicans: all these warnings I say, are so many warnings to us all, that the judgement of that Day will be far other in many respects, than we might have imagined. Let us consider, in this way, the words with which our Blessed Lord both began and ended the parable: "Many that are first shall be last, and the last shall be first." "So the last shall be first, and the first last; for many be called, but few chosen."

I will take the last words first: "Many are called, but few chosen." All Christians of course are called; every one who on this or any other day comes into this or any other Church is called to be a Christian: he is called first in Holy Baptism, and he is called afterwards all his life long, as often as he hears or sees any thing to put him in mind of the great truths of the Gospel: as often as any good thought comes into his heart. Some are called more loudly and clearly, some earlier, some oftener than others: but all are truly called: to all eternity they never can be as if God had left them in a mere heathen condition, dark and blind, and without any knowledge of Him. Think for once earnestly on this: you have been called over and over: your life has been made up of calls: you are called even now, at this very moment. You may go away and forget it, but it will not be as if it had never been. It will not be forgotten everywhere, nor for ever. It makes you so much more in debt to your God: it comes in to swell the account of ten thousand talents, which you are sure to hear of when the day of reckoning comes, either to be burthened with it or to be forgiven. In ordinary life, we know it is but too common for persons to get into debt, by little and little, more and more every day, and to go away each time, quite careless about the matter, and really not aware, not considering, what they are about. They have gone on so long in that dishonest way, that they do such things now without shame or fear. But for all that the debt is a real thing. It stands against them, and they are liable at any time to be called on to pay it. *Their* forgetting it does not in the least tend to blot it out of the creditor's books. Somewhat like this—alas! too nearly like it—is the conduct and condition of too many Christians in their dealings with Almighty God. God calls them over and over, and every call, if they slight or despise it, makes them more in debt to Him: and they go on adding to this debt without care or concern, until the day when it all is summed up and proved against them: and where then will they look for refuge? He has called them all their lives long, and they would would not hear, now it is their turn to call, and His to refuse hearing.

"Many are called, but few chosen." All Christians are invited to salvation, but few in comparison will be in the end chosen to obtain it. Our Lord has spoken it out quite plainly: but I know not how it is, that few persons seem really to believe His words. For what is the common notion as to who will be saved? Is it not something like this, that the ordinary sort of persons, keeping up a fair character in the world, are in a fair way to heaven? that only a few wicked persons, whom every one points at as thieves, adulterers, or blasphemers, will fail of pardon and acceptance at the last? How many of us have ever meditated, deeply meditated as we ought to do, on the danger we are ourselves in of falling into the bottomless pit? How many have considered in earnest that whenever we committed knowingly a grievous sin, though it were but in thought, we did, as it were, cast ourselves over the edge of that fearful gulf: the fire of it kindled upon our garments, and it was nothing but an Almighty Arm, which we could not see, that caught hold of us, and saved us from falling, and gave us a chance of putting out the horrid flame which had begun to consume us alive. How easily do we take it for granted, when people die, that they are gone to heaven, and when we die, that we shall go to heaven ourselves; as if it were a matter of course, like the air we breathe, or the food we eat. And so poor souls go on, encouraging themselves and one another in the ways of the world, right or wrong; and are little concerned either at the death of their neighbours, or at the thought of their own death: and because God is merciful, and keeps on calling them, they fancy that He will pardon them at last, though they have turned a deaf ear to His call as long as ever they had a choice. As if the labourers in to-day's parable had come and demanded their penny without having gone into the vineyard at all, and that, though they had been standing idle in the market place, all the time of the Master's many invitations, and had heard but refused to obey them. Of course, the Master would say to those idle persons, 'I never offered my penny except to those who would really work for me;' and so the Lord one day will say to such careless Christians, 'You never in earnest set about your task in My service, how then dare you think of expecting any reward?'

No doubt, it was in order to warn us against such careless and profane ways, that our Lord said so plainly more than once, how that those who shall be saved will be few in comparison with those who shall be lost. So that when we see any great crowd of people, when we read or hear of thousands assembling together, a religious mind may well think sadly, what a large proportion of those thousands will go wrong at the last day. Persons have been known before now to weep, when, beholding a large army they reflected that within a hundred years, at most, every person there would be but dust and ashes: and surely a Christian-minded person may well feel his heart sink within him, when he looks at a crowded town, or at any large company of people, and considers in his heart, 'Here no doubt are many souls, who are in a sure way to be ruined for all eternity: what if such and such an acquaintance of my own should be among the number? What if I should be one of them myself? Many are called, but few are chosen: I must look to it, else assuredly I shall be one of the many, not of the few.'

I say that it becomes a true believer, looking on the world around him, to have such thoughts as these, not in the way of judging others, but in the way of fearing for himself. Our Lord Himself has put such thoughts in our heart, by His well known and most awful words near the end of His Sermon on the Mount, "Enter ye in at the strait gate: for wide is the gate and broad is the way that leadeth to destruction, and many there be which go in thereat: because strait is the gate and narrow is the way which leadeth unto life, and few there be that find it." He could not have told us more plainly, that the saved will be few, the lost many. And why has He told it us? Not surely to make our life unhappy: not that we should despair of salvation, and give up holiness as an impossible thing: but in order to waken us up, and set us upon doing our very best for our own souls; as He declared His meaning Himself on another occasion.[a] When one asked Him, "Lord, are there few that be saved?" His reply was, "Strive to enter in at the strait gate; for many, I say unto you, will seek to enter in, and shall not be able." As if He should say, 'Yes, they are few in comparison; as I have told you before in My Sermon on the Mount: but this need not make you down-hearted: for the reason why they are but few is this, that the greater part do not strive, but only seek to enter in at the strait gate:' that is, if it were no trouble, they had rather be

[a] S. Luke xiii. 23.

good, and serve God, than not: but they will not make it an exertion and a care, they will not put themselves out of the way, they will not deny themselves for it. Therefore at the end of the world the door will be shut against them, and the Bridegroom will say, "I know you not:" and when they shall answer, "[b] We have eaten and drunk in Thy Presence and Thou hast taught in our streets;" that is, 'We have done certain easy duties, making outward profession of serving Thee,' He will say, "I never knew you: depart from Me ye that work iniquity." Alas, my brethren, how many are there, who serve God a little only, and in easy duties that cost them nothing: not really governing their passions and tempers; not denying themselves for Christ's sake anything which they have a great inclination for: not scrupling to work iniquity when the men of their acquaintance encourage them to do so! And what sentence can they expect, what sort of words will fall upon their ears, out of the Mouth of Jesus Christ? His called they are, and have been all their lives long; but how can they be His chosen at the Last Day? How can He trust them to be His servants in heaven, who have proved such unfaithful, unprofitable servants on earth? O think earnestly, if it be but for once, think in your hearts how dreadful, how intolerable it must needs be, to approach the great Master of all, surrounded as He will be by His true servants, the Saints and Angels who truly give themselves up to Him, and to ask Him your wages, and to receive no answer, but the being ordered out of His Presence for ever. Yet

[b] Ib. 26.

the miserable persons, whose lot this will be, will have nothing to say against it. They will look down on their defiled wedding garment, and be speechless. They will see and own, in spite of themselves, how simply just and right it is, that they, not having been faithful in the ordinary matters wherein God trusted them on earth, should not have committed to their trust the true riches. They have not really tried to do their work for one hour as under-servants: how should they be fit to be kings, and reign with Christ on His Throne for ever?

Considering how slothful we all naturally are, and if we have any business of our own, how unwilling we are to leave it to set about Christ's business, I should think we had great need, every one of us, very often to say to ourselves what our Lord has twice said to us all, "Many are called, but few are chosen." Assuredly the saints of God from the beginning have always said this, or something like it, to themselves. Whether they were called early in the morning, as Abel and Enoch and Noah and the first Patriarchs; or at third hour as Abraham Isaac and Jacob; or at the sixth as Moses and the people of Israel; or at the ninth as the Prophets; or at the eleventh as the whole Christian Church, the people who have come to serve God in the latter days; they have still been aware that they were called out of the world, called to be a few among many; and that unless they wrought in good earnest, not for themselves but for their Master, they could not be chosen at last to higher places, but rather would lose what they had for ever. Feeling this, the holy men of old were ever watchful and zealous about their religion: it was nothing to them, to be as good as the rest of the world, or just to keep up a fair character. They knew that the world lieth in wickedness, and that to think one's self good enough because one is no worse than it, is as if the man with the defiled wedding-garment had thought himself clean because others were no cleaner than he. They knew that in one way or another the greater part might be expected to perish: but they knew also that each one might if he would make his own calling sure. And therefore their care was, to walk with God, to be friends of God, to set God always before them, to be faithful in all His house, that is, in every work and service, little or great, which at any time He set them to do; to deny themselves, to do all to God's glory, to take up the cross daily and follow Christ. This was always the way of God's saints: not because they thought they had a call from God to be holier than their neighbours, but because knowing themselves to be sinners they were very much afraid of the end of sin, and knowing that God was their only support, they were afraid to let Him go but for a moment. They knew themselves to be called, and their one care was, to be chosen also at the last. We are called, as surely as they were: we can pray as they did: by God's special mercy, no help which they had to come near their Saviour, is now wanting to us: we may be saved through Christ as they were: only we, as they did, must labour and work and strive and wrestle for our salvation. It will not come of itself: we must really work for it, and work hard. Who would not thankfully do so, that considers in earnest that one day's work when our great Master Himself wrought our salvation at so dear a price to Himself!

SERMON II.

THE FIRST, LAST.

SEXAGESIMA.

S. MATT. xx. 16.

"So the last shall be first, and the first last; for many be called, but few chosen."

WE considered these words last Sunday, so far as they contain a warning, that such as are saved will prove at the last day but a few out of many who are called to be Christians; not because God would have it so, but because too many of us, by our wickedness, disappoint and make void His great and never-failing goodness. Now let us go on and consider the first words of the text: "The last shall be first, and the first last:" by which we are given to understand, that as it would be a great mistake to suppose that all the "called" are of course "chosen," all Christians of course saved; so it would be another mistake to imagine that those who seem most favoured here will in every case be most blessed hereafter. There will be great disappointments, overpowering surprises, when the sentence of the Almighty Judge shall be made known; not only as to the number of the saved, which will be smaller than the world thinks in comparison of the lost; but also as to the persons who will be saved and lost. Some who were very ill thought of among men will receive great praise of God: many, we may fear, who pass now for saints, will receive the sentence of incorrigible impenitent sinners. The base things of the world, and the things which were despised and passed over, as being thought worthy of no account, will then appear to have been God's chosen, and most highly honoured of Him: while that which was highly esteemed will prove many times to have been mere abomination in His sight. The poor widow with her two mites will be reckoned to have given more than all the rich men with their abundance. Many who seemed and perhaps were very eager, and ready to make great sacrifices at first, will be found to have fallen away secretly, and so will lose all the fruit of their labours. They did run well, but the devil hindered them, that they should not go on to the end obeying the truth. The very circumstance, that they did begin so well, is sometimes turned by the crafty enemy into a snare, and an occasion of falling. Our Saviour in the text seems to be warning us of this. Just recollect what it was that led Him to speak as He does here, of the surprises and disappointments, which are to be expected when He will come to judge the world. The rich young man had gone away sorrowful, on hearing that if he would have eternal life, he must part with all and follow Christ, taking up the Cross. Our Lord thereupon had pointed out to His disciples how hard it was for a rich man to overcome the temptation to trust in riches, and to enter into the kingdom of God: and S. Peter had put Him in mind, that hard as it was, it had been already done by him and the other apostles. "ᵃ Behold we *have* forsaken all and followed Thee: what shall we have therefore?" 'We have done this hard thing, have stood this trial in which this young man has failed, and in which Thou hast told us almost all men are sure to fail; surely we may hope for some great special reward.' In speaking like this S. Peter said only what would have come, I suppose, into the minds of any man whatever in his place; observe now, how graciously our Lord replies to him. First, He promises him an ample reward; that he should sit upon a throne, and reign with Him in His kingdom: for that no one who should give up the good things of this world for Christ's sake would ever be a loser by so doing, but would be rewarded a hundred-fold. And then, lest even such an one as S. Peter should think too much of himself, and depend too much on what he had already done, our Lord utters to him, and to us all, the grave words of warning which we are considering: But "many that are first shall be last, and the last shall be first." As if He had said, 'Do not rely too confidently on your good and blessed beginnings. True, you have given up all for Me: and so far you may humbly and thankfully hope for the fulfilment of My glorious promises in you and your fellows. But your trial is not at an end. You are still in a wicked world, and have to watch against the passions and frailties of your own imperfect hearts. At present certainly you are among the first; but remember there are first which shall be last, and there are last which shall be first.' Are they not most fearful and serious

ᵃ St. Matt. xix. 27.

words? And they become yet more fearful, and more serious, when we consider that one of those to whom they were spoken, Judas Iscariot, did in a very short time after quite fall away, and that another, even S. Peter himself, was in great danger, and proved himself sadly frail. Judas had been for many months, not to say years, one of the first, one of those nearest to the person of the Son of God: but our Lord knew that he would soon become one of the last; for surely so he did, when he gave up our Lord to His enemies, and when, in despair at his own guilt, he went and hanged himself. And S. Peter, though with such a willing heart he had left the ship and his father, and had followed Christ on being called by Him, yet continued so weak and frail, that a little while afterwards, when a poor maid servant charged him with being one of Christ's company, he trembled before her, and denied it again and again. Our Saviour, then, knowing all this beforehand, mercifully cautions His zealous Apostle, and all of us who should come after him, not to be over sanguine upon good beginnings; to recollect ever that there is a chance, a fearful chance, of losing His grace after all: that we may do great things, and obtain of Him glorious crowns, and yet in some unhappy moment may give the Evil one great power over us, so that on his tempting us a little more we may forfeit all our crowns, and sink into a very low place in Hell; whereas a little patience and perseverance would have kept us high in His everlasting kingdom.

Let us consider a little some of the ways, in which persons are apt to be brought to this sad and grievous end; how the first came to be last; and if, please

God, we are once thoroughly alarmed and humbled with such thoughts, then we may take comfort in the other most merciful saying, and consider also, how the last may be first.

Now in one sense, by God's special mercy, we are all first, inasmuch as we are all admitted, in our early childhood, without our knowing it, to be members of Christ, children of God, and inheritors of the kingdom of heaven. What can be higher than this? Who are "first," if we Christians are not? But too commonly, and too speedily, those who are so become last. And how does the sad and miserable change take place? Very often in some such way as this; the young child who has gone on a certain way in innocence, having been providentially kept from the knowledge of sin, is thrown among bad companions, or otherwise comes to be acquainted with evil things; the wicked spirit is at hand, to whisper to his heart, 'You have hitherto been better than you need be: you have taken no part in such and such things, which other people indulge in without scruple: why not take your portion of them, while your time lasts? God is very merciful, and in His sight you will still have goodness enough and to spare.' O wicked imagination! Yet the hearts of Christian men, beguiled by their strong passions, listen to it, not considering how very profane it is: and they sin in the first place, in order to get acquainted with sin, and then afterwards for love of its pleasures, till it has grown into a regular habit, and so thousands of the first become last. It is all the first sin over again, the sin of Eve, which you heard of in the lesson this morning: the tempter comes to us as he did to Eve, and says, You may as well *know* something of what is going on; if it is really evil, you need not partake of it; only just look, and see what kind of a thing it is; the world will laugh at you, if you go on in your present ignorance. Blessed and happy and dear to God are those, who have really struggled with this temptation, and have overcome it: innocent as yet of serious evil, because it has been their purpose and their prayer to continue ignorant of it. Most blessed and happy are they: but observe what I am going to say, for it may very greatly concern you. If any have fallen away from this first happy ignorance, and have come, through their own grievous fault, to know more of sin than they need, let them not however give themselves up in despair, as though they had lost all part in that kind of blessing: but every time they are tempted to any fresh sin, let them resolutely close their eyes against even looking at it, let them turn away all their senses from seeking to know anything of its sweetness; and so far, and for that time at least, the blessing of ignorance and innocence will be upon them: and they may humbly and cheerfully hope not to be last, although they have deserved to be so, wilfully and childishly casting away the place which God had given them among the first.

Again; persons may be, or seem to be, first, on account of some particular duty, which they have done better than others: some temptation which they have effectually resisted, some prevailing sin from which they have kept themselves pure. Sometimes others praise them, and they hear a good deal of it: and in many ways they are tempted to imagine themselves very good, and to wonder in their hearts, "What shall we have therefore?" What special reward has our Saviour in store for us, seeing that for His sake we have taken unusual pains, have denied ourselves more than is common among those who profess to serve Him? And if you once come to imagining yourself very good, the next step will be, that you will imagine yourself better than you need be, and so you will relax, and leave off watching yourself so exactly as you have done. Your fancy about your own high character will make you first proud and then careless. You will have a kind of thought in your heart, 'I have goodness enough and to spare, I have lived soberly, righteously, and in a certain sense godly through so many years, I will now take mine ease; I will eat, drink, and be merry.' And so the enemy will come upon you, and in one hour, it may be, you will lose the fruit of all your past obedience: lose it in some deadly sin, putting you down as far below others, as hitherto you may seem to have been above them. The sad and fearful fall of king David may perhaps have been owing to something of that kind. For so many years he had gone on, a true and loyal servant of his God, never in the least giving way to any kind of idolatry; true and dutiful and forgiving to his master Saul, who was always seeking his life; very earnest in his care for God's public worship, sparing no expense nor trouble, that the Lord might be served reverently and worthily. Who knows but that David might have begun to value himself on these many good works of his, and thereupon to be less particular and exact in watching against temptations of the flesh, and so the devil gained that sad advantage over him, and the first, until he had repented, was as one of the last? Nay, we cannot tell but that Judas Iscariot himself may have fallen in this way. Being so near Christ, favoured with His especial commission and blessing, seeing the fruit of his labours in great and true miracles, he very likely considered himself safe: he did not really and seriously watch, and pray: he had no religious fear of temptation; and the tempter accordingly found it no hard matter to ruin him by a very mean and ordinary enticement: the chance of helping himself now and then to a little of his Master's money was enough to make a thief and a traitor of him.

David and Judas were indeed extremely unlike in their ends. The one despaired and was lost, the other repented, and became again a man after God's own heart: but in this respect they seem to have been much alike, that being each of them most highly favoured of God, and knowing themselves to be so, they did not fear sin as they should have done, and each of them is now a warning to us, how the first may become last.

David is a warning to those especially, who are put much in the way of the world's praise. We all know what a difference there is between different persons in that respect. Two men, women or children, may be equally good, equally dutiful, when you come to know them well, but one may obtain far more approbation and love from his neighbours than the other. His goodness may be of a more showy and engaging sort, or he may providentially be put more in the way of exercising it; or those among whom he lives may be more apt to take notice of it. Such an one then is so far in more danger of being tempted and falling away. It is hard, when people are praising and admiring you, not to think well of yourself: and when you think well of yourself, the work of the Evil one is already half done with you: he has but to tempt you craftily and you are sure to fall. Here then let us put our guard: never let us hearken after the praise of men: if we chance to hear it, let us not willingly listen: above all things, let us shrink from recollecting it afterwards with pleasure and satisfaction. Now this will be a hard lesson: for praise is naturally very sweet; it sinks into men's ears like winning music: and therefore it must be met with serious thought, and prepared against with special watching and prayer. It is well, when you are praised, if you accustom yourself presently to think of your worst sins, what you are most ashamed of, and what you would least wish to be known. It is well to recollect how you may be appearing, at that very moment, in the sight of God and His saints. It is well to look on to the great unerring Judgement, so far unlike the sentence of men: to represent to ourselves the sad and shameful exposure, when the mantle of the world's praise shall be finally stripped off the undeserving, and some who are now crowding to the top of the feast, will begin with shame to take the lowest room; or rather, alas! will be turned out altogether, into that fearful outer darkness, where is weeping and gnashing of teeth. O what will it avail us in that day, to have been highly esteemed among men, and perhaps held up as patterns, if He Whose Eyes are as a flame of fire, He to Whom all things are naked and open, beholding us then from His Throne of Judgement, and not seeing His mark upon us, shall command us at once out of His sight, with all other workers of iniquity? "O consider this, ye that forget God," so far as to account yourselves wise and happy merely because men speak good of you. Bethink yourselves, when you are tempted by praise, 'How would all this sound to me, could I now see the Judge on His Throne, and feel His Eye looking down into my heart?'

Especially, and with all your might, beware of putting yourself in comparison with others; with any others whatever. The moment you begin to think, 'At any rate I am better than such a man,' that moment you are in danger: you have reason to fear that the tempter has marked you, and that he will presently be laying some grievous snare in your way. Remember the unhappy Pharisee in our Lord's parable, how he ruined and threw away all his goodness by proudly and unkindly thanking God in his heart that he was not as this Publican. What if it should prove that some of us in our prayers have often indulged like thoughts, inwardly preferring ourselves to some one or more of our brethren, and so the very time which we have spent on our knees has been wasted in pride and unkindness? My brethren, it is but too possible; else we may be sure our Lord would not so earnestly have cautioned us against it. It is but too possible that both our prayers and all our good doings may be turned into sin, and he who is first among us, may become last, for want of real, humble mistrust of ourselves. As we go on our way through the world, if we would not lose what little fruit we have borne, or can bear, in doing good and pleasing God, let us ever take with us our Blessed Lord's aweful warning to some who made, we may believe, as fair a shew as we do: "[b]Ye are they which justify yourselves before men, but God knoweth your hearts; for that which is highly esteemed among men is abomination in the sight of God."

[b] S. Luke xvi. 15.

SERMON III.

THE LAST, FIRST.

QUINQUAGESIMA.

S. Matt. xx. 16.

"So the last shall be first, and the first last: for many be called, but few chosen."

See how mercifully our Blessed Redeemer adds a word of consolation and hope to His heavy and mournful words. For what could be more mournful and heavy, than to hear from Him Who came to save us, that few would be saved in comparison of those who should be lost, and that many of those who seemed highest in God's favour, and nearest to the kingdom of heaven, would throw all their blessings away, and come to a most miserable end. Therefore He Who knows what is in our hearts, and pities His children, as a tender Father, He has not told us only that the first shall, many of them, be last, but also that the last shall be first. As on the one hand many will draw back and be lost, who seemed to be at the very door of heaven, so on the other His miraculous mercy will lay hold of many and save them, when they are on the threshold and edge of hell. As Judas fell away, being one of the chosen company of Apostles, who were nearest to heaven on earth; so that thief on the Cross, who had gone on reviling our Saviour till he was at the point of death, was nevertheless made partaker of His pardoning goodness. He received the promise "To-day shalt thou be with Me in paradise:" and so he who was in some sense the last to repent was the first to be forgiven. Not that any of us may be encouraged to delay his repentance, trusting in the mercy of Christ: but that we may be all saved from that miserable reckless despair, by which the Evil one lays hold of many, and checks them just as they are beginning to repent. Few indeed despair in such a way, as really and in good truth to look forward to everlasting burnings, and to make up their mind to dwell with the devil and his angels, in unspeakable torment of soul and body for ever. It would be too shocking: the heart of man could not bear it: and therefore when I say that many despair, I do not mean that they actually live on, thinking what hell is, and that it is sure to be their portion: but their despair comes upon them somewhat in this way. They have lived evil lives, have given themselves over to something which they know was serious sin, are now living in the guilt of it, and God sets His law before them. From time to time they hear the sayings of the Bible, and cannot hide it from themselves that those sayings are intended for such as they are. A man who is accustomed to take liberties in business, "to do wrong and defraud, and that the brethren," goes into the Church, and hears it distinctly said, "Know ye not that the unrighteous," that is the dishonest, "shall not inherit the kingdom of God;" or he opens his Bible and reads the same words; and it is just the same with the drunkard, the unclean, the covetous, the liar, the unforgiving, and with such as neglect to pray. They hear or read the saying, and cannot but take it to themselves, and it startles them more or less, and they half resolve to amend; perhaps even they begin and try to do so in some measure. But the more they look into God's law, as made known in the New Testament; in the Sermon on the Mount, for example, and in the epistles of our Lord's Apostles, the stricter do they find it to be, the higher, and more perfect the goodness which it requires of them; and here comes in a great, and sore temptation. Satan will whisper to their heart, 'This rule is too high for you, and it is no use, your thinking of obedience to it. You can no more walk by it, than you can climb up to the sun: so you may as well leave it alone, and if you hope at all, hope in God's goodness, that He will save you some other way, for in the way of strict and steady obedience surely you never can be saved.' In this way the Evil one reasons craftily with many a heart, and alas! but too successfully: and Christians are content to pass their lives in the known guilt of grievous sin, with just a faint cloudy hope, that the severe laws of Scripture were not really meant to be kept, but only to make persons more thankful, when after all they shall find themselves forgiven and saved for Christ's sake. What a frail broken reed is this for an immortal soul to lean on! Yet we have too much reason to know that thousands of those for whom Christ died have no better support. They account their enemies so mighty, that they shall never be able to prevail against them as long as they live, yet they have a kind of expectation to prevail against them at the moment of their death by the merits of Jesus Christ. I suppose it is partly against this error that the Church teaches us to pray daily, in the morning, that we may not fear the power of any adversaries, and in the evening, that being defended from the fear of our enemies, we may pass our time in rest and quietness. In those words we ask God especially for grace to fight manfully against our sins: not to make up our minds beforehand, that any of God's plain commands is too hard to be kept, any of our own habits too strong to be overcome. The devil would willingly persuade us that so it is: but Christ Himself has mercifully assured us of the contrary: as in many other gracious promises, so also in this: that the last, the very last, may by His marvellous grace be changed and come to be among the first.

Sometimes again persons are seized with something like despair, on comparing themselves with others better than themselves. They look at some bright and glorious example, either some one among their own acquaintance who is or appears to them remarkably good, or to the saints and martyrs whom they read and hear of in Church; and they say in their hearts, 'I never can be like these: I must give it up as a thing impossible: do what I will, it will always be too far beyond me. I might as well attempt to fly in the air like an angel, as to pray and repent and keep the commandments like a saint.' And so they encourage themselves to think that as

they are not the sort of people to do good and to
please God, God will deal with them according to a
different rule from that which He has plainly set
down in Scripture, by which those holy men and
women have at various times obtained His favour.
Yet God has said over and over, that He is no re-
specter of persons, and that there is but one way to
heaven—the strait and narrow way of keeping His
commandments. And if the examples which He has
set before us by His Scripture or His providence
appear too high and pure for us, and we say in our
hearts, 'How can we follow them?' He bids us
take notice of little children, and see how they set
about learning things which at first seem so very
far above them; as learning to speak for instance, or
to read, or to write. How would the child do any
of these things, if it got into a way of thinking continually to itself, 'Do what I will, I shall never, never
be able to speak like these grown up persons. It is
impossible: I may as well let it alone.' Luckily,
the simple babe has no such thoughts. He does not
trouble himself about doing it as well as others or
better; he just tries to do it in imitation of those
whom he sees or hears, because God has made it natural for him to do so: and so the young child comes
quickly to be as good and correct a speaker, perhaps,
as any of those whom at first he looked up to, and
with reason, as being then most immeasurably above
him. Only try to follow God's guidance in learning
to be good likewise, and you cannot tell what great
improvement you may come to in that also. Mark
how good men behave in the ordinary concerns of
life; how attentive they try to be at their prayers,

how they turn away their eyes and ears, and all their senses, from all that is evil; how calm they are, how sweet and how kind, under every provocation and ill usage; how patiently they suffer, how naturally they take, as of course, the lowest place: and do you try to be so far like them in the next little ordinary trial and temptation that comes upon you. You will be like a child learning to speak; your first beginnings exceedingly imperfect, yet are they the true and real beginnings, if God so please, of a very high and saintly perfection. Persevere only; indulge no thought of despondency; never draw back saying, 'It was not worth while.' How can it be other than worth while, to work and work on, however poorly and unsatisfactorily, when the great Master is looking on, working with you, promising to reward His own work in you. Use good examples when you see or read of them, to be your encouragement, not to dishearten you. What if we feel most surely and truly, that our sins have set us very much farther than we need have been at this moment from the holy ones of old? They too had small, some of them bad beginnings: they were not great saints in a moment: they had to work their way slowly upwards: they too, doubt it not, had their many and sore misgivings. They were not always first as they are now, and the same Almighty Arm is reached out to us, on Which alone they depended for their improvement. Let not then our hearts sink within us, when we read or hear of the very holy doings of others, let it rather be an encouragement to us, as a sick man would be encouraged when he heard of great and perfect cures performed on some of his acquaintance by the physician whom he was himself depending on. The grace which could do such wonders for the Blessed Virgin or S. Paul, much more may it help our weak endeavours, so far as to save us from eternal death.

But you will say, 'I have behaved so ill, I have so utterly deadened and benumbed the spring and power of that first grace: I have had good intentions before now, I have made excellent resolutions, I have even begun good practices: and now see what it is all come to! Alas! what *can* I do more than I have done, and have failed in it already?' This is a complaint but too natural: but our heavenly Teacher has provided us with a full and gracious answer to it. He says " *To-day* if ye will hear My voice, harden not your hearts. Though you have misspent former days, and thrown away the fruit of former good beginnings, yet listen, resolve, amend, to-day. You see I am not yet tired of causing My sun to rise on you, and of sending rain on your ground, both for the just and for the unjust: neither shall I be tired of giving you My Holy Spirit, to change your hearts, and amend your lives, if you will but receive Him reverently, and in good earnest. Come *to-day:* it is not yet too late: to-morrow it may be."

These are His fatherly offers, Who cannot bear to see a sinner perish. If we feel that we are last, and below the last, He will have us to know that He can and will make the last first, if they will answer His bountiful call: therefore let no man despair. Let no man despair, but let every man set heartily to work. Watch the ways of God's providence, and endeavour to walk in them with all reverence and thankfulness.

Encourage both in yourself and in others every kind of penitential beginning. The Pharisaical Jews to whom our Lord at one time specially addressed this warning about the first and the last, as they had no heart for serious repentance themselves, so they could not well endure to see its workings in their brethren. They were inclined to discourage them and put them back, with some such reproof as that in the parable: 'Thou hast wrought but one hour, and wilt thou make thyself equal to us, which have borne the burthen, and heat of the day?' Let us beware how we tread in their steps: and there are more ways than one of doing so. If a man allow himself to treat with coldness and scorn anything which may be a real token of repentance in an erring brother: or if he turn slightingly and impatiently away from the simple humble beginnings of Christian goodness in Christ's poor, or in His little ones: so far, he takes part with the Pharisees against the disciples of Jesus Christ: and in whatsoever he may now seem first, there is reason to fear that such an one will be found bye and bye among the last.

Still more, if we give any way to base envy, envy being the very opposite of that pure and heavenly charity, which the Church teaches especially to-day, "Is thine eye evil because I am good? Art thou envious because I am bountiful?" The master said it to the first labourers, when they grumbled at being paid only just the same as the last; but in purpose and meaning Christ says it to all you, my brethren, to check you in all proud discontented comparisons. He seems to say to each one of us, 'Alas! poor blinded sinner, in complaining at what is done for your neighbour, you are but in reality passing sentence upon yourself. How little can you know of your own secret sins, of your own corrupt heart, while you are thus pressing to have strict justice done. Why, if it were so, this very enviousness of yours, which you perhaps think a mere token of your love of justice, would be enough at once to forfeit your whole reward. The envious shall not inherit the kingdom of God. Those who wilfully grudge their neighbour any good thing, especially any part of the treasures of the kingdom of heaven, must expect to find bye and bye that their own share in it is finally lost.'

On the other hand, see what a cloud of glorious witnesses, what a treasure of unspeakable blessings, is prepared for those who make a right use of God's mercy in preparing a way for the last to be first. Such persons, in respect of their own sins, are penitents; in respect of other men, earnest helpers to repentance; in both, they have the angels with them, those loving yet holy beings, who rejoice over one sinner that was lost, and is found: and who call Christ's beloved disciples their fellow servants, because they help them in moving fallen hearts to repentance, and in charging Christians earnestly, that they sin not. It is well that we should sometimes remember this, now at the beginning of the holy season of Lent. The angels who visibly waited on Jesus Christ after His temptation, will all through Lent be our unseen friends and helpers in whatever we do, as true penitents, and helpers of others to repent. All who are or have been true penitents here on earth will be our friends and helpers also. They will pray for us, and in some sense with us. The whole air will be in a manner made fragrant with good and holy prayers, offered to God on our behalf. More than all, and above all, and as the only way to make all a blessing indeed, Jesus Christ Himself will intercede for us, He Who died both for the first and for the last, having Himself at His Incarnation made Himself last, that we, the last, might be first; He will never cease offering to the Father the sincere prayers and simple well-meant works of the men, women, and children, who come to Him according to their knowledge, in true faith. At holy times, and very particularly at this aweful season of Lent, He puts us on our trial, whether we will come to Him in earnest. Who is there among us that feels in his heart, as if he had hitherto been very low and little in the kingdom of God? Let him in seriousness employ this time as the Church directs it to be employed: and in some very blessed way which he will not himself understand, he shall be moved into a higher place; and persevering, will come to be one of the first.

SERMON IV.

THE THIEF ON THE CROSS AN EXAMPLE OF FAITH.

SEPTUAGESIMA.

S. Luke xxiii. 41.

"*And we indeed justly; for we receive the due reward of our deeds: but this Man hath done nothing amiss.*"

As the collects after the Epiphany remind us, one after another, of our Christian privileges, so now that Lent is drawing near, the great season of mortification and repentance, the Church takes the like method of recalling to our minds the great Christian duties, faith, hope, and charity: for an exercise of which in their order the collects for these three Sundays, Septuagesima, Sexagesima, Quinquagesima, are very well fitted, and were most likely intended.

And first the collect for this Sunday is such, that whoever uses it with a Christian mind must have true Gospel faith in the great doctrine of the forgiveness of sins. "O Lord, we beseech Thee favourably to receive the prayers of Thy people, that we who are justly punished for our offences, may be mercifully delivered by Thy goodness, for the glory of Thy Name, through Jesus Christ our Saviour: Who liveth and reigneth with Thee and the Holy Ghost, ever one God, world without end."

Here we are taught, first, the true temper of an acceptable penitent coming before his God in prayer; that is, to confess himself, in good earnest, justly punished for his many offences. Then we are taught where his hope is: not in himself, nor in any thing he can do, but entirely in the goodness of Almighty God, against Whom his sins were committed. Such is the meaning of that petition, "that we may be mercifully delivered by Thy goodness." Further, the penitent is here instructed which way he must look, and what he must seek, as long as his trial on earth shall last: that he may not have been forgiven in vain, he is bound henceforth to seek for, and to look to, the glory of God's Name as his chief end. Last of all, as in all our prayers, so in this truly Christian collect, we renounce all notion of merit, and profess to have no trust but only in the mediation of the Son of God; Whose unspeakable power and glory we acknowledge, as One with the Father and the Holy Ghost, as we do His inconceivable love, when we entitle Him our Saviour.

Now there is a portion of our Lord's history, which I think most exactly suitable to be read along with this collect; I mean that from which the text is taken, the account of the penitent thief upon the cross. If I do not mistake, his behaviour throughout, after he once began to repent, is a perfect living and speaking example of that blessed temper of mind, which the Church, in the prayer we have just considered, expects all her children to practise.

Do we, in repeating this collect, own ourselves justly punished for our offences? So did that suffering malefactor; in the very agonies of his bitter and shameful death, he acknowledged it was no more than he deserved. "We are in this condemnation justly, for we receive the due reward of our deeds."

Do we profess ourselves moved by punishment to think of God, and depend on His goodness? So the thief on the cross, while his companion was despairing and reviling, rebuked him with the simple expostulation, "Dost not thou fear God, seeing thou art in the same condemnation?" As if he had said, 'Though all the world besides join in treating an innocent, holy Man so cruelly, yet *we* ought to refrain; we, whom this punishment is teaching to feel God's hand heavy upon us; we, who shall be dead in a few moments, and can have no hope, but in our Maker's mercy.'

Does the collect warn men to what end, being pardoned and delivered, they must hereafter direct their whole conduct; viz., to the glory of God's Name? The whole conduct of the penitent on the cross, in first rebuking his wretched companion, then turning as he did to our Saviour, and to both witnessing that good confession, which proved him to be, as it were, a Christian even before Christianity began; the whole, I say, of this conduct might seem to be recorded on purpose that Christians might know what is meant, when they are taught and enjoined to pray that God's mercy in redeeming and forgiving them may turn to the glory of His Name.

Finally, does the collect lead men to Christ, and no

otherwhere, for deliverance and pardon? The dying malefactor turned to Jesus, with these words of faith on his lips, "Lord, remember me when Thou comest into Thy kingdom."

The parallel, then, between the two; between S. Luke's history of the behaviour of the penitent thief on the cross, and the prayer which our Church has taught us to use to-day for improvement in our Christian faith; this parallel is complete in all its parts. And no one is fit to use this collect, who is not at least with some sincerity endeavouring to bring his own mind and temper to the likeness of this true penitent, so highly favoured by the Saviour of the world, that He gave him, what we never read of His condescending to confer on any other dying sinner; He gave him an express promise of salvation, "Verily I say unto thee, To day shalt thou be with Me in paradise."

At first sight a careless reader might perhaps be inclined to think, that we individually, most of us, have little or nothing at all to do with this example of the thief on the cross. A notion prevails, too commonly, that his case answers only to that of persons beginning to repent just as they are going out of this world. But let us consider all the circumstances, as they are really set down in the Word of God. I am much mistaken if we shall not find something much nearer our case than any one might at first think.

He had been in his life a malefactor, an open and daring violator of God's law against stealing, and also of that other most express command, by which every soul among men is enjoined, under penalty of damnation, to be "obedient to the higher powers." Now, what if such and such an one, among us or any other congregation of Christians, never committed direct theft? never set himself, in discontent and sedition, against those set over him by the Almighty? There are other commandments as sacred as the eighth, and other duties as dear to the Almighty as those which a subject owes to his rulers. And dare any man indeed flatter himself, when he looks back on his past life, that he is free from great sin in regard of them all? that he has never, in thought, word, or deed brought on himself, the guilt of dishonouring his parents; of murder, adultery, or false witness? Let him understand that in whichever of these points his conscience charges him with wilful transgression, in that respect, and so far, he is like this man on the cross, or any other condemned malefactor; and whatever temper and disposition of mind pleased God in the penitent thief, with the same He will be pleased in you, who have anyhow broken His laws wilfully, though in a different way from the thief.

Again; this malefactor had Christ even in sight and in that, at least, some may think his case differed from all men's now. Yet a very little attention would show, that his seeing our Lord with the outward eyes, cannot make so much difference between our condition and his, if we, anyhow, are found to have as strong grounds for believing as he had. Now, what reason we have now for believing, every one knows who will attend to his Bible; he knows the miracles of Jesus Christ, His perfect laws, His Divine example, His unerring prophecies; how

He preached the Gospel to the poor, and with what unspeakable wisdom and goodness He has there provided for all our wants, both in this world and in the world to come. Of all these things, from our youth up, pains have been taken continually to teach us; and whatever wickedness prevails in the world, still the name of Christian is had in honour, and we have had it recommended to us in a thousand ways. This is our condition; these are the methods which God's good providence has taken to put us, before we could know any thing, in the way that leads to His Son Jesus Christ.

Now let us endeavour, as we may, to put ourselves in the place of that malefactor, and enter into his feelings, such as we may reasonably conceive them to have been, when he was brought so near to our Saviour. No doubt he had been taught, as the Jews were in general, to expect a glorious and triumphant Deliverer, who should make His people rich and great, and carry all before Him in the world. He had the same reason as the rest of his countrymen had, for doubting and drawing back from Christ, when he found Him rejected of men, a Man of sorrows and acquainted with grief; above all, when he saw Him condemned, (with himself, whose guilt he knew,) to the worst and most shameful of all deaths. And it should seem from S. Matthew's account and S. Mark's, that even after he was hanged on the cross, he continued for a while an unbeliever like the rest, and reproached our Saviour with His sufferings.

But the grace of God was still offered to him, and he did not go on to the end refusing it. It may be, that he could not resist the sight of one suffering as our Lord did, with such Divine majesty and meekness. Whatever he had seen or heard at any time of the exceeding mercy and power of our Redeemer, of His wonderful works, and of the gracious words in which He taught men all truth; all must have come over his mind at once, and, joined with what he saw and heard at the moment, must have convinced him, in spite of all appearances, that this is indeed the Saviour of the world, the only hope of lost sinners.

And being convinced, he declared his faith, he exerted himself in the midst of agony, to rebuke his fellow-sufferer and invite him to repentance, and to testify our Blessed Lord's innocence. "Dost not thou fear God, seeing thou art in the same condemnation?"

And this his effort of charity to his companion was accompanied with the most signal confession of entire trust in our dying Lord, that ever yet the world witnessed. For at that moment, when the very Apostles, all but one, had forsaken our Lord, when S. John, the only friend whom He had at that time near His Cross, kept near Him, as it should seem, because He was his beloved Master, not because he had any clear hope remaining that " this was He which should have redeemed Israel," even at such a moment as that, the penitent malefactor knew and owned Jesus of Nazareth on the cross, for his only King, Judge, and Saviour. He said unto Him, "Lord, remember me when Thou comest into Thy kingdom." This was indeed surpassing faith; it was, to use an expression of S. Paul's, "against hope, believing in hope." And the ever-merciful Redeemer accepted it accordingly; "Verily I say unto thee, To day shalt thou be with Me in paradise." He bestowed on him the greatest of all encouragements that one can imagine given to any one in this life; a direct assurance of immediate salvation and glory.

The whole account is full of matter for the deepest and most solemn meditations that can possibly enter into man's heart; but the particular remark now to be made on it is this, That if even under such circumstances the penitent thief, by God's special grace, found the way to practical faith, pleased his Saviour, and became heir of heaven, surely no circumstances whatever, in which any man now can be placed (supposing him only within sound of the Gospel), can justify him in practical unbelief. If we have Christ in sight as he had, we are not in the same danger of being shocked by the Cross of Christ. On the whole, in respect of advantages and disadvantages, his condition is enough like ours to make the example very edifying. And it has been seen before how very little, in all likelihood, we could find to flatter ourselves, if we fairly set ourselves to compare his previous character, malefactor as he was, with our own.

Consider now in what manner God dealt with him, by His providence, to call him to repentance. In this also we may find, if I mistake not, much that is like our own experience. Affliction, the punishment of the cross, was the outward instrument employed by God's providence to call this hardened sinner to a right knowledge of himself and his Saviour. His condemnation brought him to Christ. And would it be an unreasonable conjecture, if one were to suppose that by far the greater part of those who serve their Maker sincerely were first drawn to Him by cords of affliction? If no sudden or striking judgement comes on them, still the sense of loathing and weariness, which follows the best enjoyments of this world, is often felt as affliction enough; would be so always, if men would take time rightly to consider their own condition, and not keep hurrying on, from one care or pleasure to another, and driving eternity out of their minds, as fast as the mercy of God brings it in. Accordingly, the collect takes it for granted, that we, as many as join in using it, are "punished for our offences:" and so every one will find himself to be, who will only endeavour, with calmness and perseverance, to think over the matter seriously. All, like that thief by our Saviour's side, have some manner of cross to endure; and God in His mercy thinks it well if so we are led to repent like him, tempered as our pain always most surely is, with the loving-kindness of an ever-present Father.

In all these respects, then; in men's natural character and inclinations; in their being brought near Christ, and called on to believe in spite of difficulties; finally, in their being, most commonly, made serious by the chastenings of the Almighty: in all these respects, I say, the condition of every Christian man, stained with the guilt of any wilful sin, yet within reach of the means of grace, bears a close and instructive resemblance to the condition of the thief on the cross.

What then can a Christian do better, than study the example of that true penitent, and practise all his life long the same holy and heavenly dispositions, which the Saviour of mankind, beholding in him, was pleased to reward, with no less a gift than an absolute promise of receiving him, on the moment of his death, to His own rest? Which of us would not labour and strive to copy his entire faith, his seriousness, resignation, and great charity? That when our day of death comes (a cross which we must all of us bear) we may be with him and Christ in Paradise.

First, it concerns men at all times, when God is chastening them in any way, to have a serious and religious feeling of their afflictions; not to fall into that dangerous error, which the wise man meant when he said, "[a] My son, *despise* not the chastening of the Almighty." Some people are so light-minded, that not even the nearest and plainest visitations sent upon them by God's fatherly providence, not even the sickness and death of parents, relations, or friends, who ought to be dear to them, can make any impression upon them. They take every thing as it were childishly, thinking it hard and grievous at the moment, and then making haste to escape from seriousness, and get back with the least possible delay to their frivolous cares and ordinary amusements. Such persons are in greater danger than either themselves or their neighbours may imagine; for when even the chastenings of the Lord cannot make a person serious, what hope, humanly speaking, remains? I could wish to say to all such, 'Open your eyes for once in good earnest, and look to the Cross of Jesus Christ. By His side you will see one, the true pattern of the right way in which a sinner should endure God's wrath. His thought is, "finding himself in misery, should not a man fear God?" should it

[a] Prov. iii. 11.

not make a sinner very serious, when he not only hears of his Judge, and sees Him near in the affliction of others, but actually feels Him in his own person? What madness, what worse than childish folly, when such things happen,—for instance, when you have sick friends at home, to be taken up merely with trying to amuse yourself, or still worse, with your old sins!'

The next thought of the penitent thief was, to acknowledge the Justice of God, and the perfect purity of Jesus Christ. "We indeed justly; for we receive the due reward of our deeds: but this Man hath done nothing amiss." Here he furnishes another most needful lesson to all who suffer in any way, to lay the blame where they ought; to reconcile themselves to their own lot by recollecting our Lord's sufferings, innocent and holy as He was; sufferings endured for *their* sake. Believe me, there is no such consolation in this world of calamity, as when you make up your minds to cast yourself entirely on the mercy of your God and Father, to resign yourself, body and soul, to His will. There is nothing that can sooth even bodily pain like the remembrance of our Lord on the Cross. And on the other hand, there is nothing so wretched as that complaining, uneasy disposition, which would make you think all things hard. It is, in fact, as far as it goes, saying to one's self, "there is no God:" for so in fact he says to himself, who allows his own heart to wander in complaining thoughts, accusing God of injustice and unkindness.

Finally, this true penitent teaches all men, to the

end of the world, what is the perfection of true faith: to forget things present, and turn to Christ, living and dying, with this one care, That He of His mercy would be pleased to remember us, when He returns in His glorious kingdom. May it be found in the heart of us all (as, surely, God has put it in the power of us all) to follow his example, and partake of his blessing!

SERMON V.

CHRISTIAN HOPE.

SEXAGESIMA.

Rom. viii. 28.

"We know that all things work together for good to them that love God."

As the collect for last Sunday served especially to nourish faith, so that appointed for to-day is an expression of true Christian hope. "O Lord God, Who seest that we put not our trust in any thing that we do; mercifully grant, that by Thy power we may be defended against all adversity, through Jesus Christ our Lord."

Those who love to find fault with all things as they are, have not scrupled sometimes to accuse this prayer of high presumption; as if more were asked in it, than mortal man should dare to ask for. To be defended from all adversity, they say, is not the condition of sinners in this world, and therefore it is vain and wrong to pray for it. But let the right meaning of the prayer be considered, by comparison with this promise of S. Paul in the text, "that all things shall work together for good to them that love God." Such prayers and such promises do not point to an unmixed condition of nothing but enjoyment in this world, any more than those verses in the psalms: "[a]Delight thou in the Lord, and He shall give thee thy heart's desire;" and again, "[b]There shall no evil happen unto thee, neither shall any plague come nigh thy dwelling." They give no pledge to a good and religious man, that he shall be free from worldly trouble; but they do give a most distinct pledge, resting on the faithfulness of God Almighty, that all his troubles will turn to the best. So that he will most surely perceive in the end, that it was "good for him to have been in trouble."

The language, then, and the meaning of Scripture, is plain. But do we always find indeed, in real life and actual experience, that such as trust God in earnest, are, in this sense, defended against adversity? Do we always find them less afflicted, or sooner comforted after affliction, than the children of this world are?

In the first place, we do not know for certain, none but the All-seeing Father knows, who they are that trust God in earnest. It may be that many persons, who appear to us religious and good, are nourishing some secret discontent, charging God foolishly in their hearts. That melancholy and lowness of spirits, of which so much is to be seen, even among men of blameless character, men attentive to the ordinances of outward religion, much of it must needs be ascribed to the wilfulness of corrupt man, who will not make up his mind to let God do what He knows to be best. So far, then, God's word is sure; if such men have not their hearts' desire, they must not complain, as

[a] Ps. xxxvii. 4.   [b] Ib. xci. 10.

if they were ill-used; for they have not qualified themselves for the blessing, they have not learned to "delight themselves in the Lord."

Again, as we cannot certainly know who they are that trust in God, so neither can we tell accurately what is affliction and what is not, even in this present world. Things turn out so very differently from what beforehand we should have looked for, short and imperfect as our sight is, that very often in respect of worldly comfort the loss most lamented proves the greatest gain. Every person at all advanced in life, provided he be also used to take things not as a mere unbeliever would, but to refer all to the providence of God, every such person, I think, must remember instances within his own experience, of sorrows turning into blessings, instances too of such a kind, that people around him knew nothing of them; according to the most true observation of king Solomon, "ᶜThe heart knoweth his own bitterness, and a stranger doth not intermeddle with his joy."

Thus our very ignorance, it appears, should in all reason reconcile us to whatever we might at first think hard in the course of God's all-ruling providence. We see that even in this unequal world He has ten thousand ways, secret to us, of making "all things work together for good to such as love Him in earnest."

And ignorant as we are of the mysteries of providence, even we may sometimes discern enough of these His wonderful doings, to make us, if we have a spark of faith, give credit to them where we see

ᶜ Prov. xiv. 10.

them not. The Holy Spirit in the Bible history has, as it were, lifted up the curtain, to show us, by some remarkable instances, the hand of the Almighty ordering all things, even the least and what seem the most untoward, to the good of those who love and trust Him. Take, for a first instance, that which cannot fail to win the heart, even of every little child, who is but beginning to think of God; take the story of Joseph and his brethren. What could be a greater misfortune, than to be envied, hated, and sold for a slave, by one's own brethren, thirsting for one's blood? and yet this was the very thing which led to Joseph's glory in Egypt, and caused him to be remembered, in all ages, as a proverb of God's protecting favour. Or, to take an instance yet more wonderful, and not to be mentioned but with deep awe and reverence; who could have expected that the treachery of Judas, the dishonesty of Pilate, the malice of the Jews, should turn out to be the direct way of bringing our Divine Saviour to the unspeakable joy and glory set before Him? These things whoever remembers, how can he choose but make up his mind to believe all God's promises to the faithful, how contrary soever to present appearances? How can he possibly doubt in his heart, that the God and Father of our Lord Jesus Christ has ways and means ever at hand, to make the worst turn out for the best?

This then is a Christian's hope, and this is what he means and professes, when he prays to Almighty God to be evermore defended from all adversity. He prays that he may have such a mind, that God would give him such a spirit, as to take out the sting of all that may happen, which would otherwise be most grievous to him. He prays that his Father, for Christ's sake, would lighten the sorrows of this life, according as He knows him able to bear; and would turn them, by His unfailing grace, into so many joys and comforts in regard of the life which is to come. And this prayer he is sure will be granted, if asked in the right Christian temper.

And what is the right Christian temper? The collect tells us what it is not; it is, "not putting our trust and confidence in any thing that we do ourselves." The Apostle in the text tells us what it is; it is, in one word, "loving God." Let these two expressions be fairly considered, and it will be seen at once but too clearly, why the real life of Christians, such as one witnesses every day, is so very unlike what one should expect in persons favoured with such gracious promises.

First, profess as often as they may that they put not their trust in any thing that they do, much of their conduct bears testimony against them, that they continue still in heart self-sufficient. Why are they so ready to sink and despond, when their projects in life are disappointed, if it were not that at first setting out they depended too much on their own success, they did not with a true religious mind commit their work and counsel to the Lord?

Why are they so often discontented and unthankful, even when they have won their aims, except because they expected to be happy in them? that is, they expected far more than is to be had in this life; they thought to choose out their own happiness, instead of leaving it in the hands of their Creator. Why are they so full of bitter comparisons between their own losses and disappointments, and what they choose to call and imagine the happier lot of other men? It is because they do not lay to heart, that neither themselves, nor those whom they envy, can have any sure ground of hope, any real or abiding happiness, but in God the Fountain of all good, through His Son Jesus Christ. Once make up your mind to that, and the temptation to envy is gone; for who that knows he has a treasure in heaven, could be grieved or angry, because another has more of some trifling earthly good?

The envy, therefore, and vexation, and discontent, which prevail so generally among men, shews clearly that they still keep their hope and confidence in the wrong place: they will persist in depending on what they can gain for themselves here, what they can do by their own strength. No wonder if such are disappointed, and find all their hope, in the end, mere "vanity and vexation of spirit." No wonder if they pray in vain to be defended against all adversity, who will not trust themselves so far with God, as to let Him judge for them, what is adversity and what not.

But all the world, you will say, is not entirely taken up with envy and repining. Some appear gay and sprightly, pleased with themselves and not displeased with others; and whatever happens, they will not let it vex them. There are, indeed, many such, and so far as their natural cheerfulness is concerned, they have a great cause of thankfulness, and much to answer for to Almighty God. They have to watch and pray for His grace, in order to improve this great blessing of a light heart, which He has given them, to Christian purposes of charity and thanksgiving. It will be a great mistake indeed, if they give themselves credit for Christian hope, merely because they feel easy and unconcerned, and care little about the future. And yet a thoughtful person may well fear that there are many such in the world; people who have spent their best years in driving away care, as it is called; who have hardly known what it is to be serious, and when their hour of account draws on, give themselves credit for cheerful hearts, and true resignation to the will of God. But let us not deceive ourselves; this sort of sanguine temper is as far from true Christian hope, as the thoughtlessness of a child from the steadiness of an experienced soldier. How can he have Christian hope, who avoids the thought of heaven, because it is a grave, serious thought: who turns away from the remembrance of death, as something too melancholy to be endured? Besides, it is even too plain, that many who seem cheerful and contented, trust in themselves, and not in the Almighty. I would not rashly charge men thus, merely on account of their way of talking; for it is easy to get into a tone, without any pious meaning at heart; and no doubt the fear of doing so keeps many who have good thoughts, from uttering them in their ordinary conversation: yet it is due to the glory of our God and Saviour, when the occasion fairly calls for it, not to be afraid or ashamed to speak of Him. And they who never do so, betray, I fear, very often, great and dangerous irreligion of heart. Of such, it would appear, S. James was speaking, in that grave rebuke of his, " Go to now, ye that say, To-day or to-morrow we will go into such a place, and continue there a year, and buy and sell, and get gain: whereas ye know not what shall be on the morrow. For that ye ought to say, If the Lord will, we shall live, and do this, or that." Did S. James mean, that on all common occasions we should introduce the most holy Name of God, and make express mention of His providence? I do not so understand him, but surely he could not mean less than this; namely, to reprove the light, unthinking way in which men lay out their schemes for the future, or talk over past events, with an evident forgetfulness of Him, on Whom, however the whole depends. It is within the reach of every man's own experience and judgement, whether or no this godless temper be common among those who ought to know better; and especially if they be cheerful, and thriving in the world. The fact is, their prosperity is spoiling them; they are fast learning the fatal lesson, too welcome to their fallen natures, to trust in what they do themselves, their own wisdom, their own favour, their own strength, their own riches; upon these all their thoughts run; and in too many instances they are not afraid openly to avow their self-sufficiency, by neglecting the holy ordinances of their Maker. They feel no need of Him, therefore they do not come near Him in prayer; it is no satisfaction to them to find themselves often in the Church and congregation, where He has promised to be; they are "not weary, nor heavy-laden," therefore they never so much as think of approaching Him in the holy Sacrifice and Sacrament of His Body and Blood.

Thus we see how far they are from true Christian

hope, who are either over anxious and dejected, or else always elate and thoughtless, about worldly matters, good or evil; we see that the only ground and root of consolation and courage in our trials here, is to be thoroughly and sincerely weaned from putting our trust in any thing that we do. Once obtain that good mind, once put off your earthly trust, and let trust in God take its place; and you are in the way of that greatest of blessings, which the Holy Ghost in the text has promised to all such. Trusting in God, entirely and continually, you cannot but grow in the love of Him. And in proportion as you do so, all things, you are told, both in heaven and in earth, sad or joyful, quiet or troublesome, all are even now so ordered as to be working together for your good. It is a thought indeed too high, too vast a great deal, to be comprehended by our weak understandings, how one thing should be so chained to another in the world and kingdom of the Almighty; yet, we are sure, so it is. And let it be a comfort to all poor sufferers, who in their dejection may be tempted to think that they are too mean, too insignificant, to be thought of by the God of heaven and earth. He who orders the least things, and can turn the greatest which way He will, be sure He never can forget any one of the immortal souls, redeemed by His Son Jesus Christ with His own precious Blood. The forgiveness of sins, the comfort of the Holy Ghost, the promise of defence in all adversities, and most of all, eternal life, is provided for the least as well as the greatest of those who desire and try to love God.

And why should it be thought a thing impossible, too high, or too hard, for the poorest and least instructed of us all, to love such a Father as the Almighty, such a friend as Jesus Christ? It is true, you cannot do so of yourself; no more can the wisest, and most abundant in outward advantages: corrupt nature and bad habit will be too strong for every one who shall set himself to serve and love his Maker, as if it were a lesson soon learned, a thing which might be taken easily, and put off from time to time. If you would love God, you must pray to Him in earnest, pray to Him to grant you the Spirit of love; and earnest prayer is not a thing which a man may learn with a little practice. It requires continual severe watchfulness, to keep your mind turned towards God, while you are on your knees before Him; it requires a resolute, conscientious temper, to recall your thoughts at once when you find them wandering, as they too often will, with your best endeavours. Then, again, you must take pains to understand and remember your own infirmity; you must daily pray and hourly labour, that God, Who knows you, would not suffer you to put your trust in any thing that you do; and this of itself will give you more trouble than such as have never tried can imagine. So many temptations are to be found, both in the world around us and in our hearts within us, to fill men with a miserable self-sufficiency. Last and hardest of all, the love of God will never be learned, without a sincere and hearty endeavour to please Him by doing His will. For that is the way to have delight in His Presence; the only sure proof of love. Now, whether habitual obedience be an easy lesson, or soon learned by a sinner in the midst of a wicked world, every one can judge for himself.

It is not, then, a thing presently to be done, an easy task, to love God acceptably; but it is a thing which may be done, through His unspeakable mercy through Christ, by all who, in earnest, wish to do it. Neither poverty nor ignorance need hinder it; for why should a poor ignorant man be less able than a rich and learned one to think of God while he is praying, to trust in Christ and not in himself, to keep God's commandments when he knows them, instead of pleasing his own fancy?

You see your calling, Christian brethren; it is simply this, that by keeping the commandments for Christ's sake, you learn to love God in Christ. You see the crown set before you: to be, in such a sense, His chosen, that all "things shall work together for your good." Remember these things, and remember also, that the time of trial is short, the eyes of the Judge unerring, and that of him to whom much has been given, many means of grace, many opportunities of becoming holy, of him, we are certain, much will be required.

SERMON VI.

CHRISTIAN CHARITY.

QUINQUAGESIMA.

1 Tim. i. 5.

"The end of the commandment is charity, out of a pure heart, and of a good conscience, and of faith unfeigned."

FAITH, hope, and charity, taken together, make up the whole of a Christian's life; the whole of what we are bound to practise, that we may not forfeit our Gospel privileges; the whole of the duties we must bear in mind, when we are reviewing our past conduct, with a view to entire repentance and amendment. With good reason, therefore, our holy Church, in passing from Epiphany to Lent, from Christian thankfulness to Christian mortification, reminds us, by her collects and other services, on three successive Sundays, of these three evangelical graces, faith, hope, and charity. For the two last Sundays, I have endeavoured to explain how she has taught us, in the words of her prayers, to practise faith and hope towards God. To-day her services speak for themselves, so plainly, that a child may understand them, teaching us, by S. Paul's words and our Saviour's example, what true charity is, and framing for us, almost in those words, the following prayer to Almighty God. "O Lord, who hast taught us that all our doings without charity are nothing worth; Send Thy Holy Ghost, and pour into our hearts that most excellent gift of charity, the very bond of peace and of all virtues, without which whosoever liveth is counted dead before Thee: Grant this for Thine only Son Jesus Christ's sake. Amen."

You see by this collect how much stress we are to lay on this one grace of charity; how absolutely necessary to salvation it is, and how excellent beyond all others.

First, charity is absolutely necessary to salvation; in such a sense necessary, that "without it all our doings are nothing worth." So we are taught, most expressly, in the Epistle for this day. "Though I speak with the tongues of men and of angels:" though I, or any other man, have in perfection the gift of tongues; the power of teaching all nations the truth in the very words of the Holy Ghost, yet if "I have not charity, I am become as sounding brass, or a tinkling cymbal," my words are no better than mere unmeaning sounds. And again, "though I have the gift of prophecy, and understand all mysteries and all knowledge;" whatever height and depth of understanding God has given one in divine things; "and though I have all faith, so that I could remove mountains," that is, though one had received from God's Spirit the power of working the most wonderful miracles, yet "without charity, it is nothing." Yet again, and more than all; "Though I bestow all my goods to feed the poor, and though I give my body to be burned," suffering even martyrdom for the sake of Christ, "and have not charity, it profiteth me nothing." So expressly are we taught, in the word of God, that "all our doings without charity are nothing worth."

Again, the collect says, that "without charity whatsoever liveth is counted dead before God;" which is, in other words, the same as we are taught by S. James, "Faith, without works, is dead, being alone." Believe as firmly as you may the things of God, and of another world, you have no more power to please God, than a dead man has to do the works of a living man, except so far as you have charity; that is, so far as you desire to please Him. This you may readily understand, by what happens every day within the experience of every family. What is the fault of undutiful children? the reason why their parents are displeased with them? Not their disbelieving who their parents are, nor their doubting what they would have them do; but their not caring to please and obey them. What is it which satisfies a father or mother, and makes them account a child really dutiful? Not the child's barely doing as he is bidden, but his doing it with a cheerful and affectionate mind. Whoever will consider this for a moment, will easily understand how charity, that is, a hearty desire to please God, comes to be so praised in the Gospel, and why the very best of works are no better than dead and useless, in the sight of Him Who knows the heart, if that desire be entirely wanting.

But Holy Scripture teaches us, secondly, the absolute excellency of this charity. Without it, all else is nothing; with it, every thing is right. Therefore it is called, both in the collect and in the Scriptures, the most excellent gift of the Holy Spirit: the very bond of peace, and of all virtues. It is called "the most excellent gift of charity," upon the authority of S. Paul himself; who having reckoned up all the most glorious of those gifts, which the Holy Ghost, sent down by our Saviour, poured so abundantly on the Church; Apostolic, prophetic, pastoral, grace; the powers of miracles, of healing, of tongues; follows up all with this notice, "And yet shew I unto you a more excellent way." And what is that more excellent way? It is no other than charity, of which we speak; which is declared, in the Epistle for this day, to be not only better than miracles and prophecy, but better even than faith and hope.

And whereas it is also entitled in the collect, "the very bond of peace, and of all virtues;" this is no more than S. Paul teaches us when he exhorts the Colossians "above all things" to "put on charity, which is the bond of perfectness;" and when he beseeches the Ephesians to "endeavour to keep the unity of the Spirit in the bond of peace." That is, he would have men understand that charity, the true love of God in Christ, in whatever heart it is really found, ensures the practice of all other virtues, all good, pure, and kind dispositions. And why? because he who loves another, of course does what he knows will please the object of his affection; watches continually for opportunities of doing so. He, therefore who loves God in earnest, will never neglect or slight his prayers; because God has encouraged him to pray, and is "near to all such as call upon Him faithfully." He will seek God's favour through Christ, knowing that in Him alone the Father can be well-pleased with sinners. He will never take God's Name in vain, for he has learned concerning all such, that God will not hold them guiltless. He will remember God's holy days; to do otherwise, is more especially to please himself instead of his Maker. He will honour his parents, for so God has commanded him; will be kind to his brethren, and to all mankind, as being made in the image of God; will strive and pray to be pure in heart, that he may see God by faith here, and enjoy Him in heaven hereafter. He will not steal, for it is breaking God's order; nor will he slander, for it is abusing God's best gift; nor will he indulge himself in covetous and discontented thoughts, for that is affronting the all-seeing God, as if He did not know our hearts. Thus you see, that whoever has the love of God in his heart, has that in him which will make him carefully obey all the commandments with a willing mind; and therefore it is well said of charity, that it is the bond of perfectness and of all virtues.

The necessity, then, and the excellency of charity, being thus plainly set forth in the words of the Holy Ghost, it is no wonder that all Christians, from the beginning, with one voice, should have agreed to praise and recommend charity beyond all other graces; no wonder, again, that the enemy of Christ and of Christians should have contrived abundance of counterfeits, many false pretenders to charity, many ways of deceiving souls, and flattering sinners with a false peace.

Against all such the Apostle in the text may furnish, if you will mark him, sufficient warning. "The end," says he, "of the commandment," the practical purpose, drift, and meaning, of all the instructions you receive from the Almighty, now or at any other time, from my mouth or in any other way, all may be summed up in one word, "charity." But then, as if by providing expressly against the wilful and careless mistakes, into which Christians, in all times, would be tempted, concerning the true notion of charity, he explains it by three distinct marks. No temper of mind, no course of conduct, deserves the sacred name of charity, unless it proceed from "a pure heart," and from "a good conscience," and from "faith unfeigned." Let us consider what errors most abound and prevail among men on this matter of charity, and we shall find full warning against them in these few words of S. Paul.

1. It is no unusual mistake, especially among young people, whose education has not been sufficiently serious, to confound charity with mere good-nature. Men are pleased with themselves and others for cheerful spirits and an obliging manner, and they too hastily take it for granted, that Almighty God in this respect is even such an one as themselves. But cheerful spirits and an obliging manner, though real blessings as far as they go, are not yet Christian graces, except they be inwardly sustained and encouraged by a true thankfulness to God our Saviour, and thorough dependence on His mercy through Christ. Then, they become part of charity; that heavenly grace, of which, among other things, we read that "she is kind, not easily provoked, seeketh

not her own, thinketh no evil;" not out of fancy or humour, but in order to please the God of love and peace, and to resemble His Son, our meek and merciful Redeemer. But if a man's good humour and kindness have nothing to do with the fear of God, in the first place they cannot be depended upon; disappointment, ill health, or strong provocation, may spoil and embitter such a temper: and in the next place, as it looks no farther than this present world, so *in* this present world, in the praise and love of acquaintance and friends, it will take out all its reward. The praise and love of God Almighty is too high and holy a blessing to be granted hereafter to those who care not for it, merely because they were good-tempered and friendly.

This most serious truth is intimated by the first caution of S. Paul in the text, that the charity which fulfils the law of God arises " out of a pure heart." Whereas it appears but too clearly, from the experience of every day, that the spurious charity of ordinary men, mere good-humour and obligingness of manner, is easily reconcileable with a defiled heart, with base pleasures, and abominable practices. "[a]The harp, and the viol, and the tabret, and pipe, and wine, are in their feasts: but they regard not the work of the Lord, neither consider the operation of His hands." What if they seem good-tempered for the time? let their favourite pleasures be interfered with, whether it be by God or man, and it will quickly be seen how little such good temper, depending entirely on mere temper, and not at all rooted on principle, is able to withstand disappointment or restraint. Let

[a] Is. v. 12.

the providence of God interfere, and we shall see how the intemperate man, who seemed perhaps so agreeable in his hours of enjoyment, can bear a sick bed, or the cravings of poverty; how fretfully, how churlishly he will behave himself, for want of a little sound religious principle to keep him patient and contented. Or suppose his course of riot is checked by some one having authority over him; what most commonly in such a case becomes of his boasted good-nature and kindness? These are plain, familiar instances. Many more might be given, but these are sufficient to convince any one, who will consider them with the slightest attention, that no impure heart can be depended on for even the outward show of charity; that is, a gracious and obliging demeanour. And as for the substance itself of this divine virtue, the love of God in Jesus Christ, it is a perfect enemy to all impurity; no heart can cherish the two together. Nothing, on the one hand, so deadens devotion, so entirely indisposes the soul for prayer, as being given up to those things, of which the Spirit of God has declared, that they are not fit to be named among Christians. And, on the other hand, the sincere and constant endeavour to keep yourself pure from these, will leave you open to the holy impressions, the heavenly hopes and desires, which the same good Spirit would put into your heart. Would you then learn the love of God, and so become fit for heaven? Begin by turning resolutely away from whatever you know will corrupt your imagination. You will soon find this task so hard that you will need continual prayer to accomplish it. That prayer, sincerely offered in the name of Jesus Christ, will draw down a blessing on your next endeavour: and thus by insensible degrees you will go on, increasing in purity and charity at once. These are the sober and devout exercises by which you may draw towards the end of the commandment, not mere inconsiderate cheerfulness and good-humour.

2. Neither, again, is Christian charity rightly esteemed of by those persons, who, when it is named, think directly of almsgiving, and such other outward favours; which indeed is perhaps the commonest notion of any concerning it. For what says the Apostle with respect to almsgiving? I have already observed what care he has taken to keep men from confounding it with charity; where he gives us to understand that it is conceivable for a man to give all to feed the poor, and yet to be without charity. A thing much to be reflected on by those, who think they have done great things, if they have spent part of their substance in that way. But concerning the giving of alms, and all other outward acts of kindness, they are part of charity, if they proceed from the love of God, not else; but the substance and essence of charity, the love of God itself, is within, and cometh, as S. Paul tells us, in the second place, of "a good conscience," and no other way. That is, the love of God is then perfect, when a man delights to have God near him, out of a humble and reasonable hope that his conduct is such as God approves of. That is the composed and steady devotion, which the commandments of God were intended to produce in you. And therefore it is here called " the end of the commandment;" and the way to come nearer and nearer to it, the way to have pleasure in God's

aweful Presence, is to use yourselves to keep the commandments; just as the way for a son or daughter to have pleasure in a parent's presence is to do what the parent would have done, even when he is out of sight. And that so much the more, as God can never be out of sight, can never cease for one moment to witness your thoughts, words, or deeds. So that to think seriously of Him, without a good and approving conscience, is more than the spirit of a man can long endure.

Take it, then, for a second warning, that men must not think they have Christian charity, the end of God's commandments, because they give such and such alms, or do such and such kind actions; but they must look to it that the answer of their consciences be encouraging in these and all other respects. For charity cometh "of a good conscience;" we love God, when we rejoice in the recollection that He is near us; and we cannot so rejoice, except we are conscious of trying to please Him.

3. But here a difficulty arises. Stained and imperfect as in reality the best duties of sinful man are, how dare he talk of an approving conscience? how can he presume, at his very best, to take pleasure in the thought of his Judge looking on? The difficulty is answered by the last words of the text. Charity comes not only of a pure heart, and of a good conscience, but also "of faith unfeigned:" faith and trust in the merciful wonders, which the God and Father of our Lord Jesus Christ has provided in His Gospel for penitent sinners. Take them into the account; lift up your eyes to the Cross of Christ; accept, with contrite and believing hearts, the cross

which He lays upon you, that you may not forfeit the reconciliation purchased long since by His precious Blood; take also into your account the offered grace of His Holy Spirit, to keep your hearts pure and your consciences calm for the future; and then the accusing remembrances of the past, though they must needs make you tremble at the presence of your Judge, yet need not make you turn away from it. The hope of pardon may accompany the bitter sense of transgression, and the full purpose of amendment of life may render us composed and calm in God's sight, while the recollection of past failures should keep us humble and afraid of ourselves. And when our thoughts turn towards our brethren, we shall heartily wish them all the good which Christ died to purchase for them. This is true Christian charity, to be practised in prayers and communions, and all purity and kindness on earth; and finally to be made perfect in heaven.

SERMON VII.

ALMIGHTY GOD NOTES THE USE WHICH WE MAKE OF HIS GIFTS.

SEPTUAGESIMA.

Ps. xciv. 9.

" He that planted the ear, shall He not hear? or He that made the eye, shall He not see?"

WE are come to Septuagesima Sunday, and are preparing for Lent. Lent, as you know, is a time of repentance: a time to clear one's conscience by humble confession, earnest prayer, and the best resolutions we can make. Septuagesima, and two more weeks, are appointed for special consideration, to make us ready for the great Lenten work of repentance. And we are directed at this time to think very much of the creation of the world. The history of it is appointed for the first Lesson this morning. When God's Church would turn our hearts to more serious and entire repentance, one of the first things she does is to put us in mind *Who* created us and all things, and *how* He created us.

Now, why should this be? How has the creation of the world so much to do with the repentance of Christian people, with your sins and mine, and with the searchings of our heart when we try to get free from our sins? Repentance comes of real, deep self-examination, and it is made up of sorrow for sin, confession of it, and real conversion to God in all holy obedience. What is there in the creation of heaven and earth to touch men's hearts so thoroughly and give them such a turn?

In the first place, when we think of creation, we think of the world and of every thing in it, as God's world, and not as our own. The light by which we see things, the air we breathe, the food on which we live, the animals that serve us, most of all our own souls and bodies, so wonderfully created after God's own Image, are so many precious talents intrusted to us. They are not our own, they are freely given us of One, Who had power to give or no, and now He has given, hath power to take away. We cannot keep any of them a moment longer than He approves of. And He gave them to us, not at random, but for His own great and good ends: according to the counsel of His own will. He gave us the light, which by His word He caused to shine out of darkness, that we by it might see how to do His work: not the work of His enemy, but His own work. He gave us the air, that breathing in it, we might spend all our breath to His praise and honour. He caused food to spring out of the earth, that we might be kept in life and strength until our appointed task was done. He made the sun, moon, and stars, and set them for lights, and for signs, that we might know our time, and walk orderly, serving Him and helping one another, in the way that He knew to be best. He formed all kinds of living creatures, some out of the water, some out of the dry land, that man being served and waited on by them, might the more freely put out all his strength in serving and waiting upon his God. Lastly He made man himself out "[a]of the dust of the earth, and breathed into his nostrils the breath of life," that he knowing something of God, might by his obedience become qualified to know more and more, to draw nearer and nearer to Him. The more we think on each day's work, the more plainly we see that every part of creation is a trust put by Almighty God into the hands of man whom He last created, to be used for His own glory, and for the good of man's soul. Whoever then has misused any part of it in any way, especially whoever has misused his own precious soul and body, which were made in God's own Image, must expect one day to suffer as those do, who have been greatly trusted and have broken their trust. As they have been unfaithful in what was another's, even His, He will not allow them to have any thing of their own. Only, He gives us time: time to repent, and if we will, time to amend. He allows us Lent, and the days before Lent, that we may make up our accounts, see how things stand, and do what we can to better ourselves, before we draw near to Him at Easter. This is one way, in which the history of creation may help to prepare us for that entire penitence and pardon, which, if we are sincere, will be granted us in the Holy week, and at Easter.

[a] Gen. ii. 7.

Another penitential lesson to be learned from the history of the creation is this: that He Who made the world, and Who made man last of all things, and left him on his trial, to see how he would use the world, has not however so left us, as not still to abide with us, witnessing every part of our behaviour. This is according to the Psalmist's reasoning in the text, "He that planted the ear, shall He not hear? He that formed the eye, shall He not see?" For we need Him to preserve, as much as we needed Him to create us. Without Him none of us could any more continue in being, than we could at first come into being without Him. Therefore, whenever any one of us exercises any of our outward senses, or of the inward powers of our souls, God is there, to behold and know how we do so, just as surely as when He gave Adam that sense or that power at first. You may be sure that the All-seeing is aware of every glance of your eye, every thought of your heart, because if He were not there, enabling you to look and to think, you could not look or think at all. And so as to hearing: He Who so formed *our* ears, that we might understand the sounds which others make with their tongues: did also form *their* tongues and endue them with power to utter sounds which our ears might understand: both powers, both of speaking and hearing, are of Him, and cannot be exercised without Him: He is therefore close at hand, marking both what men speak, and how they hear: He marks, and He cannot forget.

Now, my brethren, do you suppose there is any one of us, who has thoroughly and entirely considered this matter, and carried the remembrance of it into his daily and hourly life? He that made the eye with such nice and curious art, as all the most skilful persons on earth, I do not say can in no wise equal, but cannot even quite comprehend: He hath told us, and we know for certain, that He watches over and takes account of the use we make of that precious gift. As He seeth all things, so especially He seeth how we employ the eyes which He hath given us. He notices which way we turn them: what we look on, and from what we withdraw our looks. And this, when we reflect on it, will be found to make up a great part of our trial. I mean that if any Christian person, especially any young person, could come to have the complete command of his eyes, so as never to let them dwell for a moment on objects which our Lord hath forbidden, nor to express wrong tempers and passions, such an one would have made a great step towards real Christian perfection: he would have won a crown which cannot be won without very especial grace from God. For as of the tongue it is said by an Apostle [b], "None of the children of men can tame it;" meaning that God only can do that; and again, that "[c] if any one offend not in word, he is a perfect man, and able to bridle the whole body:" so, or very nearly so, might one speak of the eye of man; as it has been said by a very wise and holy writer: "[d] Remember that a wicked eye is an evil thing, and what is created more wicked than an eye?" Of course then, he whose eyes were at all times ordered by God's commandments, might be said to have overcome one of the worst enemies of his soul.

[b] S. James iii. 8.   [c] Ib. 2.   [d] Ecclus. xxxi. 13.

You know, my brethren, to how great an extent we naturally judge of people by their eyes, that is by what we observe of their looks. It helps us more than anything perhaps to make real acquaintance with them: especially when for any reason their outward actions are under restraint in our presence. Children, e. g. and others who dare not answer again, shew us generally what is in their hearts most plainly by the look of their eyes: and so even do dumb creatures, when one has any experience of them. And there is no one thing which we more constantly employ in making up our minds about strangers when we meet them. Well then, as we judge of our fellow creatures by the turn and expressions of their eyes, so, and to be sure much more certainly, does Almighty God judge of us.

There seem to be four commandments especially, to the keeping of which the command of the eye is absolutely needful. The first, the sixth, the seventh, and the tenth. For the proud man sins against the first commandment, making himself his own trust, and in a manner his own god: and the word of truth has said, "ᵉ Whoso hath a proud look and high stomach, I will not suffer him." A proud look: observe that, my brethren. Pride is very often seen in man's looks, and is disagreeable to their neighbours who see it: how much more is it hateful to God! Again, the sixth commandment may be very grievously broken by the eye: for hear how it was with Cain, when he first began to bear malice against his brother Abel: Cain, we read, "was very wroth and his countenance fell." And the good Lord expostu-

ᵉ Ps. ci. 7.

lated with him, "Why art thou wroth, and why is thy countenance fallen?" By which we see that even such things as a cross, sulky, spiteful look if at all indulged, are serious offences against God, and may be the beginnings of murder. Then as to the seventh commandment, how sadly, and also how easily that may be broken by unchristian using of the eye, we understand at once, if we will but receive in faith the most plain and most fearful sentence of the Judge of all: "*I* say unto you, Whosoever looketh on a woman to lust after her, hath committed adultery with her already in his heart." And to mention no more commands: who can doubt that both the eighth and the tenth are continually broken in their sense and spirit by greedy or discontented persons gazing on what is not theirs, and with eye as well as heart, longing to steal it, or fretting that they cannot have it? So Ahab looked on Naboth's vineyard, Gehazi on the presents offered to his master, Achan on the forbidden spoils at Jericho: David, from a distance on the wife of Uriah. If they had not looked, they would not have touched: if they had not gazed and coveted, they would not have stolen: if they had resolutely turned away their eyes when they found the wicked imagination rising in their hearts, what sin, what misery, would that little self-denial have saved them! My younger brethren, I speak to you especially: make yourselves quite sure of it, the guard of your senses is the best guard of your hearts. Make a covenant, like Job, with your eyes, i. e. make and keep a strict rule to withdraw them at once from improper objects: Do this one thing, not once nor twice, but constantly: do it, in no reliance on yourselves but in fear and trembling, with such prayer as that of David, "*Turn away mine eyes lest they behold vanity:*" guard your looks in earnest, and I dare promise you, your thoughts and still more your actions will be guarded by One more watchful than you are.

If you come to Church next Sunday morning, you will hear the history of the first sin, the history of Adam and Eve, how they were tempted to eat of the forbidden fruit; and that will shew you plainly enough, if you attend to it, how exceedingly it concerns us to set a guard upon our senses, more particularly on our eyes. For if Eve, when she heard that first evil word of the devil, "Ye shall not surely die," had refused to listen any longer, remembering that He Who planted the ear was invisibly at hand and heard Himself so contradicted, and could not be pleased with her for listening, she had saved herself and her husband from that grievous sin. And if even when he had finished his wicked speech she had still turned her eyes from the tempting tree, saying to herself, "He that made the eye, shall He not see?" Will He not notice which way I look, and punish me if I look and long for what He has forbidden?—If Eve had been guided by wise and good thoughts like these, then the sin which was just beginning would have been stayed *in* the beginning. Sight would not have led to touching, nor touching to tasting, nor tasting to the world's ruin. As it was then, so it has been ever since. Those have pleased God best, have been most guarded from deadly sin, who in humble fear have curbed their

---
f Ps. cxix. 37.

eyes and ears, refusing **to look** upon or listen **to evil:** and those who without scruple have listened to and looked **at** every thing they fancied, have made **fearful shipwreck** of **their** innocency: and if they *are* **saved, will be saved** "ᵍ **so as by fire,"** not **without anxious** repentance and bitter suffering.

Indeed, my brethren, **all our senses and powers, both inward** and outward, **but especially our sight and hearing, our eyes** and our ears, **are a great** and fearful trust from our Maker. They are in some sense a portion of the wonderful Image of Himself in which He made **us. As** He heareth **and** seeth all things, and judgeth them according to what He heareth and seeth, so hath He given to each one of us, mankind, **ears, eyes and a conscience:** ears to hear, **eyes to see, and a sense of right and wrong** to give judgement on what we hear and see. We then, even in **these** our outward senses, are in some **sort** an image **of Him:** and woe be unto us, if we defile and profane His Image. Nay more; **by virtue of that mystical Union, whereby we are made, all of us, true members of** Jesus Christ, **our very outward limbs, our eyes and** ears, are truly **the** eyes and ears of Jesus **Christ:** how dare we then put them to unclean or undutiful uses? **Whatever** we listen to, whichever **way** we look, **He is there.** And as surely as He **in silence is continually watching** and listening to **us** now, so **surely the time will come, and that** before very long, when **we too** on our part shall **see Him** and hear openly. **We** shall **see His Face: will it look on** us sternly **or** in love? **We** shall hear His **voice:** will it bid us draw nigh **or** depart? Which-

ᵍ 1 Cor. iii. 15.

ever of the two words be, it will stand for ever. It will be true and just: we shall not be able to gainsay it. And it will depend in great measure on the words we have listened to, and the sights we have looked upon, in this our time of trial, in our youth especially. Every word then, every look, is of consequence: and we had need pray with all our hearts 'God be in our ears and in our hearing: God be in our eyes and in our seeing: God be in our minds and in our thinking: God so vouchsafe to be with us in this world, that we fail not to be with Him in the world to come.'

SERMON VIII.

FAITH THE FOUNDATION OF ALL RELIGION.

SEPTUAGESIMA.

HEB. xi. 6.

"*Without faith it is impossible to please Him: for he that cometh to God must believe that He is, and that He is a rewarder of them that diligently seek Him.*"

THESE two things, that God is, and that He is a Rewarder, are the beginning of all religion: and therefore, as you heard this morning, they stand at the very threshold of the whole Bible: they are taught us in the very first chapter of God's Holy Book. "In the beginning God created the heaven and the earth:" i. e. God IS, one great Almighty Eternal Being; before all things, and by Whom all things consist. That is the first verse of this wonderful lesson, and the last is like unto it. "God saw all that He had made, and behold it was very good." On these two verses, as I said, hangs all that we mean when we speak of religion, the whole of man's service done to God, both inward and outward. God is, else we could not serve Him: God maketh and loveth what is good, He abhorreth and putteth down what is evil, else it were not worth while to serve Him. Again, God is, and therefore the world was and is governed by Him: God is good, and therefore the world is *so* governed, as that it will surely be in the end well with the righteous and ill with the wicked.

These, as I said, are the foundation points, the very alphabet, of all religion: and both of these, as S. Paul tells us in the text, require our faith. "He that cometh to God must believe that He is, and that He is a rewarder of them that diligently seek Him." He must *believe*: he cannot see it with his eyes, but with his mind's eye he must so look at, as if he could see it in very deed; he must not at all permit himself to doubt it. This is what Scripture means by faith: for as S. Paul had said just before, "faith is the substance," the realizing, as it is sometimes called, "of things hoped for, the evidence of things not seen," i. e. venturing all upon them, as if you could see them. We do not use to say, we believe things which are in sight; no one in his senses would say, I believe it is now day and not night: we *see*, we *know*, we are *sure* of, such things as that: but "what a man actually seeth, why doth he yet believe and hope for?" Now of course we cannot see God: no man may see His Face and live; no man hath seen Him as He is at any time: there were indeed those who saw Him in the form of the Man Christ Jesus, when He went in and out among us in the days of His flesh: but they did not see Him *as* God: and of them, as of all as the rest, it might be said, God made Himself known to them not by sight but by faith. We must believe, then, for we cannot see, that God is: and we must also believe, for we cannot see, that He is always on the side of the good the dutiful, the obedient, a Rewarder of those that diligently seek Him. Certainly it does not always appear so : certainly there are and always have been occasions wherein even the most contented and faithful spirits have been sorely tempted to cry out with the prophet Jeremiah, "ᵃWherefore doth the way of the wicked prosper? wherefore are all they happy that deal very treacherously?" or with the Psalmist, " I cleansed my heart in vain, and washed my hands in innocency." But faith helps us to endure all this, as it has all along helped the holy martyrs and saints of God: teaching us to look not to the things which are seen, and which are merely for a time, but to the things unseen, which are for ever. Faith assures us of a day when He will come and judge the world in righteousness: He to Whom the promise is made, "I will put all things under His feet:" then and not till then shall we see with our eyes that " He is a Rewarder of them that diligently seek Him," but in the mean time "we see not yet all things put under Him." God's perfect righteousness, as the just Governor of all—this, as well as His Being, is out of sight, and will be so as long as this imperfect world endures. He that cometh to God must *believe*, for he cannot *see*, that God is: he must *believe*, for he cannot see, that He is one Who never fails to reward His dutiful servants.

Most plain therefore it is, that without believing there can be no religion at all, " without faith it is impossible to please God." Then comes the serious question, Whether you and I, whether each particular Christian, has or has not faith. A serious question

ᵃ Jer. xii. 1.

indeed, on the answer to which the very life and welfare of our souls entirely depends. Observe, I say that the life and welfare of our souls depends on our *having* true faith: I do not say it depends on our *knowing* that we have it; for very often, I well know, good men's minds are so overclouded, by ill health, or low spirits, or something which God permits to disturb and bewilder them for the time, that they feel as if they had no belief at all, while they are nevertheless endeavouring to give the right scriptural proof before God and man that they are believers: and what is that right scriptural proof? You may judge of it by certain cases which occur continually in men's worldly and temporal lives. E.g. a sum of money is promised to a man, on his applying to such a person, or performing such and such a work: the journey or work, puts him more or less out of his way: it costs him money, time, trouble, for the present: nevertheless he makes the venture, travels so many miles, works hard so many hours, lays out such and such a sum, with a view of obtaining the larger sum which is promised. Why? because he has faith in the person promising: the benefit is all to come, it is all out of sight, but he believes in it, therefore he takes pains about it: and when you meet him on his journey, or see him at his work, or become aware of his putting himself to expense, then you judge him, of course, to be a real believer in what he has been told and taught. Or a person is ill, very ill: and his friends and himself have faith in a particular physician: how do we know they have faith? not simply by their talking in praise of him, how many he has cured, and how he cured them, or recommending other people to seek to him: but if they have money to pay him, they actually call him in, and put the case under his direction. Nothing short of this would convince the neighbours that they really thought so well of him as they professed. In short, life is full of such cases and in every one of them one may truly say, that men shew their faith by their works, and that their faith and feelings and convictions, if not acted on, could not possibly do them any good, and might as well not exist at all. Just so it is, Holy Scripture informs us, in respect of religious faith. Your Lord and Saviour promises you, not a sum of money, but unfailing treasure in the heavens, if you will only apply for it in earnest. You say you believe, you speak earnestly about it to others, you wonder how they can reject such gracious offers, you dwell with a sort of pleasure on the merciful invitation He sends you, and the fair and noble accounts of that blessed home which He hath caused to be written for your learning: but you do not apply to Him in earnest. Why? Because you have given your heart to some poor transitory matter, some one or more of the treasures which men try to lay up for themselves on earth, and you do not in good earnest make heaven and the love of Christ the principal thing.

Or again: you are sick, very sick, not perhaps in body but in mind and heart: you have met with troubles and disappointments in life, God has denied you something on which your heart was set, or has brought on you the thing of which you were greatly afraid, or if you have outwardly seemed to succeed and have your own way, the sweetness has in a manner turned to bitterness in the very enjoyment, as Solomon in the midst of his wealth and pleasure cried out, over and over again, "Vanity of vanities, all is vanity." One way or another, you are sorely sick at heart: yet there is One near, close at hand, present in the very deep of your heart and soul, of Whom you say, that you believe Him to be your Saviour, i. e. an infallible Physician, able and willing to cure all the diseases of your soul. Why do you not in all seriousness go to Him, lay yourself and your troubles at His Feet, hearken what He shall say concerning you, what in His loving wisdom He may prescribe for your healing, and simply take His medicines and avoid what He forbids: as those did who came to Him of old to be cured of leprosy, or any other evil disease? Alas, you have not the heart to do so. You know in your secret soul that it is the only way, but you have gone on so long in the custom of keeping at a distance from Him, that you feel as if you *could* not draw near to Him, could not ask Him to help you to do so. And what is saddest of all, too often there is something amiss, something contrary to His holy law, which you cannot as yet prevail on yourself to give up: so in spite of your inward convictions, you go on wilfully miserable and far from Christ: and the chances are that you will so go on to the end.

Yet you call yourself a Christian, and think you have faith and expect to be saved by your faith. But the Scripture plainly asks, Will such faith save you? Nay, it is dead, being alone. It is as when a person has been struck with a palsy in some limb: he has the limb, he knows he has it, but he can do himself no good with it, for it is paralysed. The faith of him who has no heart to *behave* like one who believes, who just cries, 'Lord, Lord,' with a certain feeling in his heart at the moment, but does not the things which our Lord says, do you know what such faith is likened to in the word of God? It is an aweful saying, "ᵃ Thou believest that there is one God, thou doest well, the devils also believe and tremble." The Evil spirits, lost as they are for ever, they believe with an undoubting certainty that there is One God and none other but Him; they cannot help believing, for they feel it by His just and severe punishments: but it is a faith which does them no good, nor ever will do them any, they only tremble when they think of it. Is it not fearful, my brethren, to think that this is what we are drawing nearer to, every time we sin against our own better knowledge? Pharaoh had such faith as this: he was forced against his will to know and believe that wherein he dealt proudly the Lord was above him, that the Lord was righteous but he and his people were wicked. But it was a dead faith: it did not in any measure soften his heart or subdue his will. And so, when he *had* been forced to yield a sort of outward obedience to the terrors of the Lord, he did but fly back the more eagerly to his former wickedness as soon as ever he had opportunity. Felix had a touch of such faith as this: when he heard S. Paul reasoning of justice, temperance, and judgement to come, he being the most unrighteous of judges, and an open adulterer, trembled: but his trembling was too much like that of the devils, and so it would seem, was his faith,

---

ᵃ S. James ii. 19.

what faith he had: for nothing came of it but this, that he ordered the Apostle away till a more convenient season. And, saddest of all, Judas had a touch of this faith: he could not but know and believe, in a way, what power his Master has, how He hates sin, how true all His words are sure to prove: with his own ears he heard Christ declare it were good for the man who should betray Him if that man had never been born: yet he went on from bad to worse: his belief, such as it was, only took him farther and farther from the love of Christ, till it drove him to despair and self-murder.

So it is, brethren; people who are in love with any sin, and are yet aware of our Lord's sentence pronounced against all wilful and obstinate sin, cannot endure the remembrance of what they too well know they are hastening towards; and accordingly they get as near as they can into a kind of unbelief, believing in God as their Creator and Preserver, but not believing in Him as a Righteous Judge, Who will cause all our sins to find us out. They try to cheat themselves as the devil cheated Eve, with the saying, "ye shall not surely die." The prophet Balaam, fallen as he was, yet knew better than they: for he declared, "[b] God is not a man, that He should lie, nor the son of man that He should repent: hath He said and shall He not do it? or hath He spoken and shall He not make it good?" But they say,—too many around us, who think themselves believers do in effect say, 'God does lie, and God will repent,' in respect of the punishment He has threatened against certain sins: He has said concerning all uncleanness, they

[b] Num. xix. 23.

who do such things shall not inherit the kingdom of God. But ye say, When a man and woman are betrothed, it is no longer deadly sin, but a pardonable fault: God will lightly pass over it. And again, God has said plainly, Thou shalt not steal, servants must not purloin: and in that terrible case of Judas He has set his mark especially upon the sin of persons in trust, when they take a very little at a time, thinking it will not be missed, and does not signify. But ye, more or less commonly, say, I fear, among yourselves, 'It is a matter of course, almost all help themselves occasionally, some to one thing, some to another, we will not believe that it is so very serious a sin.'

By these instances you may plainly see how the love of any sin, the continued love of it after warning, leads to unbelief and hardness of heart. If they will go on making light of sin, there is no help for it, they must needs be withdrawing themselves from Christ. For a while you may appear to yourself to be as much a true believer as before: but you may depend on it that as soon as ever you have been warned of a sin and made light of it, you have made a great step downwards, not only towards that particular sin, but towards general irreligion and unbelief. You see this plainly enough in respect of sins to which you are not particularly tempted. The drunkard sees how bad it is for the covetous to make light of covetousness, and the covetous man wonders how the drunkard can possibly think of ever going to heaven. Only let each apply to himself the caution which he would be ready to apply to the other. Let him say to himself, not to his neighbour, 'How can I do this great wickedness? If I do it, where is my faith?' And where any have been graciously preserved from ill and helped in goodness, let them never forget nor doubt, that as their innocency is God's gift, so, to preserve it, they must go to Him Who gave it. They must go to Him continually by faith and prayer. If they trust to themselves they are lost.

SERMON IX.

WORK THE LAW OF OUR LORD'S KINGDOM, BOTH NATURAL AND SPIRITUAL.

SEPTUAGESIMA.

S. MATTHEW xx. 6.

"Why stand ye here all the day idle?"

"MAN goeth forth to his work and to his labour until the evening[a]." It was the law made in the beginning. Even before the fall, when Adam and Eve were as yet pure and happy in the garden of Eden, they had their appointed task. They were set there to dress it and to keep it. After the fall, the same law continued, man was still to work; only having become a sinner he was now to work as it were in chains; and what was before his refreshment and exercise, brought weariness of body and mind, the sweat of the brow, and a painful sense that whether he will or no, he must work unless he is to starve. In no condition, at no time, is it our Maker's will that we should be idle. From the beginning each one of us has had a task and a time to do it in. And

[a] Psalm civ. 23.

if persons neglect their task, and let their time run out unemployed, their Master's voice is heard sooner or later, "Why stand ye here all the day idle?" Either their own hearts reprove them, or their neighbours remark on them, or some one who has a care for them stirs them up, and if they will not attend, they sink down into all manner of mischief and misery even in this present world: as it is written Idleness "[b] shall clothe a man with rags."

But our God is not a hard Master, such as that wicked servant in the parable imagined Him, "reaping where He has not sown:" but as He appointed His creatures their work from the beginning, so it pleased Him to appoint Himself a work also: the work of preserving and providentially ordering all things which Himself had made: and when sin had thrown all into confusion, the work of recovering and renewing all: for so the Redeemer Himself spake, "[c] My Father worketh hitherto, and I work:" My Father in preserving the world which He had made: I in redeeming or preparing to redeem, the lost fallen race of Adam.

Yes, my brethren, herein is love: love unspeakable, inconceivable; that at the very time when our Lord and Judge came down from heaven, and called Adam and Eve out of their hiding-place, and passed that sentence upon our whole sinful race, "Cursed is the ground for thy sake;" "In the sweat of thy face shalt thou eat bread;" at the very time that He assigned us our portion of hard work, He also vouchsafed to set Himself a task, the task of redeeming us, and He lost no time in it. Even before the sentence was

[b] Proverbs xxiii. 21.   [c] S. John v. 17.

passed, the very chapter which gives the account of man's fall, gives also the first promise of his Redemption: "[d] I will put enmity between" the serpent "and the woman, and between thy seed and her seed: it shall bruise thy head, and thou shalt bruise his heel." Thus, very early in the morning, did the Good Householder begin to go out to hire labourers unto His vineyard: even to our sinful father and mother He gave the offer, admitting them to hope and repentance, though He drove them out of Paradise; but still they were to work; not only outwardly, to till the earth from which they were taken, but spiritually also, as penitents, to serve and please Him as well as they could for the remaining hours of their day of life. So very early did the Son of God say in a manner to His Father, "[e] A Body hast Thou prepared Me.... lo, I come to do Thy will, O God:" that will whereby in due time all believers were to be "[f] sanctified through the offering of the Body of Jesus Christ once for all."

And as He began early, so He went on. He continued to hire and employ labourers to work under Him for the good of His people, and for His Father's glory, quite down to the time when He was to be Himself Incarnate, and to set up His true vineyard, the Holy Catholic Church in the world. All the whole chain and succession of holy men and women, the congregation of saints of the Old Testament, from the first to the last: from Abel to S. John Baptist, were so many labourers hired one after another to work for their day in the vineyard of the Lord of Hosts: in the holy patriarchal families first, after-

[d] Gen. iii. 15. [e] Heb. x. 5. 7. [f] Ib. 10.

wards in the holy nation and peculiar people: as He saith, "⁵ The vineyard of the Lord of Hosts is the house of Israel, and the men of Judah His pleasant plant." Each one had his proper task; as Noah to build the Ark, Abraham to be the father and pattern of the faithful, Moses to bring the people out of Egypt, and Joshua to bring them into Canaan, David to establish the kingdom and prepare for the temple, Solomon to build the same temple, the Prophets to give each his own message, S. John Baptist to prepare the way of the Lord. And when the Lord came and His kingdom was set up, still the law was just the same. The Son of Man, when He went into that far country, gave certain commissions to His servants, and to every man his work. Every Christian has his own special work in addition to the common work and duty imposed upon all, To fear God and keep His commandments. It is grace indeed from beginning to end, yet still so, that we are to do our part. For as an ancient saint said, " He that made us, and redeemed us, and regenerated us, without ourselves, will not save us without ourselves." And so, as the welfare of this outward and visible world depends on our doing our part in it, by His help, and under His providence, so in a manner does the welfare of His spiritual kingdom. He hath said, "Six days shalt thou labour, and do all thy work." Those words are quite as much a part of the fourth commandment, as that which comes after, "The seventh day is the sabbath." We might as well think to please Him by merely resting on one day, and living all the other days at random, as we may

⁵ Is. v. 7.

think to save our souls by leaving them to Him and taking no care for them ourselves. In all generations, and to every one of us, the word of the Lord is fulfilled which He spake in this day's Gospel. He is ever hiring labourers into His vineyard, setting to each a task, appointing to each a time, promising to each a reward.

All are hired by the Great Householder, but not all at the same time. To some He cometh early in the morning, to some at the third, sixth, or ninth, or even at the eleventh hour: i. e. to some at the beginning of life, to others when their time in this world is more or less of it passed away. To all of *us* I suppose it would be true to say, He came early in the morning: even when we were newly born, He took us up in His Arms and made us members of Himself, and at the same time we agreed with Him by a plain and strong covenant, to go and work the whole day, i. e. the whole of our life, in His Vineyard the Church.

We have all been hired and our reward set plainly before us. As those workmen in the parable could not doubt that they should receive their penny at the end of the day, in recompense of their day's work faithfully done, so to every one of us it has been plainly said from the beginning, 'You have been made a member of Christ, a child of God, and an inheritor of the kingdom of heaven. The kingdom of heaven is yours by free gift, if you will not throw it away. While so many of your fellow creatures all over the wide world are never hired at all, and of those who have been hired, so many have had to wait until half, or more than half, of their hours for working were over, you, as soon as ever you were born, were engaged in this best of works: this God has been your God from your birth; will you not have Him for your Guide until death?"

We have been all hired and we know it: how is it that so many of us have not as yet begun our day's work? I say, not yet begun: for you know very well, my brethren, that neither good nor reward will come of your professing and calling yourselves Christians, if you are not really trying to love and serve your Saviour with all your heart, mind, soul and strength. That is the vineyard you are to cultivate, the blessed kingdom of God within you, "righteousness, peace, and joy in the Holy Ghost." If you are not constantly striving and praying for this, you are no workmen, but idlers, and have already forfeited your wages. You may say, 'We are not heathens, we are within the vineyard, we are not standing idle in the market place.' Nay, but how will that help you? What signifies your being in the vineyard, if you are doing nothing there? He who is standing idle, will he be pardoned because he is in the vineyard, and not in the market place, in the Church and not in the heathen world? Nay, rather his case is the worst of the two, there is something so very wilful in standing by your work and not putting your hand to it. You cannot say, as those last workmen in the parable, that it is because no man hath hired you. No: you were hired, as I have shown you, years ago: and more than that, your gracious Master the good Lord of the vineyard, has been with you all along, by His Almighty Spirit and by the voice of His Church, calling upon you from time to time to consider, before it be too late how fast the hours are wearing away, and your work hardly yet begun. To some He cometh especially at the third, to some at the sixth, to some at the ninth hour: and what is yet more wonderful and gracious, He cometh again and again, hour after hour, to the same persons. As long as you continue in this world and are able to work, He doth not altogether give you up. Men scorn Him at the third hour, and go on standing idle, and yet He cometh again at the sixth, ninth, nay even at the eleventh hour. But observe, brethren, that either of these hours may be the eleventh or last hour to any one of us. Our sun may go down while it is yet day: and if we be found then standing idle, our time, our work, and our reward will be gone for ever, and what can we expect but the sentence of the unprofitable servant, "[h] Cast him into outer darkness; there shall be weeping and gnashing of teeth."

There are some in this place, to whom especially one might say at the time, "It is the third hour, and the Master is come and calleth you." Who are they? The young persons who are now of age to be confirmed. That age or near it is just the time meant by the third hour. I will try and explain this to you. You know there are twelve hours of work, and when the third of those hours is over, of course one quarter of the work time is done. The third hour then answers to that point in a man's life in which according to God's usual providence he may be considered to have spent a quarter of his time. Allow seventy years for his whole time, and the

[h] S. Matt. xxv. 30.

third hour will be about seventeen: about the age, as you know, when men are summoned to receive God's blessing in Confirmation that they may be able to work steadily in His vineyard. This then is the case of those among you, whether youths or maidens, who are now invited to be confirmed. It is the third hour, and you are standing in the vineyard, the most part of you, alas! standing idle: for few indeed begin in earnest to turn to God in the early morning of their lives: few indeed are the Christian children who tread in the steps of the Holy Child Jesus, from the very first dawn of understanding, increasing in wisdom as in stature, "and in favour with God and man." So it is unhappily, that when the great Householder comes to you at the third hour, and calls you to be confirmed, He most commonly finds you standing idle: but will you go on doing so after He has called you? Thou hearest Him saying "ʲSon, go work to-day in My vineyard:" canst thou find in thy heart to say to Him, "I will not?" Alas! too many do so: too many even in our days, which pride themselves in their light and knowledge, refuse to hear the voice of the charmer, stop their ears, openly and on purpose, against their Saviour's loving invitation: they say to Him, "ᵏDepart from us, for we desire not the knowledge of Thy ways." They make up their minds, for the present at least, not to set about His work at all: they had rather be turned out of the vineyard altogether. Hereafter, some day or other, they may repent and go, but at this time their mind is, simply to say, "I will not." There are not, I hope, very many such, but too certainly there

---

ʲ S. Matt. xxi. 28.   ᵏ Job xxi. 14.

are some: and **surely they** are in great danger: surely all good Christians **who** know of any such **are** bound to pity and pray for them: surely we ought **to** remember them both in our Litanies and **in** Holy Communion, and beseech the great Intercessor by His **grace to** deliver **them from hardness of heart and contempt of** His word and commandment.

To some it may seem mere boyish **lightness** when **youths of fifteen, eighteen, or twenty, put off** our Lord's instruction from them, and say they care not **to be** confirmed, nor to come nearer to their Saviour. But have not those youths souls? and can those souls be saved without Christ? **And** will He **save them** if they refuse **to come** near Him? What if they should die to-day, or tomorrow, while they are still standing idle? **What** will then become of them? It will be as if they were turned **out** of the vineyard, **no other** work found for them, **their penny a** day **forfeited, and they with nothing to live upon for** eternity.

Others have so far had better thoughts **that they** have answered His Fatherly call, and when **He said** "Go work in My vineyard," **work** in My Church, and household, and in the saving of **thine** own soul, **for the rest of** this **day,** this life of thine: they have **made the proper answer "I go sir:"** but are they **all** going in earnest? **They have given in their** names **to** be confirmed: but do **they really consider** that in so doing **they were in fact** giving in their names to Christ, enlisting, so to speak, for harder **and** more dangerous duty in His service; setting **about** great things, and therefore seeking a double **portion of His Spirit?** I would it might be so: but it is the very shame and grief of the Church that in all Confirmations there are so many who come for form's sake, or because other young people do; there is no seriousness of heart in them: they do not make their coming a matter of prayer: they have never set their hearts in earnest to contemplate the awful Presence of Him before Whom they are so soon to stand in order to make their vows to Him, and to kneel in order to receive His blessing. They are not watching themselves from day to day: they are not learning to love and fear Him in earnest: they are not vexing themselves more than they used to do, about their daily sins, and backslidings, and negligences: each night when they lie down they are so much nearer their Confirmation, but they are not the better prepared for it. And what will the end be? When they go back, seemingly to their work in the vineyard, will they not be found yet standing idle, or worse, doing all sorts of mischief? It is a sad story, but too common. But let us hope and pray, that there may be some, and those more and more, who will suffer their hearts to be touched by the grace which their good Lord now so kindly offers them. Let us hope and pray that when the day of Confirmation comes, as Jesus Christ will be surely here, with His servant the Bishop, waiting to lay His Hands on you, and His Holy Spirit to enter in and dwell in your souls, and His blessed Angels to witness, and record all, so there will be many a young heart reverently and lovingly submitting itself wholly to Him, earnestly desiring to be His for ever, and daily to increase in His Holy Spirit. Oh, how will Jesus, beholding, love them! with what courage and modesty will they go forth on their way, through the troublesome world! how will they long for the Angels' Food, of which thenceforth they will be invited and privileged to partake! and how, if they cast not themselves away, will it strengthen and refresh them more and more, until they come to His everlasting kingdom! The good Lord increase the number of such worthy and happy candidates for His holy Confirmation: and to those (alas! too many) who might have been such and were not, may He grant the grace of an earnest and timely repentance: that if so be, we may serve and please Him, though it be at the eleventh hour.

SERMON X.

HOW TO PROFIT BY SAINTLY EXAMPLES.

SEPTUAGESIMA.

S. MATTHEW x. 41.

"*He that receiveth a righteous man* in the name of a *Righteous Man, shall receive a righteous man's reward.*"

FOR three weeks before Lent, the Church seems in a manner to keep reminding us that Lent is coming, by the very names of the Sundays, Septuagesima, Sexagesima, Quinquagesima; all which mean, so long before Easter; whereas we had now for some Sundays been looking backwards to the Epiphany.

Why is this change made? Because Lent is a time of particular trial, and the Church in her charity would have all her children prepare themselves against it with good thoughts and prayers.

The time of Lent, as you know, is a space of forty days before Easter, during which all Christians are to withdraw themselves, as best they may, from the world, and to get ready, by fasting and prayer, by self-examination and confession, by all kinds of holy mortification, for the holy week of our Lord's Passion and Resurrection.

Lent, therefore, is a time in which we endeavour to draw nearer to God than ever we have been yet, and to keep ourselves at a greater distance from sin. It is a time of conversion, a time of renouncing the world, a time of taking up the cross and following Christ. It is in its measure as really and truly a great trial for every one of us, as our Lord's forty days in the wilderness were a trial and temptation to Him. As He was led up there of the Spirit to be tempted of the devil, so the Holy Ghost is even now about to call us every one out of the world; and the Evil one will, of course, be busy in tempting us to despise that call, and throw the blessed opportunity away. Lent cannot leave us just as it found us: if we are not the better for it, we shall be the worse.

Therefore the Church, in great love and care for our souls, gives us notice for some time before, as our Saviour gave notice to His disciples of the coming of the Holy Ghost. The gift is very precious and Divine, and we had need prepare ourselves for it with very serious and reverential thoughts.

What I mean will be the better understood, by imagining for a moment how we should feel, if Almighty God had given us notice that some great saint was to come visibly among us at such and such a time, to stay just so long, and that, on purpose that we might have a chance of becoming better by his holy example, by praying and fasting with him, and hearing his Divine instructions. Suppose we had notice from S. Paul, as the Corinthians had, "I will come to you and tarry a time with you, if the Lord permit:" would it not make us very thoughtful? Should we not have a fear and anxiety in our hearts, lest so great a saint should come among us, and we prove never the better for his presence? Now the annual return of Lent is like the coming of a saint among us. A holy time is a token of Christ's nearer Presence, as a holy person would be.

And now that visible and outward holiness seems in so great measure to have passed away from the earth, now that we know not who are saints, and have seldom reason to think that any such come near us, it seems so much the greater mercy of God, as often as the season of repentance and holy self-denial comes round. It stands to us, if we have grace so to take it, instead of a saint's presence; it is a true token from Almighty God to the penitent, bringing fragrance and comfort from heaven; a token that He is with us; that we may have good hope, that we are not cut off from Him as we deserved. If we have not very unthankful, irreverent hearts, surely we shall have it in our thoughts before it comes, we shall wish and pray to be made worthy of the heavenly guest.

But now there are many persons, too many, who seem to think that they for their part have little or nothing to do with Lent. They account it, perhaps, very well that it was observed in the olden times: they have no doubt there are persons in the world who may be much the better for it; but somehow or another they persuade themselves that it was not intended for them.

Now these same persons, if they saw a holy man or woman, a true saint of God, coming among them, how would they behave in regard of that favoured one? Would they really try to be the better for his presence? Would they think it was a token from God, which could not safely be neglected? Or would they pass it over, as something very wonderful, perhaps, but not immediately concerning them?

For example, suppose again what I said just now; suppose the blessed Apostle S. Paul were actually to come here and live awhile in this place; no doubt it would cause a great deal of talk: there would be great anxiety to see and hear him, much wondering how he would go on, talkings and questionings and reports concerning him in every company, and by every fireside; but when his ways of life came to be known, how many would think it necessary to follow him? I do not mean to follow him exactly, but according to their own measure. How many would esteem it their duty to live by the same principles as S. Paul?

For instance; S. Paul would not "lead about a sister, a wife," that he might be free to serve God the more perfectly: how many of us, for the same reason, would refrain from any thing which they thought they might take without sin? S. Paul "kept under" his own body, dealt rudely with it, afflicted it with fastings and watchings, that it might be more entirely under the command of his spirit: but do not the generality of Christians, without scruple, allow themselves all pleasures which are not positively wicked?

In short, we may judge a little what effect the presence of a real saint would have among us, by observing how men behave towards those, whom they, rightly or wrongly, esteem in comparison saints. Every one of us would be able at once to name some few among his acquaintance, whom he considers to be more religious, stricter, more serious, more particular than the rest. What are our thoughts regarding such persons? Do we at all bring their example home to ourselves? Is not this too commonly the case, that we either coldly admire them at a great distance, or (though it be shocking to utter the words) actually come to scorn, or envy, or dislike them?

Some sort of goodness it is impossible to help admiring; as, for instance, extreme charity to the poor, unwearied kindness in waiting on the sick, courage and faithfulness in standing by those who are put under our care, whatever it may cost us. Those who have the least heart to spend their own money, or to put themselves into danger, must yet in their hearts feel that there is something great and noble in such behaviour: they naturally respect it, and in most cases it disposes them kindly towards those who practise it.

But the misfortune is, they think it nothing to them. It is too far above them, too high out of their sight. Just as we may imagine any rich man in Jerusalem, when he was told of the first Christians, how at the preaching of S. Peter they sold their possessions and goods, and laid the money at the Apostles' feet, to be distributed to all men according to their needs. Worldly persons, hearing it, might wonder, and say it was noble, but there would be an end: they would never dream of altering their own practice at all in consequence of it: they would say it was quite out of their way.

Surely, we are all too apt to put up with thoughts

of this kind, whenever we hear or read of any act of high Christian devotion or goodness, which we cannot help admiring, but have not the heart to imitate. We say to ourselves, "It is natural for such and such a person to do so; he has a call to it, a taste for it; but I have no such call, it is not therefore necessary for me:" and so we let the whole matter pass, and are never the better for the great and noble patterns which God's providence throws in our way.

But there are other cases again more painful than these: cases in which, as I just now said, we are tempted even to scorn, if not to hate, those whom we feel to be better than ourselves. Irreligious, hardhearted persons, naturally scorn the faithful and devout. To be always looking to something out of sight appears to them a kind of madness. The sinners of the old world no doubt scoffed at Noah when they saw him building the ark: the proud, worldly-minded Romans and Athenians said, with a sneer, to S. Paul, "*May we know what this new doctrine, whereof thou speakest, is?" And again, "Paul, thou art beside thyself: much learning doth make thee mad."

With this kind of scorn, very commonly, men treat those who try to be strict in matters regarding their bodily appetites. A thoughtful Christian, considering our Lord's own cautions, will be afraid not only of sin, but of temptation. He will turn away his eyes, lest they behold vanity. He will not run wilfully into the danger of committing adultery in his heart. He will stay away from many companies, will deny himself many sights which ordinarily men

* Acts xvii. 19.

are accustomed to indulge in without scruple. Again, he will be exact in his diet, knowing that he has passions to keep in order, sins to punish himself for, prayers to offer, which do not so well agree with fulness of bread. He will, in some sense or other, fast; soberly and discreetly, and as much as possible, in secret, but yet really he will fast. Now the self-indulgent world cannot endure this. Any one who practises it, must lay his account with a certain degree of scorn and dislike. They will say to him, in effect, what Pharaoh said to Moses, when he wanted to be rid of the Israelites: "Be gone, and bless me also." Pharaoh said it partly in fear, but it truly expresses the contemptuous way in which strict self-denying persons are apt to be treated by their looser and more careless acquaintance.

John the Baptist came neither eating bread nor drinking wine, and they said, "He hath a devil." Of course they kept at a distance from him; they looked at him with a sort of amazement, half contemptuous, half pitying. When he came among them, they would long to say to him, 'Give us your blessing and be gone.' Is not this too true an account of the thoughts and feelings of the generality of people, Christian people, in our time and country, in respect of such seasons as Lent, and of persons who live severer lives than they approve of? Do not they wish such times and persons out of the way, and speak or think of them, more or less, in scorn?

Or if they know better than that, yet are they not too easily tempted to say in their hearts, 'Lent, perhaps, is a holy season, a time of consolation and improvement, to a certain high sort of people, who have a taste for severe and strict living; but it does not suit me, I am not the person to keep it with advantage?' And again, of the examples of self-denying persons, they will say, 'I wish I could be like him; but I cannot, and there is an end of it.'

Now to correct this whole way of thinking, Holy Scripture gives us clearly to understand, that all Christians, and not a select few only, have an interest, and a deep interest, in the strictness and holiness of the better sort. Our way of behaving to those persons, whom we feel and know to be better than ourselves, is one of God's chief means for trying us, whether we are meet for His kingdom or no. As our Lord distinctly says in the text, "He that receiveth a righteous man in the name of a Righteous Man, shall receive a righteous man's reward."

By "receiving," He there means, in the first place, receiving into their houses; being kind and hospitable to His messengers, because they belong to Him. But no doubt the saying has its force, in respect of all other sorts of kindness also. And it seems plainly to tell us as follows:—

'If men have not courage at once to believe and confess Jesus Christ, yet the merely shewing kindness to His ministers and messengers, receiving them into shelter, supplying their wants, helping them in danger, shall do them some good; it will tell in their favour in God's book, it will entitle them, by His great mercy, to some sort of portion in their reward. So also, if men have not the heart, or the power, to walk themselves by the severer rules of the Gospel, if they dare not regularly fast themselves, or use other self-denials, yet let them not hinder, in any way, nor embarrass, nor discourage, their brethren who try to do so; let them put down, as direct temptations from the Evil one, all hard and scornful thoughts of that way of living: let them be sure that there must be something very wrong and intolerable in themselves, if they are disposed to think contemptuously of that which Christ so highly approved, and so strongly recommended.'

"[b] He that is able to receive it, let him receive it." Our Lord spoke the words concerning those, who resolve to live single for His sake; but they will apply also to those, who deny themselves regularly in their diet, or who make themselves poor, or in any way give up any great earthly blessing, for His sake. "He that is able to receive it, let him receive it;" and he that cannot receive it himself, let him not hinder his brother or sister, whose heart God perhaps has touched, but let him by all means encourage and help him to be holy. It will be worth his while to do so, were it only for the greater benefit of the prayers which the other will offer up for him.

The Holy Scripture is full of examples of blessings given to weaker and more imperfect persons, because of their dutiful and respectful waiting on the saints and servants of God. Abraham first, and afterwards Isaac, sojourned in the land of the Philistines, and by their prayers obtained blessings for the country, when they were treated as friends. Potiphar trusted Joseph, and the Lord blessed the Egyptian's house for Joseph's sake. The same Joseph was afterwards honoured by Pharaoh, and made ruler over all Egypt; and the whole land was thereby saved

[b] S. Matt. xix. 12.

from famine. Indeed, throughout the book of Genesis, God's word to the heathen is the same as that in the psalm: "[c] He suffered no man to do them wrong, but reproved even kings for their sakes;" "[d] Touch not Mine anointed, and do My prophets no harm." Rahab the harlot, because she had so much faith as to receive the messengers of Joshua, and conceal them when in danger of their lives, was alone saved from the burning of Jericho, and became a mother in Israel; nay, Christ Himself, after the flesh, was her descendant. The rich woman, the Shunammite, did but provide a lodging for Elisha, and treated him honourably, when God's prophets were little thought of; and for a reward her only child was raised from the dead. Cyrus, king of Persia, protected the children of Israel, and let them go free, from their long captivity in Babylon; and he seems to have been so specially favoured, as to have come nearer the worship of the one true God than any other heathen whatever. The good centurion in the Gospel had praise and a blessing from our Lord Himself, because, among other things, he loved God's people, the Jews, and built them a synagogue. Another centurion in the Acts, Cornelius, was chosen out to be the first Gentile Christian, because he "gave much alms to the people," the Jews, "and prayed to God alway." And a third centurion in the end of the book of the Acts, Julius, who had the care of S. Paul on his voyage to Rome, entreated him courteously, and helped to save his life; and what was the consequence? His own life and the lives of all the crew were preserved in that fearful shipwreck.

[c] Ps. cv. 14.   [d] ib. 15.

"God," said the angel, "hath given thee the lives of all them that sail with thee." By these few, out of many instances, we see how surely God sends a blessing, when any wait upon His saints, for His sake, though at ever such an humble distance, though they give them but a cup of cold water.

And not only Scripture, but daily experience shews, if men look in faith at what they see, that in proportion as people lead strict and self-denying lives, they have a silent influence for blessing and improvement on those for whom they care and pray, on their own families and neighbourhoods; provided only they be not treated with scorn. Those who fear, and as yet perhaps reasonably, themselves to draw very near to God, are still encouraged, and gradually changed, through God's blessing, till they too become in their measure good and holy. "The friend of the bridegroom, which standeth and heareth him, rejoiceth greatly because of the bridegroom's voice." To "make much of them that fear the Lord," is one of the marks and tokens of those, whom God in His good time will cause to "dwell in His tabernacle," and to "rest upon His holy hill."

Let us then open our hearts, more and more, to the holy influences of good men's example, wheresoever we see it around us. Let us for ever have done with the unbrotherly, unchristian notion, that their goodness is nothing to us, because we feel that it is as yet too good for us; or again, because it seems strange and unaccountable, and we feel tempted to scorn it.

Let us, for example, in this coming Lent, should God spare us to that holy season, try to have some such thoughts as these; 'Although I am not perhaps able, and therefore not called, to deny myself at the same rate as some whom I may read or hear of, yet surely Lent was intended for me as well as for other Christians. I will keep the saints in view, though I cannot yet tread in their steps. I will try gradually to become stricter and more self-denying, as other duties may permit; remembering always, that among those duties is the care of one's health, and obedience to those in authority. And God forbid that I should scorn or slight the more perfect vows and more courageous endeavours of others. Whatever is become of my own innocency, God forbid that I should ever be a stumbling-block to any of these little ones. And let me at least try to be a doorkeeper in this holy house of my God, the house of penitential fasting and mourning, which will shortly be opened for me. Let me do *something* in the way of self-denial, more than I have done hitherto. And God make me all along most careful neither to despise those who fast more than myself, nor to judge them who fast less.'

May God give us all, though unworthy, a portion with His saints in their watchings and fastings, in their holy sighs and tears, that we may at some great distance, through the merits of their Lord and ours, partake of their everlasting joy!

SERMON XI.

THE FIRST AND SECOND CREATION OF MAN.

SEPTUAGESIMA.

Gen. ii. 7.

"The Lord God formed man of the dust of the ground, and breathed into his nostrils the breath of life, and man became a living soul."

To-day the holy Church takes us back to the beginning, the very birthday of man's nature and of the world: causing us to hear from the mouth of God Himself how we came into this our being, Who brought us here, and what are His great purposes towards us. Now this is what we never could have known of ourselves. We find ourselves each in his own place, so many men, women and children, every one with a soul and body of his own, and God has given the power and the disposition to think upon it all, at least sometimes; and not to take everything which happens, as the dumb creatures seem to do, without consideration or reflection. Who and where am I? How came I here? And what is to become of me? These are questions which in one shape or another every child of man that is not senseless cannot help asking himself: and God has answered them for him. Know thyself, O child of Adam: know thine own high birth, and at the same time know thy meanness. Thou didst not make thyself; that thou knowest very well: neither did thy parents create thee; they were but God's instruments for bringing thee into the world. But in order to know thine own beginning, thou must go back to a time when instead of these millions of men women and children there was not yet a single man upon the earth. Thou must go back to the last of the six days of creation, to the first Friday that ever was. All the rest was now set in order: the light divided from the darkness, the sea from the dry land: the earth furnished with trees and herbs, the heavens with sun moon and stars, the waters with fish, the air with birds, the dry land with beasts and cattle and creeping things. Then, last of all, God sets Himself to make man. Hear Him, hear the Most Holy Trinity, in a manner taking counsel together: as though some greater thing than before were about to be done, some more especial preparation necessary: "Let Us make man in Our Image, after Our likeness." It is like what our Lord did at the marriage feast: He kept the good wine until last. All His other works were indeed very good: when He beheld them, He delighted in them: but of this alone it is said, "In the Image of God created He them." "In the Image of God created He them," because as you heard just now, when the great gap was to be filled up, and a creature provided who should use aright all these wonderful treasures of the first six days, who should be capable of knowing God and loving Him; and should be in

God's stead, bearing rule and having "dominion over the fish of the sea, and over the fowl of the air, and over the cattle, and over all the earth, and over every creeping thing that creepeth upon the earth," it pleased Him not to send an Angel down for that purpose, not to create a pure spirit only, but to make one who should in part belong even to the gross earthly world. "God formed man of the dust of the ground," not many men, but one man; for it was His will that we should all come from one root. And how did He form him? "of the dust of the ground" of the same material as He had formed the cattle before him: as it is written "God said, Let the earth bring forth the living creature after his kind, cattle and creeping thing, and beast of the earth after his kind: and it was so." "Out of the ground the Lord God framed every beast of the field." It was the body of man, not of course his soul, which was thus formed out of the dust of the earth. And so you see that in respect of that part of our being, the wisest, the noblest, the best of us all is akin to the beasts that perish. Except it were for a special act of our Almighty Creator, keeping us alive, the saying of Job might be any moment fulfilled in us. "[a] I have said to corruption, Thou art my father: to the worm, Thou art my mother and my sister." *That* is your kindred and mine by *body*: and we know how deeply from the beginning the holiest among God's people have felt this. Abraham after so many special promises confessed how bold it was that he should take upon him to speak unto the Lord, who was "[b] but dust and ashes." Job when God's hand was heavy upon him sat down among the

[a] Job xvii. 14.   [b] Gen. xviii. 27.

ashes: and yet more when the judgement had done its work upon his soul, and he had learned the more to abhor himself as being more acquainted with God, his word was "ᵉI repent in dust and ashes." Joshua and the elders of Israel "ᵈ put dust on their heads" when they felt God's hand smiting some of them before their enemies. David's comfort was to think that God "ᵉ knoweth whereof we are made; He remembereth that we are but dust." Solomon's preaching was, "ᶠAll go unto one place; all are of the dust, and all turn to dust again." And sad experience proves it daily: the most unbelieving is forced to confess it: for why else should he bury his dead out of his sight? See then, brethren, what becomes of the pride of beauty, and of the desires and pleasures which so entrance and carry away man's poor deceivable heart: look on a few years, it may be a few days, and consider what they must all come to: creeping things, noisome creatures and worms; this would be all, if our bodies were all: and how many, alas! if the truth were told, are even now living as if their bodies were all!

And yet they know, they cannot be ignorant, what a different lesson the Word of God teaches them; yes, and their own heart and conscience too, would they but listen to its still small voice. Surely "she," or he that most lives "in pleasure" must now and then have inward misgivings that there is something better worth living for: and then how plain is the Scripture, He that formed man's body of the dust of the ground " breathed into his nostrils the breath

<small>ᶜ Job xlii. 6.   ᵈ Josh. vii. 6.   ᵉ Ps. ciii. 14.
ᶠ Eccl. iii. 20.</small>

of life." Think of that, dear brethren, think of it till your hearts tremble within you, and you are amazed at yourselves that you have not thought of it more. What is this soul of yours, which makes you to be alive and not dead? which neither you nor any one else ever saw, but which you feel and know to be within you just as certainly as you feel and know anything. Here you are, my brethren, in this Church, sitting before God as His people [g]: you know whether you are attending or not, whether you like to be here or not, whether you wish you were somewhere else: you know all this and can think of it, but an inferior animal, a dumb creature, if there were one in the Church, would know nothing of the sort: he would not be able to think of what he feels. What is it in you which makes you able thus to think when the beast is not able? It is your soul, my brethren, the breath of life which God breathed into your nostrils as He did into Adam's: and so "man became a living soul." The beasts and all living have something in them by which they live, and this too is called their *soul;* as it is written "[h] Who knoweth the spirit of man that goeth upward, and the spirit of the beast that goeth downward to the earth?" But nowhere is it said that God breathed it into them, as it is said of Adam: and, O my brethren, let us make much of the saying: for by this Divinely breathed soul we are akin to the glorious spirits in heaven, who are all His spiritual creatures and children: nay, and we are more immediately akin to the great God Himself, Who "[i] is a Spirit,"

[g] Ezek. xxxiii. 31. [h] Eccles. iii. 21. [i] S. John iv. 24.

and "¹the Father of spirits." In this part of our being especially He made us after His own Image: in His own Image, after His likeness, in the Image of God created He man; male and female created He mankind; and both in His own Image. Alas! that ever male and female should agree to corrupt one another and change by uncleanness that Image of God into an image of the "ᵐ beasts that perish:" nay worse, of foul and filthy devils, spirits of fornication, defilers of soul and body!

But let us look once more at man—at our first father Adam, such as he was originally created. No doubt his body was beautiful and perfect in its kind: and his soul! who can imagine its beauty and perfection, fresh breathed as it was from the very Breath of the Lord God: and the man, observe, *was* the soul: for it is not said, man *received* a living soul, or was gifted with it, or the like; but man, Adam, "*became* a living soul:" the living soul, breathed into the body by the Holy Spirit from on high, that was the man, the man's very self. How beautiful and glorious soever might be the body, corruptible or incorruptible, it was not, it could not be, Adam's proper self. No more, my brethren, can it be yours. Your soul is yourself, not your body: and when death comes, and the soul and body are parted, it is not *you* that will lie dead, and be buried, and crumble away in the forlorn grave—not you—O no: your friends and neighbours, your parents if you leave them behind, your brothers and sisters and companions will look sadly towards your grave and say perhaps, "There lies such an one, poor thing," but you will not be in earnest lying

¹ Heb. xii. 9.　　ᵐ Ps. xlix. 12.

there; your **soul,** the living soul which at the beginning had been breathed by the breath of the Almighty into your mortal body, that precious soul, if you died in God's fear and favour, will be far from dreariness and decay, with God Who gave it, in perfect rest from its own works, from the works of the world and the body, from evil and mischief, in the true sabbath, in the blessed paradise of God, in sure and certain hope of the resurrection to eternal life, when **your body,** the appointed friend and servant of your redeemed spirit, will be raised and joined to it again, and become the partner of your true self again never more to be divided. Therefore be not too much cast down when you look on to your own death or when you look back on the death of any one dear to you in our Lord. Remember what He Himself said of such an one, "ⁿ Weep not; she is not dead, but sleepeth." "º The souls of the righteous are in the hand of God, and there shall no torment touch them."

But then, brethren, we must never, never forget what this consolation depends upon: this comfort wherewith we are bidden to comfort ourselves in all our troubles of soul and body, even to the parting of the two. This comfort depends entirely not upon the first creation of man in the person of the first Adam, whereby he was made a living soul, but upon the second or new creation of man in the Person of the second Adam, i. e. our Lord Jesus Christ, whereby He, God Incarnate, became to us a quickening Spirit. "ᵖ The first man Adam was made a living soul; the last Adam was made a quickening spirit." You have heard these words, most of you perhaps,

ⁿ S. Luke viii. 52. º Wisd. iii. 1. ᵖ 1 Cor. xv. 45.

in the Burial service. I beg of you to take particular notice of those words, whenever you hear or read them. For they have in them the very secret of your eternal life. The first Adam was made a living soul. You heard how *that* was, in the lesson to-day. "God breathed into his nostrils the breath of life and man became a living soul." It was the free gift of God, and an unspeakable gift it was: the very perfection of the life of this world before man fell. But alas! man *did* fall, as we know too well: fell shamefully, sorrowfully, and had he been left to himself incurably. What then did our blessed and most merciful Saviour? He became the second Adam, to undo the mischief done by the first Adam. There was a second and a far more wonderful creation; the Incarnation of our Lord Jesus Christ. In that astonishing moment described in the first chapter of S. Luke, when the Holy Ghost descended upon the Blessed Virgin Mary and the Power of the Highest overshadowed her, and she conceived in her womb, and so became the Mother of God: in that moment came to pass that of which the creation of Adam was, as it were, a type and shadow: the Lord God formed a Man, the Man Christ Jesus, of the substance of blessed Mary; which substance itself came, through Adam, of the dust of the ground: and God breathed into that sacred Body the Soul pure and holy beyond thought, and the Eternal Word, the Son of God, Very and Eternal God, took to Himself in the same moment that Human Body and Soul, never to be parted from Him, and so became a quickening Spirit; a Divine Spirit so joined to an unspotted Human Soul and Body, that through Him as Man, eternal life and all things pertaining thereunto should pass for ever to all His fallen brethren of mankind, who did not themselves reject Him. This is the good news, the Gospel of Jesus Christ. In Adam, one and all, we were dead: but here is another Adam in Whom one and all, He offers to make us alive. And why do I say He offers? nay, He has already done it, in respect of all who have been made members of Him by His Spirit in Baptism, for of such it is written, "ᑫ we are members of His Body, of His Flesh, and of His Bones." And this is again, a third creation, a new creation for each one of us separately: when we are one by one brought to Christ, when we put on Christ, when we are grafted into Christ, when we are made members of His mystical Body the Church, when we are put in a way to be nourished by the heavenly Food which He invites us to, His very own Body and Blood.

Behold then and see, if there be any privileges like unto your privileges, to whom the Almighty Father has given His own Son for a life-giving Spirit, to cure the death and ruin which you had brought upon yourselves by defiling the soul and body which He gave you at the first. What could have been done more for you, that our good God has not done? A body "ʳfearfully and wonderfully made," a living soul to quicken that body with the life of this world, His own Son, your second Adam, to quicken both soul and body with a better life, that is a heavenly; a task to do in His vineyard, His Spirit to help you to do it, everlasting joy with Him your exceeding great Reward. "ˢ What could have been done more

ᑫ Eph. v. 30.   ʳ Ps. cxxxix. 14.   ˢ Is. v. 4.

in My vineyard, that I have not done in it?" Alas! my brethren, what will be the end of it all? What will come at last of these worldly and ungodly lives, these days and nights without true prayer, these oaths and hypocrisies, Sundays profaned and weekdays wasted, this great disregard of parents, masters, elders and all in authority? this anger and quarrelling and envy, this uncleanness fornication and excess; this thieving and cheating, this lying, slander, covetousness, fretfulness, which we day by day make a shew of before Christ and His holy Angels, here in the midst of His new creation? You know what came of our father Adam's fall from the purity of the first creation. What if you should fall at last, fall wilfully, fall incurably, from your place in Christ's own Body? And you are in great danger. Believe me, you are. Believe not him who says, "Ye shall not surely die." But rather believe Him Whose word is, "'let him that thinketh he standeth take heed lest he fall." O, look around, is there no bad example? look inward, are there no lusts of the flesh? look onward, are no temptations before you? and then, lest you despond, look upward: and tell me do you see nothing, do you discern no One there to encourage you? O yes: look up steadily, look up in faith and you will certainly have a glimpse of Him. He Who found a remedy for your father Adam, desires, be sure, to save you. He waits to be gracious unto you. If you live so long, He will be here this very Lent, as in former Lents, to turn your heart if you will let Him. It is His appointed time, His day of salvation. O, prepare for Him: do not cast all away.

† 1 Cor. 12.

SERMON XII.

NOT SIN ALONE, BUT THE OCCASIONS OF SIN TO BE AVOIDED.

SEXAGESIMA.

Gen. iii. 3.

"*Neither shall ye touch it, lest ye die.*"

Two thoughts there are by which, more commonly perhaps than any others the Evil one entices Christian souls down the broad way into deadly sin. One is, when he prevails with us to doubt whether such and such behaviour is grievous sin or no. The other, still more ordinary and more dangerous, when we indulge the thought that we may commit the sin and yet somehow escape the penalty of it. For no one is at once as bad as he can be: and when the crafty tempter would beguile you into the deeds which he knows will be your ruin, he does it by degrees, hiding his own foulness, and appearing sometimes even as an angel of light. And these two, as I said, are two of his principal devices: to raise doubts, 1. whether what he suggests be a grievous sin or no; 2. whether supposing it a sin, God will really punish it, or no. So it was in the first sin of man, you have heard the warning to day. The tempter first suggested to Eve, that perhaps God had not really forbidden that one tree. "*Hath* God said, ye shall not eat?" are you quite sure He said it? The thought to which he was prompting her was was a thought of unbelief. That however she resisted: she well knew, and distinctly repeated, the law which the Lord had laid upon her: " we may eat of the fruit of the trees of the garden: but of the fruit of the tree which is in the midst of the garden, God hath said, ye shall not eat of it, neither shall ye touch it, lest ye die." Then he went on, but too successfully as we know, to set her upon questioning whether the punishment would be so sure to follow the sin. "The serpent said unto the woman, Ye shall not surely die." She listened; and what followed is but too familiar to us all. She fell, and with her we all. By her giving ear to that one false and wicked saying, "ye shall not surely die," "[a] sin entered into the world, and death by sin, and so death" and all kinds of misery " passed upon all men, for that all have sinned."

Now Eve did not sin in ignorance; what she did amiss was not at all for want of knowing better. She was like a person answering out of the catechism, and giving a true account, not only of the words of the commandment, but also of the drift and meaning thereof: and then going on with her eyes open to break it. I say the meaning as well as the words: for whereas God had said, "Thou shalt not eat of it," her account of His words is, Ye shall not eat of it, *neither shall ye touch it*. She was quite aware that in forbidding it to be eaten, the Lord forbade it to be touched also. Therefore, when she went on

[a] Rom. v. 12.

afterwards to listen to the devil's advice, and look towards the tree, and consider with herself how desirable and tempting it seemed, and when she was putting forth her hand to touch it, she was sinning with her eyes open, as truly so as when she was actually eating it and giving it to her husband. She was sinning, in that she knowingly put herself into the way of sin; she did not avoid the occasion of it, as she knew it was her duty to do. Thus her sad history becomes a most solemn warning to us all, as against all that is wrong, so especially against the disposition to tamper with sin, and look after it, and dwell on it in our thoughts, wondering what it is, and having a sort of blind wish to know more about it: and so to draw nearer and nearer to it, and take liberties one after another, until we actually lose ourselves in it. People think they can stop themselves when they will: that they can say to their own bad passions, Thus far shalt thou go and no farther. They might as well think of staying by a wish the rushing of water, when they have withdrawn that which pent it in, and have nothing to put in its place. The water will flow on in spite of their wishes and regrets: and so will our sins, if we get into a way of half indulging them, of going as far in them as we dare. He Who alone can help us will not go on to offer us His restraining grace, when He sees that we care so little for Him: and what should the end of such a man be, but that the devil will have his own way with him? Therefore, as the Wise man says of strife, so we may say of all other sins, 'the beginning of them is as when one letteth out water.' Leave them off before they be meddled with: turn away from them at once, as soon as ever you know they are sins. Seek not to know any more about them: it is enough to know that they are sins, hateful to God, and poisonous to the soul of man. Again, do not trifle and play with them: keep yourself afar not only from the sin, but from all that is near to it, and like it; give no way to the restless feeling which urges you to take this or that liberty, though your conscience whispers to you that you are getting beyond bounds, going too near to such and such a fault. Particularly, as you hope to avoid sin, do not willingly be familiar and intimate with sinners: be on your guard, treat them with reserve, as soon as ever your conscience whispers to you, that they are in a way to break any one of God's plain commandments. Be kind and charitable to all, and always, but do not for pleasure or for neighbourhood's sake make friends and companions of any, whom you see to be going on in any thing forbidden of the Almighty. And thirdly, let each one as well as he can, find out and watch against his own particular occasion of and temptations to sin.

I will try to speak a word or two, in order, upon each of these three rules: for indeed, my brethren, it is as much as our souls are worth, that we keep ourselves, by God's gracious help, not only from eating but from touching: not only from sin but all near occasions of it.

First of all, it is most perilous to seek to *know* more than we can help about forbidden things. The very tree that ruined us all was the Tree of knowledge: the knowledge of evil as well as good. As long as man was contented to know good only, he was safe and happy: all the good trees were at his command, and most especially the Tree of Life, but as soon as ever he indulged the desire of being made (as he thought) *wise*, by the knowledge of evil also, that very moment his mischief and misery began. Do not imagine that this was the case of our first parents only: it is in a great measure the case of every one of us Christians in turn. For as we are admitted into a sort of paradise when God makes us members of His Son; put within reach of the Tree of Life and of every thing else which is pleasant to the eye of faith and good for the food of our souls, so after a time we find that we are within reach of the forbidden tree, the tree of Knowledge also. For a time God's providence keeps men from actual sin, simply as being in ignorance of it. As soon as ever they come to know that there are at hand within reach things which they are to have nothing to do with, presently the devil begins whispering to them, 'Would you not like to know something more of these various sorts of things, to be like other people, understanding both evil and good? Why should you go on in ignorance?' Thus he acts on the natural restlessness and curiosity of young people; corrupt and fallen nature inclines them to listen to him; they get ashamed and uneasy at not knowing as much as others: perhaps they are sometimes laughed at for their childishness in being so ignorant of what is going on in the world: and so they turn aside from the safe way in which God's Holy Spirit had begun to lead them: they look this way or that after things which they know in their hearts they had better have nothing to do with; they are uneasy till they have forfeited the great blessing of child-like simplicity: they enter themselves, as it were, in the devil's school, as if it were a great point for them to learn how to sin; although perhaps they flatter themselves that they shall never fall into the sin. Alas! and what is it at all, but touching the forbidden fruit, with their minds and thoughts at least? And what can come of it, but one of two things, bitter repentance, or eternal, incurable ruin? The time will come, —God grant it may not come too late—when we shall wish and long with all our hearts that we had from the beginning turned ourselves away altogether from the polluting wisdom and knowledge of this world, and had taken our lot with those few blessed ones who try steadily to keep themselves pure from the very dream and imagination of things hateful to God. For why? they believe what is written, "[b]the knowledge of wickedness is not wisdom, neither at any time the counsel of sinners prudence." And so they look on that sin, which they cannot help seeing, as the sun in heaven, or the saints and Angels look on it, taking no pollution at all, only pitying the sinner, and hating the sin itself.

But if we are not to touch the forbidden thing so much as in seeking knowledge of it, much less may we in act or in word or even in thought venture near it when known. If we are not to inquire about it, much less may we tamper and trifle with it, hovering round it as a moth round a candle, going as near the edge of it as we dare. What is your feeling when as often happens you see a young child rush across the road, braving the danger as it were, just in front of a carriage which is driving furiously? So and

[b] Ecclus. xix. 22.

much more frightful would it be, could our eyes be opened to see things truly, when a Christian wilfully puts himself in the way of temptation: going on purpose where he will see sights or hear words which will kindle the flame of evil desire within him. "[c] Who," says the wise man, "will pity a charmer that is bitten by a serpent?" i. e. If a man take upon himself to play with poisonous snakes and tame them, and sometimes gets bitten by one, all will say it was what he might reasonably expect, many will think it was no more than he deserved for so foolish an undertaking: "so one that goeth to a sinner and is defiled with him in his sins, who will pity?" We pray night and morning, and as often as we say our prayers, that God would lead us not into temptation. What a sad mockery would it be of this our holy prayer, if when we rise from our knees we were to go forth to our sins; the thief to his stealing and cheating, the drunkard to his drunkenness, the unchaste to his shameful and defiling ways, the malicious to his spite and quarrelling: and yet, is it not too often the case, that Christians quickly forgetting their prayers, do without any necessity go forth into company or set about employments, or haunt places, which they know will prove very tempting to them? They are so far more guilty than Eve, in that the Tree of knowledge was by God's providence set in the midst of the garden, in her sight, and within her reach. God allowed it to be there, to try her: but our custom too often is to go *out of our way* to look for the temptation which He has graciously kept far from us: as if the fatal tree had been planted somewhere

[c] Ecclus. xii. 13.

beyond the borders of paradise, and Adam and Eve had broken bounds and gone out of paradise in order to look for it. This is what the Church especially warned us against, causing us each one in our Baptism to renounce the sinful lusts of the flesh, so as neither to follow nor be led by them; but we, unhappy and inexcusable! how many of us before now have sought our enemies out, and gone among them on purpose: how many have tempted themselves, and then have pretended to excuse their sin because the temptation was so strong! And so they have gone on, sinning most times they said a prayer; for they prayed not in faith; i. e. they had no steady intention to use the grace they prayed for; they secretly wished to be in temptation when they were praying not to be led into it. How can that man think to receive any thing of the Lord?

God forbid that we should be such; and in order that we may not be such, take notice, I beseech you, my brethren, of one thing which God particularly expects of us: that we should each one watch himself, each find out his own particular danger. For as no two persons are exactly alike, it may well happen that places, employments, diversions, which are not tempting and dangerous to most men, may be tempting and dangerous to you or me: we may have proved it by sad experience. Well then, you and I must be on our guard against those dangerous occasions; we must quietly avoid them if we can, and if we cannot avoid them, must earnestly prepare ourselves to meet them. For example, there are some persons of unhappy temper, who find themselves continually put out by matters which to most of us are no disturbance at all: this is a sad temptation to anger and sulleness, and they cannot escape it, it meets them at every turn: they cannot escape it, but by the grace of God they may overcome it: and how? They must commit themselves beforehand to the meek Lamb of God, when they are going into company in which they are likely to be provoked: they must endeavour silently to think of Him when the provocation really occurs; they must promise Him beforehand to try and restrain black looks, angry gestures, peevish and violent tones of voice, and when the dark feeling comes over them, they must, as well as they can, keep their promise. In this way, after a time, by slow degrees and with many distressing failures, the proud sullen temper will be soothed and tamed, and instead of making ourselves miserable with a fancy that every one is affronting us, we shall open our hearts to receive thankfully all tokens of love from God and man, and to make the best of all that is not love.

This way of amendment will answer, by the blessing of God, in the cure and avoidance of any other sin, as well as of ill-temper and proud wrath. There are three things you see, to be done: first, earnestly pray and strive to know no more of sin than you can help: and this rule holds most especially in the case of shameful, carnal sins. Secondly, on no account tempt yourself to sin; do not touch the tree of which you are forbidden to eat; do not look at it; turn yourself another way, both your eyes and your thoughts. Play not at all with temptation: it is like children playing with fire, even with the sparks of hell fire. Especially, I beseech you, break away from tempting companions; it is not unkind; it is the greatest kindness both to them and to yourself. And lastly, find out and watch what are particularly occasions of sin to yourself: (every man has some of his own), pray against them, decline them if you can; if not, prepare yourself to deal with them as a Christian ought.

Say not, It will be such incessant trouble: *how can I do all this?* Nay, how can you help doing it, if you have but a spark of love for Him Who loved you and gave Himself for you: if you have but a little care for your precious souls? Love could not bear to be always taking liberties, always venturing as near as it dares to what the beloved cannot endure. Holy fear and care for our souls would keep you as far as possible from the edge of the bottomless pit. You would shrink, not only from sin, but from all that would be likely to make you sin. If this rule seem to you too particular, depend upon it you are not yet in earnest, whatever good feelings you may have sometimes. Remember Balaam, how near he was to God, how he wished to die the death of the righteous, how he refused to curse those whom the Lord had blessed, yet how sadly, how completely he fell. Why? Because he trifled with the sin, he wished it might be allowed him, he put himself, as much as he could, in the way of it. And on the other hand, remember Joseph; how it is written of him, that when he was so sorely tempted, he not only shrank from deadly sin, but also from all kind of companionship which might at all lead to it. When the wicked woman spake to him day by day, "he hearkened not unto her," saith the Scripture, "to lie by her, or to be with her." Again, Job made a covenant with his eyes, set them a strict rule, that not one of them should go out of order. David did but once forget the rule, and we know what sin and misery followed. Which will you be like, my brethren? Will you by God's help guard yourselves from the first beginnings, temptations, occasions of sin? Or will you suffer it to have its way with you until you are almost or altogether ruined? Will you for the love of Christ be careful and exact in trying to please Christ? Or will you in a thankless heedless way seek to please yourself in every thing that you think you can short of deadly sin? Lent is very near at hand. God's time, the time of consideration, will soon be here: if the holy season with its blessed opportunities is indeed to do you good, you had need set your conscience to work in earnest. Look back on your past time: look around you: consider your ways: search your heart with earnest prayer, to find out what is your chief sin, and where and when and how it besets you most, and having found, if you can, avoid being tempted, if you cannot, bravely fight against the temptation. Your Lord will be with you, and you will not fight nor labour in vain.

SERMON XIII.

GOD'S MERCIFUL CALLS, AND HOW TO ANSWER THEM.

SEXAGESIMA.

GENESIS iii. 9.

"*The Lord God called unto Adam, and said unto him, Where art thou?*"

I SUPPOSE that few persons can read or hear this third chapter of Genesis with any real thought at all, and not seem to themselves to be reading some of their own history: the sad history of their own first fall from the purity and innocence which God gave them in their Baptism. And when we read in this verse, how God called unto Adam, then we see a clear token of His never-failing mercy to us sinners. We hide from Him, but He calls unto us. He will not leave us to perish in our sins. Every thing depends on our way of receiving these His merciful calls. If we answer them, we may have hope: if we reject them, we are lost for ever.

All this is brought clearly before us in the simple yet aweful history, which was read to us this morning out of the first lesson. Let us try and fix our minds upon it, for what can concern us more? Too surely we also have sinned: we have sinned, most of us, quite enough to forfeit our paradise. And most surely also, our God is very merciful, and has not hitherto passed by and left us to perish in our sins. Even now He is preparing us for one of His great yearly calls. Lent is coming; ten days more and it will be here. The time of repentance is at hand. If we live over those ten days, He will call upon us once more, as He has already for so many years. And what shall we do? Shall we hide ourselves from Him or no?

Consider how it was with our first father, at the moment when the Lord God called unto him, for the first time after he had sinned, and said, "Where art thou?" Why did He so call unto him? Because Adam was hiding himself. Instead of hastening out, as in former and happier days they perhaps might have done, to meet the heavenly Friend and Visitor, Adam and his wife had hidden themselves from the Presence of the Lord God. They heard His voice, as though of one walking in the garden in the cool of the day. The garden was as fair as ever; the morning breeze, or wind of the day, was as sweet and cool and refreshing as ever: the God Who had kept them all the night long, and had brought them safe to the beginning of that day, and was showering His blessings upon them as in all former days: He is come down to visit them as usual: He hath not withdrawn Himself: they hear His voice, and they know it; but alas? they hide themselves from His Presence. All else is as it had been, but their hearts and consciences are changed. Their own hearts and consciences tell them plainly, that they have sinned:

they have broken, wilfully and knowingly broken, the one command which their **Lord** had given them to try them: and now they are too miserably certain, that they **are** quite unfit and unworthy to appear before Him: and so, **when they hear** His voice, they set about hiding themselves from **His** Presence.

Whatever else in the Bible is hard to understand, surely we may almost all of us, understand this but too easily. For only think for one moment of the dismal, hardening, miserable effect of the first serious sin which a Christian who has known his **duty** may have been tempted to commit: **the** first deliberate lie, or theft, or wilful and conscious indulgence, **for** any time, of **impure thoughts. Is it not too well** known, that **when after** such a miserable **fall the** voice of God is again heard calling men to self-examination and **prayer,** they feel a strange unwillingness to answer the call? The Evil one whispers to them, 'Never mind your prayers for this time: **you may set** about them bye and **bye, but you know you are not fit to pray now, so you may just as well go** on and enjoy **yourself** a little more.' Or if they are not yet so bad as to listen **to such** direct temptation, **still he too** easily prevails upon them to shrink from the **pain and trouble of** looking into their own hearts, **finding out how bad their** sins were, and humbling themselves **for them before God** accordingly. And **what is this, but** hiding themselves, **as** Adam did, from **the** Presence of the Lord God?

There are different ways of doing this. Not seldom, men who have so defiled their consciences get into a general dislike of prayer and all religious exercises: **they sink** altogether into **an** unbelieving way: they cannot bear the thought of God, or of death, or of eternity, or of what shall be hereafter. It is all dismal and melancholy, and they get away from it as fast as they can.

This is the ordinary way of ungodly people. But there is another more subtle way, which Satan often tries upon us but too successfully. Those who have been well brought up, and used to devotional ways, should they unhappily fall into grievous sin, many times cannot find it in their hearts to slight their devotions altogether; yet neither can they make up their minds to the only true and safe way, that is, to humble and courageous confession and amendment: and so they try if they can find a middle way; saying their prayers, and confessing their sins in a way, and going on with their duties in general, ninety nine of them, perhaps, out of a hundred, but with a wilful sort of blindness, passing over the hundredth; passing over the one whereof their conscience is afraid. This again is hiding ourselves from the Presence of the Lord God. He indeed sees all, and we cannot conceal ourselves for a moment from Him: but sin, so far as men give way to it, makes them very foolish in all their behaviour with Him, and they go on behaving as if they could hide themselves, as some kinds of silly birds are said to hide their head in a bush, and so imagine that they are out of sight. Like to this are our dealings with God, as often as we play the hypocrite with Him, as if we could beguile Him not to punish our one grievous unrepented sin, because, as we fancy, we are in other respects good and devout.

Observe where Adam hid himself from God. It

was among the trees of the garden. He did not hurry out of paradise, out of God's sight and earthly dwelling place: he did not quit it altogether, but was very desirous, no doubt, of staying in it: moreover, the trees of the garden, among which he and his wife hid themselves, were God's own gracious gift to them: for out of the ground of that garden the Lord God had caused to grow every tree that was pleasant to the sight and good for food, and had told him to dress and keep them, eating freely of their fruit. Adam therefore in some sense was still continuing in the way of his duty: still looking after the good gifts which God had committed to his charge, and making believe, perhaps, to be so busy among them, that he could not at once answer God's call, saying unto him, "Where art thou?" And so it may have been, or may yet be, with some of us. A man may have done right in many things, may have set about serving God in many good works, but in some one thing he may be still going greatly amiss, and his conscience may be whispering to him in secret that so it is: just as a person may be in good general health, but may be aware of something wrong in some particular limb. If he neglect it, who can say what the consequences may be: and much more certainly, if a Christian neglect any one of the commandments, trusting to his zeal in some others, we know by the Gospel that he is guilty of all. It is as if Adam should have said to himself, when he was hiding among the trees, 'Here I am in the garden, looking after the plants which God gave me to dress and to keep: What if I did transgress in that one thing?' and so had determined to trouble himself no more about it. Alas, my brethren, I fear there are not a few, perhaps there may be some here present, who hide themselves in this way from God's presence among the trees of the garden: that is, they take refuge from the remembrance of their past sins, not, in earnest and continual repentance, but in the decencies and comforts of the life which they are now leading. They do not go on humbling themselves before their God; they have little or no bitter remembrance of their past sinful years; yea rather they turn away on purpose from thoughts of that kind: seldom or never coming to the Holy Communion because they have a feeling, that in order to do so, they must examine themselves about all this bad part of their life, and confess it particularly to God, and vex themselves for it; seldom or never denying themselves any thing, because they do not feel as they ought, that such as they have been are unworthy of indulgence; seldom or never quieting themselves, when they are ill-used, with the thought, surely I have deserved it all, and much worse. This, I fear, is no such very uncommon state of mind, even among decent and orderly persons, who are far from intending to be altogether irreligious. They were wild, perhaps, for more or less of their time; they were given in their youth to drinking, or to other vain and wicked pleasures: now it is so no longer with them: but have they truly and sorrowfully repented? Are they leading penitent lives? If they were, surely they would be found regularly there, where is the only true comfort for penitent sinners, at the foot of their Saviour's Cross, before His Altar, humbly preparing themselves to partake of His Body and Blood. Yes, good brethren, it is indeed so. You may be decent men, you may have left off many wrong ways, you may be going on now in a way for all men to speak well of you: but where is your real hearty horror of sin? Where is your love of your dying Saviour, and deep shame that you should have been so ungrateful to Him, robbing Him of all the best years of your life? Where is your broken and contrite heart, your earnest care to judge yourselves, that you be not finally judged of the Lord? O, if indeed these were the thoughts of your heart, should not we your pastors see more of you, not only in this place, but as coming in private to open your minds to us, and to ask our counsel about making your repentance perfect? and would not your God and Saviour see more of you kneeling at His Altar, and partaking of His best gifts? Depend upon it, wherever you see decent orderly domestic people, shrinking from self-examination and confession and Holy Communion, then you see something very like Adam and Eve hiding themselves from God's voice among the trees of the garden.

And consider this one thing more, which must come, I should think, into many persons' minds, in reading this history of our first parents. What if the Lord God, walking that day in the garden, had passed by the place where they were hiding themselves, taking no notice, not vouchsafing to call them at all? What would the consequence have been, to them and to us? We are not told: but we know without being told, what becomes of poor sinners, if God in His just judgement withdraws His grace, leaves off calling them, and suffers them to walk altogether in their own ways. There is no chance but they will go from bad to worse, and be lost for ever in the bottomless pit of fire. So it must have been with those first sinners, if the Lord had passed them by, and suffered them to go on hiding themselves. As it was, being called, they made answer, and having in some sort confessed their sin, and being truly ashamed of it, were invited to repentance by the promise of one Who should redeem them by destroying their enemy the serpent; that is, by the promise of God's only Son to come in the flesh. The Almighty was so merciful, that as soon as ever they had sinned, He shewed them in part what a deliverance He was preparing. All this they would have lost, and would have lost themselves too for ever, had they gone on hiding themselves when He called them from among the trees. And all their posterity, for ought we can tell, would have been lost with them.

Now, God is calling to each one of us, as He called to our first parents: and we, so far as we are putting off the work of earnest and entire religion with worldly excuses, so far we are like Adam and Eve hiding ourselves among the trees of the garden. I asked, just now, What if God had passed by Adam, and what if Adam had refused to answer God's call? Now I would wish that we should every one ask himself, 'What if God should pass by me in His calls? and what if I should be yet hiding myself, yet turning but half an ear to them? As yet, He has not passed me by: I heard Him this morning even when this Scripture was read: I hear Him now, that I am being reminded of it: I have been too apt to shun the thought of His heart-searching Presence, to wrap myself up in vain excuses: yet He has not passed me by: this very day He has, as it were, called me by name, and has said, Where art thou? Wherefore hide thyself away from thy heavenly Friend? What has happened? What art thou doing, that thou comest not unto Me with all thine heart?' Thus our Lord has called unto each one of us; we are sure of it, in that He by His good providence has caused us to read or hear this lesson to day. We are sure then (O how can we thank Him for it enough?) that He has not yet passed by us, has not yet cast us away. We may if we will, come forth, as our first parents did in their sad penitential way, and may make our humble confession, and meekly and thankfully submit ourselves to His just judgement: and so when we have undergone our penalty, as they did, we may by His infinite mercy and merit be forgiven, as they doubtless were, at the last. We may have the blessing of penitents, now: but if we let Him pass by this time, and choose rather to remain hid among the leaves; among our vain excuses, and earthly comforts: how do we know that He will ever call to us again? The world may last another twelvemonth, the preparation for Lent and Lent itself, may return, and the Lord may utter His voice as He is now uttering it, and may say, "Where art thou?" but we may be gone out of hearing: our souls may by that time be in another world, where it is too late to confess and amend and do any work of repentance. Or if we be still in this world, another year's neglect of God may have quite hardened our hearts, so that we shall not even seem to hear when our Lord calls. Who can tell but it may be so with any one, who now hides himself from his God? Who can tell but it may be so with himself? God forbid! but so it will surely be, sooner or later, if we do not come out of our hiding places when He calls: that is, if we do not attend in earnest, and put off our foolish excuses.

Yes, you will say, but it is a hard thing, a grievous thing, to turn away from our worldly supports and comforts, and open up our old sins, one by one, alone with our God. Well, it is a hard thing, a grievous thing: but will it not be much harder and more grievous to do the same at the last day? *Now* if you do it in earnest, and dutifully, you have the comfortable hope of perfect remission and forgiveness: but if you put it off till then, there will be many times more pain, with no hope at all.

Come then, sinful brethren, out of your hiding places. Seek not, as Adam did at first, to cover your iniquity, but come forth, as Adam did afterwards, in answer to your Judge's call, and make your humble and particular confession to your Judge. Suffer not this Lent, this one more merciful call from your God, to pass away, without your carefully going over the whole of your life past, so far as you can remember it, and spreading it out as it were before the Lord, to be blotted out, if it so please Him by the most precious Blood of His dear and only Son: you in the meanwhile humbly submitting yourself to any pain, or grief, or disgrace, which it may please Him to lay on you; as Eve submitted to the pangs of travail, and Adam to the hardships of labour, and both, to the sentence of temporal death. If you have not done this in former Lents, do it now: if you have done it imperfectly, try to supply what was wanting. Answer His call now sincerely and dutifully, and He will answer you mercifully, when you call on Him in death and in judgement.

SERMON XIV.

NECESSITY OF CONFESSION.

SEXAGESIMA.

Gen. iii. 8, 9.

"*And they heard the voice of the Lord God walking in the garden in the cool of the day: and Adam and his wife hid themselves from the presence of the Lord God amongst the trees of the garden. And the Lord God called unto Adam, and said unto him, Where art thou?*"

As the account of Eve's temptation and fall truly represents the course of corruption and sin, the way in which the devil daily and hourly beguiles and ruins Christian souls in the Church of God, now His earthly paradise; so the behaviour of our first parents afterwards may be understood but too easily by most of us; it answers so exactly to the feelings and conduct of those who have unhappily forfeited their baptismal innocency, and have permitted the Evil one to seduce them into wilful sin. Their first feeling was an indistinct sense of shame, a desire to hide themselves from one another and from all the world. Their eyes, both of them, were opened, and they knew that they were naked, and they sewed fig-leaves together, and made themselves aprons. Until then they had been like little children, not knowing shame, because they knew not sin; but from that day forward they and their posterity had to carry both sin and shame about with them whereever they went.

That was the first miserable effect of their transgression. The second and most miserable was, that it separated between them and their God. When He next vouchsafed to come near to them with His gracious presence, instead of hastening, like dutiful children, to meet Him, they shrank away, and tried to get as far from Him as they could. "They heard the voice of the Lord God walking in the garden in the cool of the day: and Adam and his wife hid themselves from the presence of the Lord God amongst the trees of the garden. And the Lord God called unto Adam, and said unto him, Where art thou?"

I wish this place were harder than it is to understand. Would to God the lives and hearts of too many of us did not furnish too plain an account of its most sad and miserable meaning! For it is not only that we feel in ourselves the corruption which caused Adam so to behave, but so far as we have wilfully sinned, we are, or have been, doing the same thing which Adam then did.

How can it possibly be otherwise, as long as sin, and shame, and belief in God go together? For shame makes the sinner shrink and draw back, and not endure to have his thoughts and doings watched or seen by any eye whatever. And belief in God tells him that there is an all-seeing eye about his path, and about his bed, and spying out all his ways;

to which the darkness and light are both alike; and an all-hearing ear which knows altogether every word on his tongue. As often then as he sins wilfully, if he thinks of God at all, he must secretly wish there were no God to see him; and he will be tempted to do all that he can to make himself forget God, and so in a manner hide himself for a time from His presence; as some large birds are said to run for shelter where there are thick bushes, and hide their heads in one of them, and so appear to fancy that no one can see them at all.

Thus any one sin, wilfully indulged, leads to profaneness and unbelief, and tends to blot the very thought of God out of our hearts. But if people cannot quite come to this, (as indeed the Almighty is very gracious, and takes possession of our minds beforehand, and fills the world with tokens of Himself, and seems as if He would not permit us quite to forget Him, do what we will,) then the Evil one teaches us a more subtle way of hiding from Him, as he taught Adam in paradise; for we are not to doubt, that after that first sin the tempter, though out of sight, was at hand to lead our first parents into further mischief; he encouraged them in their natural feeling, to hide themselves from God among the trees. We that have been brought up in God's Church are so far like them in paradise, that we know in our hearts that God is near us: so near, that none of our secrets are hidden from Him; as no doubt our first father, when he hid himself from God, yet knew that he could not really hide himself; but he got among the trees, as the lost ones will call on the rocks and mountains to cover them in the last day, because it was something like hiding himself.

Much in the same way are backsliding Christians led to invent or accept notions of God and His judgement, as though He in His mercy permitted them to be hidden and covered, when in truth they cannot be so. If they have strong feelings of repentance, however late, if they earnestly put their trust in Jesus Christ, God, they imagine, will cast all their sins, even their wilful and deadly sins, whereby they have broken their baptismal vows, God will cast them all behind His back; and the hope of this encourages them to go on, as if even now what they are doing were out of God's sight. This is hypocrisy, so far like that of the Pharisees, that it has great reason to dread the woe pronounced on them. It is behaving towards God as if we could hide ourselves from Him.

And the same temper naturally leads us to be more or less false towards men also, trying to seem better than we are; delighting to be praised, though we know how little we deserve it; talking, and looking, and moving about, as if we had some remarkably good purpose in our minds, while perhaps inwardly we allow the Evil one to have his way in our hearts in respect of some secret corruption; malice, or covetousness, or pride, or lust.

Among particular sins, it would seem that two in particular dispose the heart towards this kind of falseness; that is to say, first, sensuality, or undue indulgence of the lusts of the flesh; and next dishonesty, what tempts men to cheating and stealing. Both these, at least in their first beginnings, are, in an especial sense, "works of darkness;" as they are described in the book of Job [a], "The eye of the adulterer waiteth for the twilight, saying, No eye shall see me; and disguiseth his face." That is the nature of sins of wantonness. And in the next verse he says the same of sins of dishonesty. "In the dark they dig through houses which they had marked for themselves in the day-time; they know not the light: for the morning is to them even as the shadow of death; if one know them, they are in the terrors of the shadow of death." The unclean person, and the thief, these are the kinds of sinners who shrink from being seen, more earnestly, perhaps, than most others, and to whom, therefore, the thought of God's presence is most especially oppressive and irksome.

How many hearts will bear witness to this hereafter, in the day when their secrets shall be laid open; and when, according to our Judge's positive saying, "[b] there is nothing covered that shall not be revealed, nor hid that shall not be known!" Then shall it be seen how bitter and acute was the feeling, when young people, christianly brought up, first permitted themselves to wander in secret from the pure and undefiled commands of God; to indulge any sinful desire, the lust of the flesh or the lust of the eyes, or to take what did not belong to them.

How ashamed and angry with themselves did they feel! How uneasy, in a kind of imagination, that other persons might know or suspect their fall! How busy, too often, in mean and miserable contrivances, false and lying words and deeds, to hide from man what they knew in their hearts that God all the while was looking at! And thus, too often, their consciences were hardened and they went on with

[a] Job xxiv. 15, 16.   [b] S. Luke xii. 2.

less and less scruple to repeat the same sins or commit worse. But if they had permitted their natural shame to work a good work in them, if they had confessed, and humbled and chastened themselves before God, and had remembered their sin, not to hide, and excuse, and repeat it, but to punish themselves secretly for it, denying themselves praise and pleasure; this would have stopped the evil in the bud, would have secured to them the continued gracious aid of the most Holy Spirit, to resist the devil when he should next approach. He would have given them tears of true penitence, to wash out the stain before it was ingrained in their garments; and they might hope to feel more and more, that God was calling to them, though severely, yet in mercy: as to fallen and erring children, yet as to children, and that, as such, they might still venture near Him.

Such was probably our first father's mind when the Lord God had called him from among the trees, and had mercifully expostulated with him. Think how it would have been, what misery to him and to us, had the Almighty Judge suffered him to remain there hiding himself, and had not called him out to confession and repentance! Had God left Adam as he then was, the whole of mankind had been lost for ever. But He mercifully called him, and Adam heard the call; and it was generally believed among the first Christians (though I do not know that it is any where expressively set down in the Bible), that both he and our mother Eve truly repented, and are now at rest, through Him Who then came to judge, and promised in due time to come and redeem them.

So, too, my brethren, when any Christian person has fallen unhappily from his pure Christian beginnings, and is fain to hide himself from the Presence of God in the trees of the garden, i. e. in whatever comes in his way, that may seem to leave him quiet and free for the moment; God is generally so merciful, that He will not let them be at ease and forget Him. They hear His voice walking in the garden, i. e. they discern the tokens of His peculiar Presence in the Church, and they hide themselves. But He calls them out of their hiding-place, as He called Adam from among the trees: He forces them to hear Him, saying, "Where art thou?" Then begins that long and painful strife, in which so many of the best years of so many of our lives are passed; when instead of obeying His voice at once and for ever, and passing all our time in penitence and obedience, we take license to sin again; and He calls us again, and we would again hide ourselves from Him; and so, if we are not lost in the end, in that very course of sin (which the greater part, it may be feared, are), yet our fruit is but little and scanty, and it is a miracle if we turn out any better than unprofitable servants.

We cannot be at any loss to know *when* God is so calling to us, and not permitting us to shrink from Him.

He calls us by our parents and teachers: the very sight of them, and the sound of their voices, is a reproof and check to us in the beginning of our bad ways; and that as much or more, when they are kind and indulgent, as when they see something to reprove in us; for what can be more bitter to a young mind, that is at all affectionate or honest, than to be treated by a parent, or elder friend, or teacher, or pastor, with their usual open, unsuspecting kindness, when, if they knew how it was with you, they would be mourning over you as one sadly fallen, or warning you away, as unworthy to join in holy things?

This feeling, when any person has it, is a real and true call from God, a token that He is not leaving us to ourselves. And the devil if we permit him, will teach us to shrink from it accordingly. Do we not see how he prevails on young people, when they have once set out in sin, ever so secretly, to avoid the company and conversation even of their parents, because it is a silent reproof to them? Do we not see how they draw away by degrees from the more innocent and simple among their friends, and rather get into that kind of society, which will keep them in countenance, instead of making them secretly ashamed; how, if one of a family grows wild and wicked, he cares not to be much with his more dutiful and considerate brethren; how his very home, and the things and places which he was used to in the days of his innocence, grow wearisome to him, and seem as if they silently reproached him? These are all so many signs of the Lord God walking in the garden, drawing near to us in our daily resorts, and in our daily work, and of our hiding ourselves from Him.

But if secret guilt makes men shy of their earthly friends, much more of Him Who is our heavenly Friend, of Him Who came into the world on purpose to destroy sin. And, therefore, no wonder, if young persons, losing their innocence, lose, at the same time, in great measure, their relish, what they had, for holy and devout exercises; for their prayers, night and morning; for reading the Holy Scriptures, or the writings of good and devout men; and most especially, for serving God really in His Church.

I say, serving Him *really*, because, no doubt, there is a way of coming to Church, and of joining in the service there, which persons somehow appear to practise without misgiving, even when they are loving their sin. Like people in a sort of intoxication, they try to go on as if nothing was the matter; but this does not last long: when the first wild excitement of their wickedness is over, the prayers and holy lessons of the Church, and all the sure tokens of God's majestic Presence there, must surely become irksome to them; and if for any reason they still come outwardly, yet inwardly in their hearts they try to be far away.

This, I much fear, is too true an account of the irreverent, profane behaviour of many young persons in holy places; they have that in their hearts which would make them ashamed and uneasy, if they began to think seriously of Him in Whose Presence they are; and others, it may be, know it of them, and would mock them, and call them hypocrites; and so, though for custom or obedience sake, they come into the Presence of the Lord, and perhaps would be afraid entirely to stay away, yet they too easily allow and encourage the Evil one to direct their minds to something else. Their looking about them, their whisperings and gazings, their irreverent postures, and entire inattention to the service, are then but so many endeavours to cover their transgression, like Adam; to withdraw their thoughts from that aweful Presence, which, by the very act of coming to Church, they are all the while acknowledging.

Of course it is to be expected, that persons in this mind should keep back as much as possible from the holy ordinances of the Church, and from regular devout preparation for them. Confirmation and the Holy Communion, and the strict and aweful self-examination which they both require, how should they be other than intolerable to a man just fresh from his sins, and not beginning truly to repent of them? This is one sad, but most real reason, why it is so difficult to prevail on young persons, after they are grown up, and are at all gone out in the world, to submit themselves to the Church's pastoral care and teaching, and to be trained and prepared either for Confirmation or the Communion. Our inviting them thither is the Lord's call to Adam; but Adam has sinned, and is hiding himself among the trees. Well would it be for him, if he would come out of his hiding-place, leave all his vain excuses, force himself to confess his sins and forsake them; but this, few of us have courage to do, and therefore our repentance is in general so imperfect and unstable even when we do repent.

If men would oftener follow the charitable advice of the Church, which directs that when a man cannot quiet his own conscience, but finds it troubled with any weighty matter, he should confess it to the priest, who shall absolve him in Christ's Name: if men would oftener do this, we should have, I dare to say, fewer of those most grievous cases, where people slide back and are lost, after seeming repentance in sorrow and sickness. But so it is: people's false shame hinders them from really confessing, even before God's ministers; and since He has promised to be with His ministers in their office, this, too, in some measure, is trying to hide themselves from God.

But He is so merciful, that He will not withdraw Himself, nor be silent, nor leave us at ease in our sins, grievously as we provoke Him to do so. He calls us by the events of His providence: pain, perhaps, and sickness come upon us; we are disappointed in something on which we set our hearts, (and this is a kind of call which early youth is particularly alive to), or we lose some dear friend, and conscience tells us, that if we are ever to be happy with him again, we must quite entirely change our way of life; nay, the very same false ways which people resort to for hiding their sins, are sometimes turned by Him into occasions of amendment. As, for instance, outward shame and fear of discovery may drive an adulterer or a thief to Church, and there he may hear some lesson, or prayer, or sermon, which may do him good, and fill his heart with God's fear.

In a word, man is not more busy in ruining himself, and hiding from the face of his Maker, than He, our gracious Saviour, is watchful to awaken and save us. His calls we cannot but hear: every thing depends on our way of taking them. We may, if we will, hide ourselves from His Presence for awhile: Adam might have done so, might have refused to obey His summons, had he been as hardened as too many of his wilful descendants. Had he so done, he would not indeed have received at that moment (so far as we know) the reproof of the Judge, and the sentence of death and pain; but neither would he have heard the first gracious promise of a Saviour, Who should come to bruise the serpent's head. We may, if we will, withdraw ourselves; we may refuse to come forth from our guilty hiding-places, to confess our sins to God and His Church, to exercise ourselves in true penitence, as the Scriptures require; we may go on in our sin a little longer, avoiding present pain, and shame, and self-denial; but what will be the end? To such the serpent's head will not be bruised, nor the curse taken from off the ground; they have refused Christ for their Judge in this life, and therefore He will be no Saviour to them in the life to come: "ᶜIn their trespass which they have trespassed, and in their sin which they have sinned, in them shall they die."

ᶜ Ezek. xviii. 24.

SERMON XV.

THE SOWER AND THE SEED.

SEXAGESIMA.

S. MARK iv. 3.

" Hearken: Behold, a sower went forth to sow."

THE Holy Gospel here tells us of the beginning of one of our Blessed Lord's sermons. "ᵃ Much people were gathered together, and were come to Him out of every city:" and when they were all in expectation, thus He began, "Hearken." You may imagine how they listened, how every eye, ear, and mind, in that great multitude was fastened on Him, wondering what He might be going to say. And can you not also imagine, that when He went on and just told them, "A sower went forth to sow," they might for a moment or two be surprised, and begin to say in their hearts, What is this? What has this to do with faith and religion and the service of God? "A sower went forth to sow!" well, that is no new thing: of course the sower goes out at the usual time of year to get the crop into the ground: and if he did not, we all know that we must do without bread: but the kingdom of God which

ᵃ S. Luke viii. 4.

this Jesus of Nazareth is preaching, we have always understood to be something new and strange, and we cannot imagine why He begins speaking of such an ordinary thing as sowing seed. They might say among themselves what was once said by the hearers of the prophet Ezekiel, "[b] Wilt thou not tell us what these things are to us, that thou sayest so?"

Our Lord we know expounded it all to His disciples. But without going on now to that explanation, which you heard in the Gospel of the day, I wish you to consider only those simple words, "Behold, a sower went forth to sow." You will find a great deal more in them than you might at first think; deep knowledge, warning of heavenly truth.

In the first place, the mere act of putting the seed into the ground is a lesson from Almighty God, to put us in mind of the fall of our first parents, and our sad condition in consequence of it. Before Adam fell, as you know, the Lord God Himself planted the trees upon the fruit whereof Adam was to live; no need for Adam to sow or set them in the ground, God caused them to grow there (as men speak) of their own accord: "every tree that was pleasant to the sight and good for food." Adam had indeed to dress and keep the garden, but it was not in the way of toil or hard work: it was rather, as we may believe, in the way of service done to Almighty God the Owner of the garden; it was pleasurable exercise, not wearisome trouble: and having so done, he had but to put forth his hand, and take of all trees but one, and freely eat. But when they had unhappily listened to the enemy—when lust had brought sin, and sin death—

[b] Ezek. xxiv. 19.

all this as you know was changed; the sentence went out immediately, "Cursed is the ground:" and ever since the rule of this world has been, "*In the sweat of thy face shalt thou eat bread.*" The ground, left to itself, as we all know, brings forth only thorns and thistles, nettles and all manner of weeds and rubbish: if you want good food out of it, "*ᵈWine that maketh glad the heart of man, and oil to make his face to shine, and bread which strengtheneth man's heart,*" there must be ploughing, raking and harrowing, planting and sowing, fencing and weeding, and all the hard and anxious work of the farm and garden. And why should it be so? What reason is there in the nature of things, why a piece of ground left to itself should not bear wheat and barley, vines or good fruits, as well as nettles and brambles and all manner of weeds? You never can find any reason, but this one, that it so pleased God. It pleased God that the ground so left to itself without any sort of cultivation, should not ordinarily bring forth the food that is needed for man's life. And why? For a token to us all how displeasing sin is to God: for a remembrance of His curse laid upon the earth for the first sinner's sake. That curse is not worn out: this world indeed appears to grow on the whole, outwardly and bodily, more and more comfortable to live in, as fresh contrivances are found out, and civilization, as it is called, goes on: but still each new generation finds, as the former generation had done, that the old sentence remains, man's life must be labour and sorrow. Earth, left to itself, will not feed him.

ᶜ Genesis iii. 19. ᵈ Psalm civ. 15.

And thus you perceive that so common a sight as a sower going out to sow his seed is, as I said, a lesson from God, to make you aware how He hates sin, and how surely the words which He has spoken against sinners will sooner or later come to pass.

But the same thing, the sight of a man sowing, is in another way a token of His great mercy. For by this parable He has taught us that this our ordinary sowing is just a type and parable of Jesus Christ the great Husbandman coming to amend this wicked and unfruitful soil—man's fallen and corrupt heart and life—whose end otherwise is to be burned. "He that soweth the good seed is the Son of Man:" He soweth, that we may reap, and then so merciful and condescending is He, that He looks forward to the harvest as to a time of joy for Himself as well as for us: "[e] that both He that soweth and he that reapeth," the Saviour and those who are saved by Him, "may rejoice together." That is, at the last day, when He will see us again, His joy, which He took in us when He first made us His children, remaining in us, and our joy made full by our entering into His joy: entering for ever into the joy of our Lord.

That will be the harvest: but now it is the seed-time: and Christ, as you have heard from Himself, is the Sower: "He that soweth the good seed is the Son of Man." Christ is the Sower: now consider what is the seed. First, the seed is the Word of God: He tells us so Himself. The Sower went forth to sow when Jesus Christ began to go about in Galilee, preaching the Gospel of the kingdom, shewing forth the glad tidings of the kingdom of God. His Ser-

[e] S. John iv. 36.

mon on the Mount, and the rest of His holy sayings, were the good seed of the Gospel, scattered here and there: like bread cast on the waters, to be found after many days. It was sown broadcast over the whole country, sometimes among the multitude, sometimes among His disciples only. And when He was gone away from us into heaven, still the same Word continued to be sown, and He to be the Sower of it. No longer indeed in His own Person, but by His Blessed Spirit coming down upon His Apostles, He filled their bosom with good seed, "f pressed down and shaken together, and running over;" and what they had freely received they were freely to give. And they did so in all peoples, nations and languages: "g their sound went out into all lands, and their words into the ends of the world." And so He has done ever since, by the same His Apostles and their successors, with whom He has promised to be always, even unto the end of the world. So He does to each one of you, my brethren, as often as you come into this Church and hear the Bible read and the meaning of it preached. At every such time it is as if God's providence spake to your inward ear and conscience, saying, 'Hearken: behold the Sower is going forth to sow.' Nay, and this is true also as often as any one of you, rich or poor, man or woman, opens his Bible in faith and humility, and reads the holy Word which the Blessed Spirit has caused to be written for his learning, whether he read it in silence to himself, or in fatherly care to his family, or in quiet friendliness to some other who cannot perhaps read it for himself.

f S. Luke vi. 38.   g Psalm xix. 4.

Such moments are very serious, and by God's help may be very blessed. For then it is indeed the Divine and gracious Saviour, sowing the very word of life: as He has been doing, publickly and from house to house, now for these 1800 years: as it is written, "[h] He hath dispersed," that is, hath sown His seed, "abroad, and given to the poor" (for "to the poor the Gospel is preached"). "His righteousness endureth for ever."

But the good seed which the Son of Man sows has yet another and a still more gracious meaning. It signifies not only the Word and doctrine, but the living souls also which hear the Word and believe the doctrine: for so we learn in another parable: "[i] He that soweth the good seed is the Son of Man: the good seed are the children of the kingdom." So that the heavenly and Divine Sower is always, night and day, sowing not only the Word but the Church upon earth. The Word He sows by preaching and teaching: the Church by holy Baptism: as the Holy Ghost tells us by S. Peter, "[k] Ye are born again, not of corruptible seed, but of incorruptible, by the Word of God which abideth for ever:" i.e. Christ Who is the Word of the Father, Himself living and enduring for ever, gives you a new birth of incorruptible seed by making you members of Himself, which we all know He does in our Baptism. Christians then, baptized persons, wherever they are found, in whatever way they are behaving, are or have been the crop and the harvest of Christ. As such He sowed them in His field, the world; as such He is ready to cherish, to water, to

[h] Ps. cxii. 9.   [i] S. Matt. xiii. 37, 38.   [k] 1 S. Peter i. 23.

protect, to fence them in by all the means of grace in His holy Church.

You, my brethren, e.g. you who are gathered together in this congregation are as a field of standing corn, which the careful and wise Husbandman has planted in His own ground, has anxiously provided for in every way: a field on which the eyes of the great Owner of all are continually fixed as on Israel of old[1], from the beginning of the year to the end of the year. You one with another make up the standing corn in this field, each one a separate plant, and from each one according to his growth the Husbandman looks for fruit in due time. Only He is not like an earthly husbandman, in that He knows each seed separately, yes every one of the innumerable plants, the millions of souls that are growing or ever have been growing on His land. He takes account of each separately, what fruit it ought to have borne, and what it really does bear. His eye detects every weed, every tare, which has intruded itself among the wheat. For the present indeed He seems to take no notice, for the harvest is not yet come: but it *will* come, and that speedily: and then you will know and feel, if you would not before, that His Eye has all the while been upon you; and what if you should also feel that you have been all the while forgetting Him?

Christ then is the Sower, and His Word and His Church are the Seed. Now you know how a man who goes out to sow feels as concerning the crop which he sows. What if he sees any one disturbing the seed on purpose? pulling up the young plants?

[1] Deut. xi. 12.

trampling them down as they grow? turning in mischievous animals? sowing or planting weeds, to choke the good corn? How should you like this, brethren, were any one to deal in this way with your field, or your garden, and that perhaps regularly year after year? Of course you would say as it is in the parable, "[m] An enemy hath done this." You would count that person your enemy, and one of the most spiteful of enemies, who should so deal with the crop on which you had set your heart; on which you had spent your labour, your time, your care. Much more if the person so wronging you should prove to be one most deeply obliged to you; one whose life you had saved; one who owed to you all he has in the world. You would say, and all your neighbours would agree with you, 'How would *he* like it if any one used him so?' Well, my brethren, do as you would be done by. Behold, here is your best friend, your only Saviour, the Good and Holy Jesus Who bought you with His own Blood, behold He has been here sowing His seed, the seed of eternal life, in your hearts, and in the hearts of all these your fellow Christians on every side of you. This parish, this congregation, is one of His fields. His corn is growing here: He will come bye and bye at the harvest to gather it in: and He would fain save it all: not one grain would He have spoiled or lost: it is a thing which He has so much at heart, that He even died the death of a malefactor that He might bring it about. If then you love Him at all, if you have the least wish to please Him, must you not be very careful not to damage this crop of His? You

[m] S. Matt. xiii. 28.

would think it very unkind if any one came into your garden, and rode or walked carelessly about among your choice herbs and flowers, for which you had paid a large sum : but you think very little of dealing carelessly with the souls for whom Christ died. You will utter your oaths and curses or other bad words in the hearing of young Christian children, or you will even come here and keep a sort of school for teaching the little ones to behave amiss in the very house of God. Is this doing as you would be done by? Do you think your Saviour cares less for the souls of these little ones than you do for your plants and flowers? Nay, He will not endure them to to be trampled on : He is even now preparing the millstone to be tied round your neck and to drown you, not in the depth of the sea but in the bottomless pit of fire, whoever you are that take a wicked pleasure in teaching these little ones to sin.

And as His anger is towards those who damage His crop, such is His tender love and favour towards those who take an interest in it. The least little token that you really care for instruction; your coming here when you can on Festivals and other week-days; your listening at lessons and sermons; your turning away from those who would disturb you at Church ; your making a rule to read in your Bible, if it be but a few verses, regularly at home; your sparing, if it be but a few pence, as often as you can for Church Missions: every one of these things, even the least little prayer and endeavour to promote the working of God's word on your own and other men's hearts, our dear Lord will take kindly ; He will not forget it : in its way it will bring you a blessing. It is said to such[a], Ye "are labourers together with God." What an honour is that, my brethren, and at the same time what a great thing to answer for! Think of it in this way! Most of you are labouring men: you work for this master and that: but remember that after all there are but two masters. Under which are you now working? Whose wages are you now earning? Do not sleep this night, until you have tried to answer this question in your own secret heart and conscience: lest you should find youself, waking, where those must go, who die scorning God's Word.

[a] 1 Cor. iii. 9.

SERMON XVI.

THE PERIL OF WEARING OUT THE LONG SUFFERING OF GOD THE HOLY GHOST.

SEXAGESIMA.

GEN. vi. 3.

"*And God said, My Spirit shall not always strive with man, for that he also is flesh; yet his days shall be a hundred and twenty years.*"

WE may well stand amazed, and consider with trembling of heart, how great the evil which one single sin may bring on, when we read over the early part of the book of Genesis. In the first lesson, for instance, this morning, is the sad account of the Fall, the first sin: and in the first lesson this afternoon, we find that within a very few generations, as the life of man then was, sin had so spread over the whole world, and so deeply infected the hearts and consciences of all men, that God was in a manner compelled to destroy the whole world by a flood of waters. And so one sin of early childhood, which one scarce perhaps thought of at the time, may have gone on defiling and corrupting the whole of a man's heart and life, so that if God leave him as he is, he is only fit to be destroyed for ever in the flood of fire, which we know will soon come on the earth. Which of us knows for certain, my brethren, that he is not even now cherishing in himself the seed and spark of some evil, some deadly inclination, which if not checked in time, will be his eternal ruin? To us perhaps as yet it seems little and trifling, and we are tempted to be angry and scornful when we are warned of it. But did not the tasting of the evil fruit, think you, appear to our mother Eve a trifling inconsiderable fault? Would she not have started back, scarce able to believe it, if she had been any how told that in a few years time the whole earth would be corrupt before God, and filled with violence, and that every imagination of the thought of man's heart would be only evil continually, and all on account of her not looking another way, but rather putting forth her hand to touch and take the forbidden fruit? O let us be wise in time, and believe what Holy Scripture here teaches us so very plainly, that any wilful sin may have consequences far beyond our measuring; miseries and corruptions reaching through all eternity. Let us be sure, there is no knowing what a burthen we heap on ourselves, whenever we purposely and knowingly give way to temptation.

But what is this, which we read next in the history of the fallen world? "[b]It repented the Lord that He had made man upon the earth, and it grieved Him at the heart." Strange and fearful saying! that the unchangeable God should repent, and change His purpose, He Who says by another pro-

[b] Gen. vi. 6.

phet, "God is not a man, that He should lie, nor the Son of man, that He should repent. Hath He said, and shall He not do it? or hath He spoken, and shall He not make it good?" These two sayings appear to contradict each other, but when we consider, we find that they exactly agree. For in both cases, whether it is said that He repents and changes His mind, or that He cannot alter or repent, it comes to this, that being in Himself All-Holy and Good, He cannot either endure men swerving to unholiness and wickedness, or forsake them as long as they try to be good and holy. Thus in the case of Abraham and his spiritual seed, the gifts and calling of God are without repentance: He cannot forsake them, because, by His grace, they keep true to Him. On the other hand, in the case of these sinners before the flood, God could not but change His mind and dealings towards them, because they had so entirely fallen away from Him. He is the same, therefore His proceedings are not the same as they were towards them who have changed: He calls Himself, *I Am that I Am*, "the Same yesterday, to day, and for ever," therefore His counsel is not with the wicked; the mercy which He shews them for a time cannot always continue: they must repent, or sooner or later He will repent of His goodness towards them. This is some account of what is meant, when we read "It repented the Lord that He had made man."

And besides this, we may well believe that this saying expresses His great and marvellous love, His fatherly affection towards the things which He hath made. "It repented the Lord that He had made man upon the earth, and it grieved Him at the heart:" as if it were said, "[c] He Who doth not afflict willingly, nor grieve the children of men," when He saw that His creatures were determined to ruin themselves, did in a manner grieve and repent that He had made them: as in after times He lamented over Judas, "Woe unto that man by whom the Son of Man is betrayed: good were it for that man if he had never been born." Thus in the very act of passing sentence, the Almighty Judge makes known His unspeakable mercy. He shews that if the sinner would yet repent of his sin, He would repent of His condemnation, and forgive him after all.

To the same purpose are the repeated notices, which we read of in this chapter, given to the wicked world, through Noah: and especially this earliest one, which I read to you as the text: "My Spirit shall not always strive with man, for that he also is flesh: yet his days shall be a hundred and twenty years." Attend to this, my brethren, I beseech you, for indeed it very nearly concerns us all. See, it is said here concerning the sinners of that old world, that for all their sins, God's Spirit was striving with them. What is that, "striving with them?" You know by your own experience, more or less, as many of you as have thought at all of what is passing between God and your own souls. You know what the feeling is, when you are set upon some wrong indulgence, and an unseen hand seems to draw you back, an unseen eye to be frowning upon you, a voice which the ear cannot hear to be whispering to you: Hold, stay your hand, go no further in that direction, pass by, look not that way, suppress the words which you are longing to utter, indulge

[c] Lam. iii. 33.

not the thoughts which are now arising in your mind. What was this secret check but the mysterious Presence of God's most Holy Spirit, striving with our own evil mind, and with the suggestions of the too crafty tempter? Again, who has not before now felt himself moved in a way he could not account for to think of the world out of sight, and of Him Who rules it; to say prayers, to attend holy services, to confess his sins, or some of them which particularly trouble him, to seek for his own soul's good the friendship and conversation of good and holy persons, to relieve the poor and afflicted, denying himself, for Christ's sake. Let us take it for a certain truth that all such good and godly motions come of the blessed Sanctifier and Guide and Comforter. They are the strivings of the Holy Spirit with the soul of man. He graciously condescends in a manner to struggle and wrestle with our unruly desires. He has done so from the very beginning: He did so, as we here read, in the times before the flood: and in all generations before Christ and after; only since the kingdom of heaven has been set up, He has yet more mightily striven with the souls in which He actually abides, having regenerated them by holy Baptism: and we are so much the more inexcusable, when we oppose or reject His strivings.

The declaration therefore of the Almighty in the text, if it was terrible to the sinners of that day, may well be infinitely more terrible to us. "My Spirit shall not always strive with man." There will be an end, bye and bye, to the forbearance which I now practise. I shall cease to invite this evil generation to repentance. They will be given over to the just punishment of their stubborness and hardness of heart. This was His warning to Noah: and He adds the reason: "for that he also is flesh," i.e., These, like the men who have gone before, one man as well as another, generally speaking; are corrupt and wilfully bad; they are selfish and sensual: they are, in one word, flesh: all made up as it were of the polluted and evil nature which they inherit from Adam: walking after it, and not after the merciful and gentle leadings of the Holy Ghost. 'My Spirit therefore shall not always strive with them. After a time, I will " give them over to their own hearts' lusts, and let them follow their own imaginations." They shall be let alone, unchecked and unreproved, to follow the wild and abominable counsels of their own blinded hearts, and of the evil spirits whom they have chosen to be their guides.' Here again, fearful as the sentence is, we may, it is likely, too many of us, know somewhat of its truth and meaning by sad experience. When any of us has wilfully given way to known sin once, twice, or three times, the thought of it, we knew not how, tormented us less, we more easily put up with the excuses which our wicked heart suggested, we more and more readily turned our minds, after committing it, to other things, just as if nothing had happened. We were by degrees inclined to be impatient of any thing which rebuked us for that sin: we listened, willing to be deceived, to the whispers of the Evil one, tempting us to think lightly of it. Alas, these were but the too certain signs of the Holy Spirit beginning to depart from us, and to cease striving with us. They were the tokens of that false and fatal peace, in the enjoyment of which he entices his deceived to the very edge of the pit of hell, persuading them all the time, that they are not altogether turning their backs on heaven. And then oftentimes, all of a sudden, having brought them, as I said, to the edge, he will try to change their false hope into a kind of reckless despair: he will say to them, 'There is no hope, none: you have sinned past forgiveness: the mercy of God has quite forsaken you, and you may just as well throw yourself over the gulph.' In this way he has tempted many to self-murder, and many more, it is to be feared, to desperate excess of unclean living. Now, as I was saying, when any one of us has gradually given way to any known sin, and has ventured to resist and silence the strivings of the Holy Ghost against that sin, he was taking the first step in this dreadful and downward course; and surely it is an unspeakable mercy, after such doings, that we are still here; still on earth, still in our place of trial, not yet in hell: permitted by His unspeakable inconceivable mercy still to have more or less hope in Him, capable through His grace of bearing the cross, of amending our lives, of seeking to please Him, of bringing forth worthy fruits of penance. Our very being here, after venturing so near to damnation, is surely a token of a very gracious purpose towards us. God is still striving with us, though we also have been flesh, have given wilful way to deadly and corrupt inclinations. God is still striving with us, therefore we may hope: but He will not always strive, therefore we must never cease to fear; therefore we must lose no time, nor grudge any burden which He lays upon us.

To those sinners before the flood He fixed a certain period, letting them know through Noah that their days would be a hundred and twenty years: that is, (as the words seem to say) that He allowed them a hundred and twenty years warning, from the time when He was speaking, before He should cut them off. Their lives, as you know, were very much longer than ours: a hundred and twenty years, though it sounds so long to us, was but about a fifth of Noah's own life at the time when he entered the ark, for that was in his sixhundredth year: a hundred and twenty years therefore was to those before the Flood much about the same in proportion as fourteen years would be to us: for our life is about seventy years, and fourteen is equal to a fifth part of seventy. Suppose now that instead of leaving us uncertain what time we should have to repent in, our merciful Judge had told us that we should have each of us fourteen years and no longer: in the first place it is plain that many young persons would think fourteen years a good deal, and would say, in their hearts at least, 'Time enough for us yet in the matter of repentance:' and so they would put it off, and put it off, until the fourteen years had passed away as in a dream, they hardly knew how: and where alas! would they be at the end of it? Again, the time being so fixed, many timid and anxious tempers would scarce be able to bear it, especially when it was drawing near: they would be like persons hurried in setting out on a journey: the very hurry and anxiety would make their preparation imperfect. For reasons like these, we may well be very thankful that Almighty God has hid from us, not only the time of the last Judgement, but also that of our own death. Knowing not when the time is, we feel ourselves the more called on to take heed, to watch and pray continually. Whereas if a certain time had been fixed, many would have been made, by knowing of it, dilatory at first, and hurried and disquieted at last.

In the meantime, though neither fourteen years, nor any set period of our life is known to be appointed for us, yet so far we do know for certain: that long before that term of years is over, which was offered to those sinners by Noah, we shall be, every one of of us, with our trial over, and our sentence determined, in the more immediate Presence of our Judge. Long before a hundred and twenty years from this time, the youngest here will be in the unseen world, his soul parted from the body, awaiting the general resurrection. And how will it be with that soul?

If this question troubles any person, who has hitherto dealt lightly with such thoughts; if it makes him anxious and uneasy, let me beseech him, for the love of Christ, and for the love he bears to his own self, to make a serious use of that trouble and anxiety; not to let it pass away, as if it had never been, but rather to pray that it may sink deep into his heart, and never leave him till God's grace have made it the means of his true repentance and final salvation. Such misgivings are no less than the strivings of the Holy Spirit, in the consciences of sinners. And since we know that He will not always strive, we may well fear that each one of such opportunities, if neglected, may prove the last. Be not then always mere flesh: do not go on giving way, as so many have done before, and as you have hitherto done, to your low and corrupt passions. The flood is coming, that flood of fire, from which no flesh, no wicked one, shall escape: and your notice is short: far shorter than the one hundred and twenty years, which were allowed to the old world. The flood is coming, but the ark also is building: the ark of Christ's Church is in your sight, the Holy Ghost is daily building it up by adding new souls to it in holy Baptism. If you have wandered from it by grievous sin or sloth, the door is yet open; return to it by timely and entire repentance. Then shall you be borne safe over or through the flood of fire: whatever you may suffer, it shall not harm you for ever. Then shall the Church see accomplished in you the loving prayer, which she offered up at your Baptism: as you were then delivered from God's wrath, and received into the ark of Christ's Church, so shall you henceforth, stedfast in faith, joyful through hope, and rooted in charity, so pass the waves of this troublesome world, and the fires of the last Judgement, that finally you shall come to the land of everlasting life, there to reign with Him world without end, through Jesus Christ our Lord.

SERMON XVII.

AS IT WAS IN THE DAYS OF NOAH.

QUINQUAGESIMA.

GEN. vii. 1.

" And the Lord said unto Noah, Come thou and all thy house into the ark, for thee have I seen righteous before Me in this generation."

LAST Sunday the Church instructed us to consider the warning which Almighty God mercifully gave the sinners of the old world, before He sent the Flood upon them. His Spirit strove with them, according to that warning, one hundred and twenty years. All that time He allowed them to repent in, if they would. All that time each person's own conscience, the secret misgivings of his own heart, reproached him more or less for going on in ways which he knew to be wicked, and hateful to God. These were the secret whisperings of the Holy Ghost: but alas! none listened to them effectually. Many, for aught we know, might be moved for a time by such thoughts: might wish themselves better, might feel, as it were in a dream, 'What if God's anger should really come upon us? what if this secret dread, which we cannot help feeling, be but the token of somewhat unspeakably horrible, daily coming nearer and nearer to us?' Such dim and shadowy fears, we may well believe, many had; but none had the heart to follow them up: none really made up their minds to cherish their good thoughts by prayer, and to turn in earnest to Him Who was warning them.

And yet they had His outward and visible warnings also. Noah was a preacher of righteousness to them: and we may well believe that his preaching was known far and wide. And at the end of the time he preached in another way, not by words only, but by making the ark in their sight. Those at least, who were living near him, could not fail to take notice of *that*: but no one of them was moved to true penitence and amendment.

Thus they went on till the ark was finished, and the hundred and twenty years were over. The days of waiting are accomplished: the Holy Spirit ceases to strive: the time of forbearance is past, and the time of judgement is at hand. What now are Noah's thoughts? and what are the thoughts of the unbelieving world around him?

As for Noah, he has done, in every point, as God had commanded him. He has finished the ark, and now he has only to wait, in faith and in fear, for the coming of the flood. Like a person to whom God's good providence has given warning of approaching death, who has prepared himself for it, made his will, taken leave of his friends, counselled his children and those depending on him, forgiven his enemies, paid his debts, and above all repented of his sins; and who now has nothing to do, but in patience and prayer to expect when God shall call him: such was Noah, that just man, when the ark was finished, and the one hundred and twenty years were over, expecting when the flood should begin. We may well imagine what his thoughts would be, how he would watch every cloud and every shower, how anxiously he would hope that some at least of the wicked and careless whom he saw around him might be led to have better minds before it was too late.

We may also imagine, for our Lord Himself has told us, how the rest of that generation were employed, even to the very time that "[a] the flood came, and swept them all away. They did eat, they drank, they bought, they sold, they planted, they builded, they married wives, they were given in marriage: and knew not," until that last fatal moment. They knew not; *that* was their sin: for they might have known: God had told them very plainly. They had heard by the preaching of Noah that at the end of one hundred and twenty years their trial would be over, and their punishment would come. But they had neglected the warning, or would not believe it, and it was now gone out of their minds. Some of them, who knows? might at first perhaps have been moved by it, and might have begun to turn their hearts to God. But the pleasures, the vanities, the mockery, of the wicked and corrupt world, had proved too powerful for those weak beginnings. They had no root in themselves, and so endured but for awhile: and now they, like the rest, are on the very edge of destruction without knowing it.

For whilst they are amusing and vexing themselves with mere matters of this world, and whilst Noah for his part is waiting in fear and in prayer,

[a] S. Matt. xxiv. 38, 39, S. Luke xvii. 27, 28.

the one hundred and twenty years being now fully completed, the awful word comes down from heaven, "Come thou and all thy house into the ark; for yet seven days, and I will cause it to rain upon the earth forty days and forty nights; and every living substance which I have made will I destroy from off the face of the earth." Here was another week of warning for those stubborn and unhappy sinners, as many of them as were in the neighbourhood of the ark: and surely it is a very remarkable warning. For now the ark, which they had seen so long in building, begins to be filled: not only Noah and his family go into it, but the lower kinds of creatures also, the beasts and birds, are seen approaching it from all quarters. As sometimes before a violent storm, we may notice how the cattle, by a kind of instinct, make for some place of shelter, being sooner aware of what is coming than we are; so, but much more remarkably, did all the kinds of living creatures on the face of the earth hasten towards the ark by pairs, as knowing in their instinct far more than the proud unbelieving men who were looking on them. If they had even then any misgivings, either they were ashamed to own them, or confounded and bewildered, or their old ways and habits were too strong for them: and the seven days were over, and the flood had actually begun, before they had effectually repented.

The seven days are over: Noah and his family, eight in number, and all the chosen remnants of every creature, are now gathered into the ark: the Lord has shut them in: and the flood begins. The fountains of the great deep are broken up, and the

windows of heaven are opened: the waters both come
down from above, and rise furiously from beneath.
We must imagine for ourselves, for no words can
paint to us, the horror and confusion of that time;
how those, who had all along had misgivings about
the coming judgement, were the first to feel that it
was really come upon them, and to wish that they
had had root in themselves: how, as the tempest
came on more and more steadily, and the waters
gradually rose, the very hardest of the unbelievers
was compelled to fear and own the truth: how they
must have longed to be received into the ark, that
ark, the building whereof they had perhaps been
scoffing at for many years. But it was too late:
the Lord had shut the door: the Lord had shut Noah
and his family in, there was no opening to any other,
however earnestly they might now wish it. It was
as in our Lord's parable of the ten virgins, "[b] When
the Bridegroom came, they who were ready went in
with Him to the marriage, and the door was shut.
Afterwards came also the other virgins, saying, Lord,
Lord, open to us. But He answered and said unto
them, Verily I say unto you, I know you not."

Even if our Lord had not told us, my brethren, I
suppose we should scarce have failed to perceive how
nearly we are concerned in this fearful picture. The
history of that world before the Flood is but too nearly
the type and shadow of our own history, our own
condition in God's sight. For what was paradise,
but an image and likeness of that blessed new creation, the holy Church and kingdom of God, when it
was first set up on earth, undefiled by heresy or

[b] S. Matt. xxv. 10. 12.

deadly sin: all truth, **pureness, unity, and** concord? We see how things are fallen **from** this: how God's **house is rent** and **divided: what false** doctrines, heresies and schisms, what open and notorious **sins** walk about boldly and uncorrected: so that what **is** said of that old world may too truly be said of the world which calls itself Christian. It is corrupt before God, and filled with violence; and all flesh **hath** corrupted its way. Again, if one inquires the **cause of this, what more** prevailing, what deadlier **mischief can be** named than sensual lust, defiling the **heart, and** leading **to all evil** communications: **much** in the same way as we read that **the great cause of** the corruption before the Flood was that " the **sons of** God (such as we all are by Baptism) saw the daugh‑ **ters** of men that they were fair, and they took unto **them wives of all** whom they chose:" observe it says, **of all whom they chose:** their own wild and wilful **choice was what** guided them; not the fear of God: not reverence, discretion, and soberness: and what was the consequence? the **world** grew more despe‑ rately bad with each succeeding generation, until **God** was even compelled **to** destroy them with **the earth.** But this He did **not,** till He had long striven with them by the godly motions of His blessed Spirit: **and in** like manner, nay, and much more graciously, He has hitherto gone on striving with us. Only, as in time He gave them **up, and it** repented Him that He had made them, so we know not how soon He may repent of bearing with a race so unworthy and ungrateful. We know not how soon His own saying may be fulfilled, "c **When the Son of** Man cometh,

c S. Luke xviii. 8.

shall He find faith on the earth?" We know that He will not always strive with such as resist Him: we have no reason to depend even upon the one hundred and twenty years, which He promised Noah, before He destroy this our world. Why should we expect a long day? I would not rashly venture on forebodings, but surely I remember no time, when the hearts of thoughtful persons seemed so moved to look anxiously after fearful things to come on the earth, as they seem just now to be in our land. Every day almost something occurs, to make religious people say to themselves, what if we should be on the point of a great breaking up of all things, such as the prophecies seem to speak of, and to say, then shall the end come? At this very time, and in this very land, the law of marriage is even now in a way to be changed: and as before the flood the sons of God saw the daughters of men that they were fair, and took them wives of all which they chose; so it seems that in our time those who profess and call themselves Christians think it hard that they may not marry those whom Holy Scripture has forbidden them to approach on the ground of nearness of kin; the wife's sister, or the husband's brother. Holy Scripture says, this is one of the abominations on account of which God was so angry with the Canaanites, so that the very land where they lived did, as it were, spue them out, not being able to endure them: yet there is great reason to fear that this abomination will soon be part of our law: part, I mean, of the law of England—it will not be the law of the Church, nor the law of God—but except the people of England shew their minds to be earnestly against it, I fear it will soon be licensed by act of parliament: and surely that will be one thing more to draw down God's anger upon all flesh as having corrupted its way upon the earth.

On the other hand, we see also that the ark of refuge is in building, the number of Christ's elect is daily being accomplished by the death of holy and penitent persons, and the baptism of innocent babes. And in one respect, we are far happier than those sinners before the flood: that we are actually in the ark: the merciful providence of Almighty God elected us out of the world to be members of His Son before we could choose or know anything. Most assuredly we are, or have been, in the saving ark: we were there presently after our Baptism: if we are not there now, if we be not found there in that day, when the last flood, the flood of fire, shall overspread the whole earth, whose fault must it be? not His surely, Who set us there by His own free mercy: not our parents', who brought us there in our infancy: not the Church's which took so great care to instruct us by Catechisms, to warn us by sermons, to use us to holy prayers, to strengthen and refresh us by Sacraments, to chasten us by fastings, to put saintly examples in our way: it cannot be the Church's fault if we are not in God's ark: it cannot in short be any one's fault but our own.

This is our burthen, fellow-christians: for this we are to answer. This is the pearl of great price, the hidden treasure instrusted to our charge, for which we must give account at the peril of our souls. What are we to do to keep it? How may we be secure against the unspeakable misery of being cast out of the ark even after admission and long continuance in it? Surely, by being such as he was, for whom and by whom the ark was first builded. Mark what reason the All-seeing God mentions, why He should have invited Noah alone into that place of refuge. "Come thou into the ark, for thee have I seen righteous before Me in this generation." Noah was righteous, truly righteous: a just man, and perfect in his generation. He was righteous before God, and not before man only. Not of course without spot or blemish, for that is not said of any child of Adam, but of Him Who being manifested to take away our sins had in Himself no sin. It is not meant that Noah had no infirmities, but that taking his whole character together, he was not only free from mortal sin, but was sincerely good and well-meaning in the sight of God, Who trieth the hearts and reins. Such must we be, free from deadly sin, either by innocence or by penitence, and sincerely endeavouring to please God, making it the rule of our lives: else shall we be found outside of the ark when the flood of fire comes on.

It is said moreover, that Noah was found righteous before God *in that generation*. In that evil and corrupt generation he alone was faithful and good. The wickedness on every side did not infect him. They might mock, scorn, persecute, threaten, entice him. It was all one to him: he went on steadily with his work. This is a very great point towards remaining finally in Christ's ark: not to be moved from what you know to be right, though all the world besides give way. To practise a good and holy stubbornness, and set your face like a flint against the enemies of your Lord, knowing that so you shall never be ashamed.

Finally, learn of Noah's example to be righteous before God even in the worst of times, and so to stay in the ark, for your family's sake, and those dear to you, as well as for your own. For thus speaks the Lord to him: "Come thou *and all thy house* into the ark." His whole house is saved, because he is found righteous. As God would have spared Sodom, had He found but ten good persons in it: as He promised S. Paul in danger of shipwreck, "[c] God hath given thee all them that sail with thee:" so here He saves Noah's house from destruction, not for their own sake, but for Noah's. Let fathers and mothers, let friends and brethren and sisters, attend very earnestly to this. As ever they truly love those who are nearest to them, and ought to be dearest, let them never grow tired of rooting sin out of their own hearts. It is unknown how far, how deep, the blessing may reach which they so gain for their families. Noah's righteousness is even to this day visibly rewarded to the good of all us his posterity, in that God's rainbow shines upon us, and is a token to us, that the seasons shall on the whole go on in the usual course, and that the waters shall never more be a flood to destroy the earth. Keep his faith and obedience in heart, make it your rule, as he did, to do all that God commanded you, and see if you be not delivered as he was. The flood of fire is coming on, but God hath shut you and your household into His ark, before long to come forth, and offer Him the sacrifice of praise to all eternity.

[c] Acts xxvii. 24.

SERMON XVIII.

THE TENDERNESS OF ALMIGHTY GOD TO HIS FALLEN CREATURES.

QUINQUAGESIMA.

GEN. iii. 21.

"*Unto Adam also and to his wife did the Lord God make coats of skins, and clothed them.*"

THAT which I pointed out to you last Sunday from Holy Scripture concerning man's *work*, answers very well to the teaching of the same Scripture concerning another point, his *clothing*. We may see in both the same just and merciful providence of Him Who is both our Saviour and our Judge. As in respect of work man's original condition was, not to be idle, but to delight and solace himself in the dressing and keeping of that happy garden, where all things grew unbidden: so in respect of clothing, as we may well suppose that our first parents needed it not to shelter them from cold and inclemency of weather, so we know that in their state of innocency they were like little children, "[a] naked" and "not ashamed."

Again as one great token of God's anger after the Fall was His so cursing the ground, that it should

[a] Gen. i. 25.

not ordinarily bring forth its strength without severe toil, on man's part painful and wearisome, and often very disappointing; as the sinner was not to eat bread except in the sweat of his face; so even before that sentence was passed, before the Lord came down to pass it, the punishment of Adam and Eve had begun by the intolerable feeling of shame and sense of nakedness. The devil had promised that their "[b] eyes" should "be opened," and they were opened indeed, the eyes of both of them, opened to feel their own shameful condition. Before, they knew good only, now they knew evil also, the evil that they had brought upon themselves, and which as far as they knew, was to cleave to them and to their seed for ever. "[c] They knew that they were naked," and they could not endure the knowledge, so they set about hiding their shame as well as they could. Is not all this sadly like the history well known to too many in every Christian congregation, of what happens when people begin to fall from Christ by deadly sin? when the first wilful and deliberate lie is told, the first gross act of impurity, malice or dishonesty? I am not now speaking of persons who have been brought up as reprobates all their time, who have been left like the heathen to live without God in the world: but of those who have been brought up in the fear of God, who have been taught the consequence of sin: what do such persons see, if they would but think of it, in that first shame of Adam and Eve, but a miserable and dreary image of their own feelings, when they came to themselves after the excitement of their first deadly sin: looking round in

[b] Gen. ii. 5.   [c] Ib. iii. 7.

vain for shelter, ready to sink into the earth, longing, if it might be, to hide themselves from God and man. But it may not be; they cannot be hid: sooner or later, sin must bring open shame: as surely as "[d] the eyes of the Lord are" now and always "in every place, beholding the evil and the good;" so surely is there "[e] nothing covered that shall not be revealed; neither hid, that shall not be known;" so surely will the hour soon be here, and the Judge "[f] to bring to light the hidden things of darkness."

As to our poor endeavours to hide our sins, they are no more to the purpose than the wretched contrivance of fig leaves, which our first parents sewed together and "[g] made themselves aprons." Alas! how vain! if they thought that so they were preparing themselves worthily to appear before the Holy and jealous God! but not vainer than your thoughts and mine, my brethren, if ever we dream of sheltering and excusing our sins by a mere veil of outward decency: if we think that many prayers will atone for unclean thoughts, or liberal alms for dishonest gains, or anything whatever in the way of moral goodness for an irreligious and profane course of life!

But Almighty God saw and pitied the wretchedness of their shame, and their poor vain efforts to hide it: as He foresaw and pitied the hardness which they must endure to get their bread: and as He turned their toil into a blessing, both to their souls and bodies, in many ways, so He made their shame and nakedness an occasion of His own great and peculiar mercy. Pitying them as they stood

[d] Prov. xv. 3.   [e] S. Luke xii. 2.   [f] 1 Cor. iv. 5.
[g] Gen. iii. 7.

before Him, so forlorn and helpless, He provided for them garments indeed. "Unto Adam also and to his wife did the Lord God make coats of skins, and clothed them." Our very clothing that we wear, as well as the ground we tread on, is indeed a token and remembrance of our fall and shame and punishment: the ground, because if let alone, it yields nothing but weeds and rubbish: our clothing, because we need it to hide our shame, which shame is the fruit of our sin: but who does not feel also the tenderness, the fatherly kindness of our God and Judge; Who when they had cast away the bright and joyous garments of purity which He had wrapt around them, and were lying exposed in their shame, not knowing which way to turn, contrived this shelter for them, not beautiful nor costly, but sufficient to cover shame? And thus the very garments we wear are to be to us as a perpetual remembrancer from Him both of the happy innocency we have lost and of the shame we must bear as our punishment, and of His mercy towards us after all. In a certain sense, we ought always to wear mourning: mourning for the pure and happy beginnings which might have been so blessed to us, but which we have recklessly spoiled and forfeited: mourning for our lost home, paradise, and our companions the Angels, and most of all mourning that we should have caused our good and gracious Saviour such bitter pains and agonies, and should since have crucified Him afresh by our falling away. Can you think earnestly on these things, and yet count it right and natural to spend much time and thought and money upon your dress? The clothing which God gave in His indulgent care for sinners, can you dare to abuse it for purposes of luxury or pride? to tempt others to sin, to get them to talk of you, to feed your own foolish vanity with what perhaps might feed many poor? Nay, hearken to Christ's Apostle, who bids you be content with "[h]food and raiment;" or rather, hearken to Christ Himself charging you not to take "[i]thought for raiment," and promising that if you will "[k]seek first the kingdom of God and His righteousness; all these things shall be added unto you."

But that first clothing, the coats of skins wherewith the Almighty condescended to provide Adam and Eve, was a token, yea a type of greater mercies by far, of spiritual clothing to be vouchsafed to their naked souls. As the sweat of Adam's face, which after the fall accompanied him in all his hard work and endeavours to get bread out of the ground, was a type and token of our Blessed Lord the second Adam, in that Agony and Bloody Sweat with which He began His saving Passion; so the nakedness and shame of those first sinners was a token and type of what He should endure Who would come to be the Saviour of sinners. He was to provide the cure of our nakedness by taking it on Himself. How did Christ take man's nakedness and shame on Himself? First by being born: for He, the Holy Child Jesus, the Son of Mary, when He was born in that stable Bethlehem, before she "[l]wrapped Him in swaddling clothes, and laid Him in a manger;" was born as other children are in this respect also, that as His servant Job had said long before, so He might say,

[h] 1 Tim. vi. 8.   [i] S. Matt. vi. 28.   [k] v. 33.
[l] S. Luke ii. 7.

"ᵐ Naked came I out of my mother's womb;" Job added, "Naked shall I return thither" (for as we bring nothing into this world, so neither do we carry anything out). And our Saviour might well take up that saying also: for this was part of His deepest humiliation, among the circumstances of His Cross and Passion, that He had to be twice stripped in the course of it: once when He was to be scourged, and afterwards when He was to be nailed to the Cross. Thus He vouchsafed to bear the shame and reproach, as well as the pain, due only to the worst of sinners, He that was brighter than the morning star, purer than the highest Angel and the nearest creature to God in heaven. Thus by His unutterable shame did our Lord earn a pardon for our most shameful sins, the sins by which men most grievously profane their bodies which are His temples, the sins which they would least wish to have known, even they shall be forgiven and spared, if truly repented of, by virtue of the shame which He bore for them when He offered Himself, stripped and quite helpless, upon the Cross.

He was to suffer thus in shame of His Body, because He had taken upon Him the whole of that nature in which we had so grievously sinned: He took it upon Him, though without the sin: for He was made true Man, true Flesh, but only in the likeness of sinful flesh. The flesh was real, the sinfulness was only in appearance: as when Jacob, who is the figure of Christ, put on his brother Esau's garments to obtain the blessing which Esau had forfeited (of which you will hear this day fortnight). It

ᵐ Job i. 21.

was but the likeness of our sin which Christ took, but He took the very reality of our sorrows; the pain of body and anguish of heart, the hunger and thirst, the weariness and painfulness, the tears and the sweat, and so also the nakedness and shame. For we know that even in beings so imperfectly pure as the very purest of men and women, the sense of bodily shame and the horror of anything like nakedness is always most keen when there is least sin to be ashamed of—(as Rebekah when she was to meet Isaac covered herself with a veil)—how much more in the Lord of all purity, when He had condescended to become Man. Depend upon it, His sufferings in that respect, as in all others, in the awful hour of His Passion, were beyond all that we can imagine.

But this His nakedness was to be our clothing and our shelter; His shame, to be our glory. He was stripped, that He might clothe us with Himself.

For so we read in many places of Scripture. There is a "[n]robe of righteousness" "[o]fine linen, clean and white" the righteousness of Christ and His saints, which is given to every one to wear, who is called to "[p]the marriage Supper of the Lamb." It is the "[q]wedding garment," which whoso lacketh may in no wise abide at the feast of the King's Son. What is this robe? The Holy Ghost plainly tells us, that it is more than Christ's righteousness, it is Christ Himself. For "[r]as many of you as have been baptized into Christ have put on Christ." And we are bidden to put on "[s]the Lord Jesus Christ, and make not provision for the flesh." Christ then comes to

[n] Isa. lxi. 10.   [o] Rev. xix. 8.   [p] v. 9.
[q] S. Matt. xxii. 21.   [r] Gal. iii. 27.   [s] Rom. xiii. 14.

be our clothing, as well as our meat and drink. He clothes us with Himself, first in holy Baptism when He takes us up in His arms and blesses us. He folds Himself as it were all around us, so that the Father looking on us beholds us not as it were in ourselves, naked and unsheltered, in all our sins and uncleanness, but as we are in Jesus Christ His Son, true members abiding in Him, therefore pardoned and saved by Him. This righteousness of Christ is as the coats of skins with which Adam and Eve were clothed. Some have thought that those skins were the skins of beasts slain in sacrifice. And it seems very likely, since we know that sacrifice was practised in Adam's family, for Abel offered unto God "'the firstlings of his flock." And Abel no doubt learned of his penitent parents how "ᵘto walk and to please God." The death of those animals therefore, whose skins the Lord put upon Adam, would be a type of the Death of Christ. For every sacrifice was a type of Christ's Death. And their putting on those skins would be a type of our putting on Christ. And as they being so clothed might venture to appear before God and man, and go on with their daily duties, in hope and patience, waiting for their more glorious apparel; so also may we Christians, clothed as we have been with Christ in Baptism. We may draw nigh unto God in private and public prayer: more solemnly in Confirmation, most solemnly in Holy Communion: we may serve Him by the help of His Spirit in all our ways with cheerful hope, waiting, as I said, for our new and glorious apparel. What will be our new and glo-

---

ᵗ Gen. iv. 4.   ᵘ 1 Thess. iv. 1.

rious apparel; Hear the promises; "[x] this corruptible must put on incorruption, and this mortal must put on immortality." He "[y] shall change our vile body, that it may be fashioned like unto His glorious Body." "[z] We have a building of God, an house not made with hands," wherewith we earnestly desire "to be clothed upon:" i. e. He is preparing for each one of us a glorious body, to be put on when we rise from the dead; a portion of His own glory such as it appeared when He was transfigured in the mount. There are in His stores and vestries "white robes" for each one of us to wear standing "[a] before the throne, and before the Lamb;" fine linen, bright and clean, to appear in at His marriage Supper. The promise is to each one of you, and the token of it is the baptismal robe given you here. Grace here, to seal you for glory hereafter.

Men may indeed, if they will, strip themselves, like persons out of their mind, like the men "[b] possessed with devils," "exceeding fierce," whom our Saviour met "coming out of the tombs," they may choose to wear "[c] no clothes," they may have made all haste to cast away the purity which Christ gave them, and may even now be wandering about in the nakedness of shameless sin: shameless before God and His Angels, however it may be hidden before men. Too many have done, and are doing so. Perhaps some of *you* may have been of the number. I cannot tell, God knoweth, and your own hearts and consciences know, whether and how far you have given way to evil lusts and unworthy desires, and so stripped your-

---

[x] 1 Cor. xv. 53.   [y] Phil. iii. 21.   [z] 2 Cor. v. 1, 2.
[a] Rev. vii. 6.   [b] S. Matt. viii. 28.   [c] S. Luke viii. 27.

selves of the holy garments which He put on you when He made you His own. I cannot tell, God knoweth: but one thing is quite certain; that such a sin cannot be a small one; cannot be a matter of course; cannot be got rid of with a slight and easy penance. Think of it for a moment, and you must see that it cannot be a slight matter to put off your baptismal innocency: for it is to put off Christ. Never comfort yourself then, when you have broken some plain and great commandment, with the thought, 'All the world does the same,' or 'There are many worse than me,' or the like. But let all your comfort be in this, "[d]I have sinned against the Lord:" but He died for me, and He has said, "[e]Him that cometh to Me I will in no wise cast out." It is not yet too late. A Lenten time is coming: it is at hand. Christ is here: He is come on purpose to meet you, as He met those two possessed men who were wandering about without garments. Do not scorn Him: do not turn away from Him. If you will let Him, He will cast out the devil entirely: and when Easter comes, you will be found at His Feast, "[f]sitting" as one who is at home and at rest; and "clothed" with robes of penitence newly washed in His Blood; and in your "right mind," resolved, by His grace, to love and serve Him, and none but Him, for ever.

[d] 2 Sam. xii. 13.   [e] S. John vi. 37.   [f] S. Mark v. 15.

SERMON XIX.

OUR NEED OF SPIRITUAL SIGHT.

QUINQUAGESIMA.

S. LUKE xviii. 42.

"And Jesus said unto him, Receive thy sight: thy faith hath saved thee."

LENT is a special time, as the Church put us in mind last week, for coming out in answer to our Lord's call: coming out of our hiding places, that is, out of the shelter of our vain excuses, and confessing our sins one by one, and humbling ourselves in true self-denial before Him Who will soon come to be our Judge. Day after day and, if it may be, hour after hour, it will be good for us now to exercise ourselves in thoughts of this kind. The more we shrink, as plainly most of us do shrink, from opening our minds and owning our faults to God's ministers, the more earnestly ought we to try and judge our own selves. The Communion Service has some very grave words about this. We are to "search and examine our own consciences, not lightly, and after the manner of dissemblers with God, but so that we come holy and clean to His heavenly Feast." This of course means that we must take a great deal of trouble about it.

It will be very dangerous for a person, just glancing over his past life, to say, 'Thank God, I see nothing particularly bad, nothing that seems to me a weighty matter, nothing that greatly troubles my conscience.' This can never be safe: for in the first place, how very forgetful we all are; and how apt to think little of a thing, merely because it happened a good while ago: as if the mere tract of time wore it out and did it away. And in the next place, if we have not been *very* particular with ourselves in time past, how can we be sure that we are not even now under the dominion of some grievous sin, blinding our mind's eye, and hindering us from truly judging of ourselves? so that we have need of deep thought, and earnest prayer, over and over again, before we can so much as find out our grievous sins: much more, before we can properly repent of them.

Now, some persons will be ready to cry out, 'How can we ever get through such a task as this? it will be so painful, so strange, to search out in this way all the dark corners of our own heart, and force ourselves to read over again the miserable history of our own evil-doings, which we had rather have forgotten both by God and man.' Yes indeed, brethren and fellow sinners; it will be very strange, very painful: and if you have ever done it once thoroughly in a true penitential spirit, I do not say that it is your duty to go over it all again so very particularly. Though even in such a case it is generally good for persons to repeat their special confessions before God at such solemn times as this of Lent, so far at least as to bring it quite home to themselves, that *they* car the persons who did such and such kind of evil things, in spite of such and such warnings: and how can they ever be humble and watchful enough? But for others, who have never told before God on their knees the sad story of their own particular sins, but have been content to call themselves miserable sinners as all others are—for such it cannot but be wholesome, yea necessary, to look back as minutely as they can over the past years of their life, and reproach themselves in the bitterness of their soul for their earliest fall from baptismal innocency: for their many relapses when God had called them to repent, for their coming unworthily to Church and perhaps to Holy Communion, for their mingling their prayers with their sins, for contriving hypocritical excuses, for turning away from the warnings of the good Spirit, for not caring how they tempted others. Alas! how shameful, how miserable a feeling it is, to go over thoughts like these in our mind, to dwell on them, to put it home to ourselves, that we, we are the persons of whom all this is true: we, we have the stain of all this guilt upon our souls: but the shame, the misery that such thoughts bring now will prove nothing, nothing at all, in comparison with what it will be to have the same wretched story read in our ears out of God's book, when we shall indeed be forced to confess it, but our confession will be too late, it will do us no good, it will be the beginning, not of true repentance, but of eternal incurable punishment. If our eyes were but really opened to see what is fast coming upon us; death and judgement, heaven or hell; Christ on His throne, the saints and Angels around Him, the graves opened and the dead raised, the judgement set and the books opened: surely we should think little in comparison of the trouble and anguish of confessing our sins here, whether it be to God or man, with the comfortable hope of having them forgiven and cured, for Jesus Christ's sake, and by the help of His Holy Spirit. If our eyes are not thus opened, if we do not as yet seem to ourselves at all to behold these great truths as they really are, surely we must in the bottom of our hearts wish that our spiritual sight were better: surely we cannot always go on well pleased with ourselves, knowing what is close at hand, yet feeling as if we could not open our eyes and see it, because our long habits of sin and carelessness have blinded us to all but worldly things. We know we are on the very edge of a steep pit, a bottomless pit: would we not wish to have our sight strengthened, that we may not fall into it unawares: that we may find and follow the paths that lead away from it? What if it be frightful to see one's danger, to see on what a hair's breadth we stand, and over what a gulph? Is it not much better than to fall over and be lost for ever? What if it be distressing and shameful to look our sins one by one in the face, in order to bid them begone in the Name of Christ: will it not be much worse if they should come bye and bye and look us in the face, never more to depart from us?

Let no man therefore be afraid of having his eyes opened to his own true condition; rather let us all come to our Lord in earnest prayer to Him, that He would "[a] enlighten our eyes, that we sleep not in death." Let us ask of Him with all our hearts to give us so far a right understanding of ourselves, that none

[a] Ps. xiii. 3.

of our serious faults may remain, this Lent, unconfessed and unrepented of: that no part of God's holy will may continue to be slighted and disobeyed by us.

If you were without bodily sight, and knew of some skilful surgeon, who would and could cure you if you applied to him, would you not make all haste to do so? Would you draw back under a notion that your eye-sight would make you acquainted with a great many disagreeable objects, and that you should then be better able to work, and consequently have more trouble? No such thought, I am sure, would have power to keep you back: the gift of eye-sight would be far too precious to you, for you to mind such trifles: you would go at once to be cured, and be very thankful. Think of those blind men by Jericho, of whom we hear in the Gospel to-day. For a long time, perhaps for years, they had been used to sit by the wayside, begging: all their care had been to ask an alms, to obtain a pittance for prolonging their poor and hard life: no thought had they of so great a blessing as recovering the use of their eyes. And so far they may perhaps be truly likened to some of us, who have gone on helpless and spiritually blind, day by day, seeking only such poor vain help as this present world can give: having perhaps, from time to time, a dim thought of something better and higher, as those blind men might have a dim remembrance of the light: but as they never expected to receive their sight, so too many Christians, I fear, go on for many years with no real hope or intention of ever being truly religious. They see and hear of others around them who find their happiness in serving and obeying

Christ, but they do not understand it at all, it seems quite beyond them, just as those blind men were surrounded with others who had the use of their eyes, but took it as a matter of course that they were not ever to recover their own.

Thus it went on, we know not how long, till on a certain happy day, appointed before by the good providence of God, our blessed Saviour passed by, on His way to Jerusalem, where He was now going to lay down His life for us: and as He drew near to Jericho, the blind man, whose name was Bartimæus, sat by the way side begging: and hearing a multitude pass by, he asked what it meant: and they told him that "Jesus of Nazareth is passing by." No doubt he had heard of Jesus of Nazareth, and God gave him a heart to believe in Him and His mighty works: and he calls earnestly on His Name: that Name, besides which there is none other under Heaven given unto men, whereby they may receive sight or health or salvation, or any good thing:—the blind man cries out, as we do in the Litany, "Thou Son of David, have mercy upon me:" and when our Lord, to try his faith, seems as though He would pass by without making him any answer, and when the bystanders sought accordingly to quiet him, rebuking him that he should hold his peace, he did but cry so much the more, "Thou Son of David, have mercy on me:" and so Jesus stood still, and commanded him to be called.

Now I say, that this affecting history, besides being a most lively instance of the care which our good Saviour takes of all His poor and afflicted people, is also a special encouragement for all those to turn to Him, who feel themselves more or less blinded in heart, bewildered by their sin and ignorance. Suppose, for instance, this very season, some one who has been all his life long blind and dead to heavenly things should find himself more than usually inclined to attend to them: this will be like Jesus of Nazareth passing by, Christ our Saviour passing by on His yearly progress from Christmas to Easter, from His birth to His cross and grave: if you feel inclined to call on Him, and ask His help as He goes along, beware how you part with such a good and holy thought: make much of it, let it not go, recall it again morning by morning: if nothing seem to come of the prayer, yet persevere, as the blind man kept on, "Son of David, have mercy upon me:" bye and bye He will shew that He regards your prayers. As He stood still, and commanded the blind man to be called, so He will put it in the hearts of His servants and ministers to say comfortable words to you, and read comfortable Scriptures: His providence will in one way or another encourage you to come near Him: as the persons round Bartimæus said, "Be of good comfort, rise, He calleth thee." And as then the blind man cast away his outer garment, that he might the more quickly and easily arise from his place on the ground and follow Jesus, so let every one who would be a true penitent make haste to get rid of his evil ways and unnecessary cares, of all that clings about him and would hinder his obeying Christ's call. For instance, one man would fain come to his Lord, and have the eyes of his soul opened, but he has some evil companion to whom he is attached, and who will perhaps ridicule him for making a change to the better: that evil companion is like the garment, whom he must cast away that he may come to Jesus. Or perhaps it is some bad custom that he has got into, of staying away from Church, or of using bad words, or of drinking rather more than he ought, or of idling away his time or his money, or of disrespect towards his elders and betters, or of not turning away his eyes when he ought: well, these bad customs are like garments which a man is used to, and which it is more or less unpleasant to him to give up: but if he wants in earnest to come to Jesus, and recover his spiritual sight, given up they must be; any one such evil habit, wilfully indulged in, is certain to keep you in blindness, and away from Christ.

And if you would know what a person loses by being so kept from his Saviour, follow in spirit along with blind Bartimæus, and see what a blessing he obtained. When he came up, our Lord asked him, "What wilt thou that I should do unto thee?" Not that the holy Jesus needed to be told, but He would try the poor man's faith, and shew it to others: even as He expects us to tell Him our wants in prayer, and our sins in confession, though He cannot but knew them full well before we ask. The blind man answers, "Lord, that I may receive my sight." Other things, no doubt, he wanted, but he did not hesitate for a moment, he was quite clear what was his principal want. He prayed to have his bodily eyes opened: and we, if we know our own good, shall pray in like manner that the eyes of our understanding may be opened to discern heavenly and spiritual things. Such a prayer, sincerely offered, our Lord Christ is sure to hear: as He heard and granted immediately the blind man's petition. "Receive thy sight," said our Lord: "thy faith hath saved thee." And immediately he received his sight: And what did he see? What was the first object on which his eyes rested? What but our gracious Saviour Himself, with His eye of divine mercy turned towards him? No wonder he was so struck with what he saw, and what had been done to him, that he could not find in his heart to part from his Divine Benefactor; no wonder the next thing we read should be, that "he followed Jesus in the way." And we too, my brethren, since at this moment Christ is inviting us to Him: since He is in a manner standing still, and commanding us to be called; let us not doubt, but hasten to Him, casting away our evil customs and fancies, and present ourselves to Him by saying our prayers earnestly, and He will assuredly command our inward eyes also to be opened; and we shall see Him by faith: we shall see Him, God made Man for us, in all His mighty and merciful works and sufferings. This very Lent will shew Him to us, from His fasting and temptation going on to His Agony and Death. May we only find grace to follow Him Whom we shall see! to follow Him, with that blind man, along the only true way, the way of the saving, life-giving Cross!

SERMON XX.

HOW TO LEARN THE LOVE OF GOD.

QUINQUAGESIMA.

1 S. John v. 3.

"This is the love of God, that we keep His commandments: and His commandments are not grievous."

The Church to-day, as you know, speaks to us very much of Charity. We are instructed by S. Paul in the epistle how precious charity is, and what are the marks of it. The Gospel sets before us the Lord Jesus Christ, the one great and perfect example of charity, in His tender compassion healing a blind man, and planning how to redeem us all by His Death. The collect is an earnest prayer that God would pour into our hearts abundance of charity, the most excellent of all His gifts, binding all our good things, if any we have, in one, and so necessary, that without it we can have no real heavenly life; we may have a name among men that we live, but in God's sight we are but dead.

Plainly then if anything in the world concerns us, it is this, that we have true charity, or at least be in the way to attain it. What then *is* this charity, this crown of all good things? And how may we know whether we have it, or at least are in a way, by God's mercy, to arrive at it?

First, it is not fine talk: it is not saying plenty of religious and beautiful words. There is something indeed very winning and engaging in such words, especially when he who speaks them seems to be affectionate and in earnest: but the Apostle tells us, they may be without charity: and then they are no better than sounding brass or a tinkling cymbal; a noise only to amuse children with.

Secondly, charity is not knowledge, nor scholarship: for S. Paul goes on to say, "ᵃ Though I understand all mysteries and all knowledge, and have not charity, I am nothing;" nothing, i. e. in God's sight, nothing, in the judgement of Him Who alone knoweth the true value of all things.

Thirdly, charity is not the being able and willing to do great things even in God's service: for S. Paul says in the third place, that a man may have all faith, so as to remove mountains, and yet not have charity.

Fourthly, neither is charity the same as giving of alms, (though many think more of that than of anything else). For a man who is without charity may nevertheless bestow all his goods to feed the poor. He may do it out of vanity, to make himself beloved or praised, and that is very far from true charity.

Nor yet again is it quite certain that a man has true charity, the true love of God and his neighbour, in his heart, though he be willing to suffer

ᵃ 1 Cor. xiii. 2.

all, even death in torments, for what he says is
God's cause. This seems a hard saying, but it is
just the plain saying of the apostle. "[b] Though I
give my body to be burned, and have not charity it
profiteth me nothing." So strange, so full of self-
deceit, is the heart of man, that there are some who
have died, rather than own Christ's Truth: some who
have died with stubborn unforgiving hearts, the
devil's martyrs rather than God's. They might
have a kind of zeal, but they had not the true love
of God and man, neither were they trying to have
it: therefore their death, how courageously soever
they bore it, was no token of their being true martyrs in the cause of our Lord and Saviour.

All these things then, martyrdom, giving away
all, miracles, knowledge, speaking with tongues,
may be without charity, and charity without them.
But what then *is* charity or the love of God? Many
seem to imagine that it means chiefly a certain
eager feeling concerning God and eternity, yearn-
ing of spirit towards the Cross and towards Him
Who suffered thereon, such as will cause a person easily to shed tears when He, His Agony and
Passion, are spoken of. The love of God in many
men's account is certain emotion of joy and satisfaction which persons to whom such grace is given,
feel on hearing or reading or thinking of Christ, in
that they are enabled to assure themselves that they
are Christ's, His dear children, His highly favoured,
and shall be finally saved by Him. But this can
hardly be a true account of what Scripture means
by the love of God. For, not to speak of other Scriptures, S. Paul surely meant his Philippians to have

[b] 1 Cor. xiii. 3.

the true love of God in their hearts, yet he bids them work out their salvation with fear and trembling: and they could not so well fear and tremble, if they were quite sure they could never fall away. Therefore the love of God, that most precious thing which can be in the heart of man, is not a mere thankful and joyful sense of salvation: it is not any mere feeling in the mind and fancy, but it is a principle, a living rule, ordering the whole heart and conduct: just as the love of her child is a living rule to a mother, accompanying her, guiding, restraining her, whatever she sets about, not coming and going, but always present with her: a part of her being, which is with her night and day, and directs and encourages her in a thousand things, often, almost, without her being aware of it herself.

In a word, my brethren, and that word taken from the lips of him who is called the Apostle of love, our Lord's own most beloved and loving disciple, "This is the love of God," this is charity, "that we keep His commandments, and His commandments are not grievous." By which we may understand that he who desires to love God cannot do so immediately upon willing to do so. Love, we all know, is a thing which cannot be forced. It cannot be learned as a child learns a lesson, or as an apprentice learns a piece of work in his trade. The love of God is indeed the first and chiefest of all the commandments, as the catechism teaches us out of the mouth of Christ: but how are we to set about learning and practising it? Surely in the same kind of way as we should use and train a child to love a nurse, companion, or teacher, to whom it was as yet unaccustomed. We should not at once bid the child love this or that person. It would be idle to do so. But we should use the child by degrees to that person. We should employ little arts and ways to recommend that person to the mind of the young child, we should use it to say loving words to him, and to think loving thoughts of him: and so by degrees the person being really amiable, the child would be brought up to love him: and loving him, would rejoice to be with him and to do what it knows will please him. Somewhat in the same way may we teach ourselves and others true charity, the true love of God, the loving Him as He requires to be loved, with heart, soul, mind, and strength. The true Scriptural method in which to learn this best of all lessons is to use yourself night and day to do say and think what you know will please God: to remember and remind yourself continually that He is close at hand, looking into your very heart; that by Him you live and move and have your being: all the comforts of your life, all your kind friends, all the helps you are conscious of against want and danger, all your innocent enjoyments, and most especially whatever pleasure you take in right and noble things, and in getting over the temptations which beset you: all, all comes from Him. He is the Parent of your parents, the Friend Who provides you with friends: in Him is that Fountain of love out of which, as so many little streams, flow all the loving and affectionate feelings which any one on earth has towards you; as one has beautifully said, "From Thee all love, all pity flows; mothers are kind because Thou art." I say, if you use yourself continually thus to see God in your daily and hourly life, this is using and training yourself to love God: and this cannot be, without the faithful keeping of His commandments.

Observe what I say, my brethren, your remembrance of God will be no lesson of love to you unless you are sincerely endeavouring to do what will please Him. You heard last Sunday how it was with our first parents, when for the first time after their sin they came to be aware that God was very near them. They could not bear it, they tried to hide themselves, their instinct was, if such a thing might be, rather to wish Him far away from them. So it has always been, and always will be. In your sin and shame you are moved to hide yourselves as it were from God, because you know that He hates such doings, and you cannot bear the thought of His eye of displeasure fixed upon you: you are tempted to drive away the remembrance of Him, to be glad when you can quite forget Him, as the wicked in Job say to Him, "ᵉ Depart from us, for we desire not the knowledge of Thy ways." But now, to be glad to forget a person, to be pleased when he is far away from you, is surely the very contrary to love. Love rejoices in the presence of the beloved: the nearer he comes, the longer he stays, the better: therefore wilful sin, causing you to shrink from God's Presence, plainly instructs and practises you in hating God; and earnest obedience, causing you to delight in God's Presence, is the very thing to train you to the love of God.

One might indeed apprehend, that earnest endea-

ᵉ Job xxxi. 14.

vours to obey would not always make the thought of God's being at hand comfortable, because there must always go along with them a painful sense of imperfection. You must feel sadly how very blemished, how sadly unworthy of Him is all you are doing: and this might seem likely to hinder you from being glad with the joy of His countenance, from being pleased at His looking upon you. But it is not so, for this reason: that such faithful endeavours to obey, such thankful acknowledgements of God in all things, are rewarded by Him with a sense of His being your Father: His Presence then is the presence of a loving Parent, Who takes pleasure in His children's efforts, how mean and weak soever: bears with their mistakes, pities and forgives their infirmities. As one who is only learning music would feel timid, having to sing or play before a person who had exquisite skill; but is encouraged and comforted again if that person be one who dearly loves him and is sure to deal gently with his errors: so is the assurance, "[d] Thou God seest me," all in all to the timid believer, striving to do right but deeply aware of his deficiencies. Awful as the Presence of God is, to such an one it is deep delight and heavenly consolation. It is his only hope to be excused the past, and to be helped to do better for the future.

Every way then we may understand how that obedience is the true and only school of love. Of course there must be prayer: without *that* there can be no real obedience. You must try and pray to do right, and you must pray that God would teach you to love Him: and then He *will* teach you to love Him:

[d] Gen. xvi. 13.

there is no doubt whatever of it. He will teach
you to love Him, though for a long time you may
not feel as though you loved Him. One great token
of your improving in His love will be, that commandments which used to be grievous to you will become less grievous: you will be better able to command your tempers, to bear with vexations, to keep
your eyes and imaginations in order, to get over bad
habits, to do as you would be done by yourselves.
Such are true fruits of love, for which, if they are
granted you, you ought to be very thankful, even
though your hearts be not lifted up to that fervour
of love which you could desire. *Dutiful* love, *that* is
the good and safe temper: that is what is especially
meant, when our Lord tells us of His yoke being
easy and His burthen light. How is it easy, seeing
that He no less surely tells us, "*e* Strait is the gate
and narrow is the way?" Why, it is love, loyal,
dutiful love, that makes the yoke and the burden
pleasant. For as Jacob's seven years of patient ser-
vitude under Laban seemed to him but a few days
for the love he bare to Laban's daughter Rachel, so
it is with the lovers of Christ; so it was with the
heroic Apostle, as you heard last Sunday: he took
"pleasure in infirmities, in reproaches, in distresses,
in persecutions, for Christ's sake." Why? Because
he loved Christ. So in our time, though of course
none of us may be compared to S. Paul, there are
not wanting, we trust, those of whom it might be
said, 'This man takes pleasure in his hard work, his
daily labour, his poor condition, for Christ's sake; he
is thankful to earn his bread by the sweat of his brow,

e S. Matt. vii. 14.

remembering that our Incarnate God was a poor carpenter at Nazareth for many years.' And again, of another it may be said, 'See that faithful, courageous young person; how in early youth, in the midst of tempting company, being free to have his own way, he keeps himself in order for Christ's sake, he is chaste in thought word and deed; he rejoices in self-denial, hoping to be pure in heart.' This, we trust, may be said of some among us; said, I mean, by the holy Angels; for of the noble virtue of chastity men are not sufficient judges. And where this *may* be said, surely that man is in a fair way to learn most perfectly the lesson of heavenly love. Another, it may be, is tried by sore affliction, and does not even pray to have it otherwise, because he would fain have no will but the will of his Father: and so, being " chastened with pain upon his bed, and the multitude of his bones with strong pain," he too, without knowing how, is daily learning to be more perfect in love. The patient sick man, the chaste young man, the contented poor man; each one of these after his own way is being taught in the school of Divine love: and not these only, but all who strive to obey Christ.

Let no man's heart fail, because of his not yet feeling distinctly that love of his Saviour which he would desire to feel: even as none should be lifted up and pleased with himself, because he thinks he *does* feel that love. Do not so much mind *feeling*, one way or the other. The great point is, are you trying in earnest to obey Christ and to pray? If you are, only go on, and bye and bye you will find the yoke easier and the burden lighter. And in His good time you shall come to perfect love: and perfect love is perfect and eternal joy.

SERMON XXI.

PREPARATION FOR HOLY COMMUNION, PREPARATION FOR DEATH AND FOR JUDGEMENT.

Amos iv. 12.

"*Prepare to meet thy God, O Israel.*"

LENT is at hand, and the trumpet will soon sound again, the great and holy trumpet, of which it is written, "^a Blow ye the trumpet in Zion, and sound an alarm in My holy mountain." The sound of it will be heard next Wednesday, by all who have ears to hear. The true and dutiful children of the Church, the loyal soldiers of Christ Jesus will next Wednesday hear the call of their Leader's trumpet, rousing them up, as on all Ash-Wednesdays, to set about His work, to fight His battle, in earnest. It will be the old note, but you will not therefore scorn it, if you are true men and brave soldiers. You know it would never do for a soldier, when the trumpet or bugle sounds in the morning, to say, 'It is only the old call over again, what I have been used to so very often; I am not going to disturb myself for that;' and so to stay quietly in his quarters. No more will it do for you, Christian warriors, to make light of your Lord's summons, now that He is calling upon

^a Joel ii. 1.

you at the opening of another Lent; another holy season of penitence self-denial and prayers. He calls you morning by morning, and morning by morning you must answer His call. And what is the note, the keen and ringing note, by which He would call you, and scatter your deadly sleep? The awakening note, the clear word of warning, is, as you know, 'Turn unto the Lord:' that is, 'Prepare.' "Prepare to meet thy God, O Israel;" so He cries aloud to the whole Church, and to every separate member of it: 'Prepare, get ready to meet Him;' as you soon must, face to face. Ready or not, you must and will meet Him, He must and will come upon you. Prepare to meet Him, as a wise builder looks on and prepares for a great work which is required of him: as a skilful commander of an army prepares to meet the enemy, whom he knows to be at hand. It is our Lord's own advice. "[b] Which of you, intending to build a tower, sitteth not down first, and counteth the cost, whether he have sufficient to finish it? . . . . . Or what king, going to make war against another king, sitteth not down first, and consulteth whether he is able with ten thousand to meet him that cometh against him with twenty thousand?"

Christ our Lord asks a question of you, my brethren. He asks it of every one of you. Christ asks you a question: had you not better think how to answer it? He says, 'I am coming, I am at hand, I shall presently be here: are you ready for Me?' How is He coming? And how are we to prepare to meet Him?

First, He is coming to each one of us in death.

[b] S. Luke xiv. 28—31.

Then, if not before, He will so come that we shall not be able to hide our eyes from Him. Here, while we are in this world, we have so many persons around us, so many things to do, all is in such a mist, hurry, and confusion, that it is as much as one can do to see his path distinctly, or to hear the still small voice of the Almighty, saying, "ᶜThis is the way, walk ye in it:" but death, when it comes, will clear all the mists away, will silence all the disturbing voices, will quiet all the throbbings and pantings of the heart after the poor vain trifles of this present world. When we die, the spirit, as the wise man said, returns straight unto God Who gave it. We die alone; however we may have lived in crowds and companies to the very last moment of our time on this earth, we die alone: our friends may be standing around us, kneeling beside us, mourning over us; but none of them all can enter into a man's heart, and know what thoughts, feelings, anxieties, what griefs or joys unutterable, are going on there at that moment. God only can tell that—only He Who reads the secrets of the soul; Who accompanies the departing spirit all through the moment of death, and beyond it, into that world where Lazarus and the rich man were. When you once come to that world, on which side soever of the great gulf you find yourself, you will be aware that God is present, in a different manner from any thing that you feel here.

Suppose you were born blind: you would have no notion of colours, nor of any of these things, beautiful or hideous, which we, the rest, see with our outward eyes. And if by His good providence you had come

ᶜ Isa. xxx. 21.

any how to obtain your sight, what a new thing, what an overpowering wonder would it be to you. And distant things (so we are told), would appear quite close, would seem even to touch your eyes. Something in this way, we may well believe, will happen to each one of us, the very moment the breath is out of our bodies. We shall understand how near God is to us, how deeply He is looking down into our very hearts, we shall feel His eye fixed upon us, in a manner quite different from anything we can experience here. You will not then have to guess, nor faintly to imagine, but you will *know* what the Holy Scripture means when it tells you of "[d] the word of God being quick and powerful, and sharper than any two edged sword, piercing even to the dividing asunder of soul and spirit, and of the joints and marrow, and is a discerner of the thoughts and intents of the heart. Neither is there any creature that is not manifest in His sight; but all things are naked and opened unto the eyes of Him with Whom we have to do." You read or hear this now, and I hope you believe it. But the moment after your death you will see and feel it. Will you not make acquaintance with that aweful light, as you may, beforehand, that you may be able to bear it when it dawns upon you?

And it may very likely dawn suddenly: you may be called without any notice at all. Death is a door which may be opened for us at any moment, and when it is opened, pass through it we must, be we never so unwilling: it is no use to hang back: pass through it we must, and see what is on the other side. As yet we are waiting round that door: every now and

[d] Heb. iv. 12.

then it opens, and some one of our friends neighbours or acquaintances is drawn out of the crowd by an unseen hand, and guided through the door, and it closes behind him: we see him no more, nor does he see us: but what then? Is it nothing at all to us? May we rightly and wisely go on with our work or our play, and think no more of that mysterious doorway, nor of the hidden things behind it? Nay, my brethren, for we know for certain that it must open for us before long, and our turn is likely enough to be the very next time it opens. Do not flatter yourself that it can hardly be so, that you may depend upon having plenty of notice: you must know better than that: I dare say there is none of us but has learned by experience how suddenly death may take any one, whether old or young. We hear the bell tolling of a morning, and we know not for whom it may be: would it not be a wise and a Christian thought, if we were always to ask ourselves, each one, 'What if it were going for me? How would it be then?'

Is there any thought more aweful, more awakening than this, 'I may be called any moment to meet my God in death?' Yes, my brethren, there is one thought yet more aweful, "ᵉ It is appointed unto all men once to die, but after that the judgement." After death comes judgement: and then we shall have to meet our God in the way which Christ has warned us of: bodily, and not in spirit only: face to face, and not only thought to thought: we shall not only feel His Presence, His Eye looking down into the deep of our hearts, but we shall have

ᵉ Heb. ix. 27.

to give account, before Him, and before His Angels, and before our brethren small and great, of all the things we have done in secret, all the hidden uncleannesses and vanities and hypocrisies, which we thought at the time no man knew of, and since had perchance quite forgotten ourselves. How will you endure that, brethren? How could you bear it, if even now whoever knows most harm of you were to stand up before the congregation and declare that harm without consideration or pity? If you think that you could not bear *that*, that you would be ready to sink into the earth—O consider what it must be to have the *whole* of your secret history read out of God's unerring book in the hearing of those holy ones! And it is no dream, it *must*, it *will* be so. For this is the word of Him Who is the truth, "'There is nothing covered which shall not be revealed:" And again, "Every idle word that men speak they shall give account thereof in the day of judgement." Oh, how shall we be able to bear it? Only in one way, and that is, by preparing for it: by providing ourselves beforehand with a Friend, Who will cast His robe, even in that hour, over the sad nakedness of our souls and consciences. And there is but one Who can do so, but one Who will support us in that intolerable confusion; and that is our Judge Himself. Acquaint yourself with Him, unite yourself to Him, now whilst there is yet time, now whilst you are on your trial; and He will clothe you, as He did our poor fallen parents standing before Him in their shame and misery. Do you your best to put on Christ here, and He will in some marvellous way clothe you with

---

ᶠ S. Matt. x. 26.

His own fine linen, the righteousness of His saints; nay, He will clothe you with Himself, He Himself will be your Righteousness, He will shelter and protect you, so that even when all your sins are made known, you shall not be ashamed at His coming.

Yes, dear brethren, you know it in your hearts, however some of you may be accustomed to make light of the thought: nevertheless you know in your hearts, that you have indeed but one thing to do in the world, and that is, to prepare to meet your God first in death, and afterwards in judgement. If you ask, How am I to do this? Give me some short rule, which I may carry away with me, and remember and practise, for I am not learned, I must have something simple and plain. If you ask me this, I will give you such a rule as you ask: but, my brethren, will you practise it? You will, if you desire to deal honestly and justly and truly with your loving Saviour Who bought you with His own Blood. But the rule is the same, whether you will mind it or no, for it is in God's own message, and when once it is delivered, upon you must be the burden of rejecting it, if you choose to do so. Well, the rule which will prepare you to meet your God in death and in judgement is simply this: You must prepare to meet Him, and really and regularly meet Him, in His own great Sacrament; you must become a worthy communicant. If your own death is to find you ready for Him, you must live in remembrance of His Death; and His Sacrament, you know, is His appointed Remembrance. And if judgement is to find you ready, you must judge yourselves in time in self-examination before the Sacrament.

Consider a moment, and you will see that it stands to reason that the Holy Communion should be *the* true way of preparing to meet Him. For it is in fact using yourself to meet Him. He has promised to be there, as often as we "do this in remembrance of" Him. For He is "[g] that Bread of life." He is there, that eating Him, we may live by Him. He is "[h] the true Vine." He is there, that we may all of us drink of His Blood, His Blood of the new Testament, shed for us and for many for the remission of sins. His priest too is there, by whose mouth He blesses the bread and wine; His priest, one of those with whom He has promised to be unto the end of the world.

You see in how many gracious ways our Lord comes to meet us in Holy Communion. In preparing therefore for Holy Communion, we are preparing to meet Him. Be ready for this Sacrament, and you are ready for death: nay, you are ready for the dreadful day of Judgement, which may happen, you know, whilst you are yet living on earth. A person coming to Holy Communion with a true penitent heart and lively faith, and charity to all men, were he to die immediately after such Communion, would be as sure of salvation as a babe just baptized and dying. Therefore, I repeat it again—it is quite plain, and quite certain, Prepare to meet Christ in communion, and you are preparing to meet Him in death and judgement.

Now the holy weeks of Lent, my brethren, are God's good gift to His Church for this especial purpose, to prepare you for death by preparing you for Holy Communion. For every Christian you know,

[g] S. John vi. 48.   [h] Ib. xv. 1.

who will keep the law of the Church, his mother, is bound to communicate at Easter: and these forty days before Easter ought to be to every one of us, days of repentance, **days of holy discipline and serious thought**, days of self-examination and confession of sins, days for searching and trying our ways, and turning again unto the Lord[i]. Now let me call upon you, dear brethren, now at least, in *this* Lent, to use the good time, and not throw it away, lest haply you should never see another. In former years, we have wasted Lents enough, God knows, and too many: God forbid it should be so again. In His Name the messengers of Christ call upon all who hear them, not to let this season pass without considering, as in God's sight, how they stand in regard of Holy Communion.

I would put it to you, dear brethren, in this way. Each one of you, from the eldest to the youngest, is either a regular communicant, or one who has more or less fallen away from being so, or one who has hitherto neglected the Communion, or he is one who not being yet confirmed, cannot by the rule of the Church, as yet communicate. Now Jesus Christ invites you, to whichever of these sorts you belong, He, your only and most loving Saviour calls upon you this very Lent, in some such way as this: 'I am coming to you at Easter: prepare to meet Me;' "prepare to meet thy God, O Israel." You that have begun and persevered hitherto, as a Christian ought, in waiting on your Lord in His Sacrament, surely you cannot be too careful, too particular, in trying yourselves, whether you have always come there

[i] Lam. iii. 40.

worthily : surely His past mercies ought to make you more anxious than ever in watching and cleansing your garments, lest after all you lose your place at the Feast. You that unhappily have begun backsliding, (alas there are too many such here, too many who had once begun to wait upon our Lord in this His appointed Sacrifice, and have now (for one reason or another,) ceased to do so, what,) think you, is Jesus Christ's message to you? Why, you may find it in the book of Revelations, and a fearful message it is. To such as you the Almighty Judge says, "[k] I have somewhat against thee, because thou hast left thy first love. Remember therefore from whence thou art fallen, and repent, and do the first works : or else I will come unto thee quickly, and remove thy candlestick out of its place, except thou repent."

But perhaps you are not a backslider, but one of those who never would communicate. He has called again and again, but for this or that reason thou wouldest not hearken. Shall it be so again ? Shall this Lent too and Easter, with so many more, be registered against thee? Not if you have faith as a grain of mustard seed : not if you really love God at all, or care for your own soul, though it be but a little. If you have but one drop of faith or love you will at least begin this Lent to think seriously of Holy Communion, and not be ashamed to speak of it to your Pastor : nay, dear brethren, for that would be being ashamed of Christ.

Lastly, to the younger and unconfirmed persons our Lord also cries out ; 'Prepare : prepare, for you too have souls : you too must give account : you too must

[k] Rev. ii. 4, 5.

die and be judged: for you too Christ died.' Think then of Christ: pray to Him: for His own sake try to learn about Him, to behave yourselves well in His Presence, to overcome your bad ways in order that He may be pleased with you[1]. Whoever you are, my brethren, you have had your call: Christ has made you hear His Voice: He now waits to hear your answer; or rather, to watch and see whether you are minding Him. And observe, He does not call you as heathens· His word is, "Prepare to meet thy God, *O Israel*." Get ready for Christ, because you are His own people. Let it not be said of any one of you, "He came unto His own, and His own received Him not." Your burden, dear brethren, is very great, as well as your blessing: your blessing, in that you are God's own people; your burden; for what a thing it would be, should God's own people become the devil's!

---

[1] [The following passage was inserted when the sermon was preached for the second time, six years afterwards, at Cockington, where there was a collection for an Infirmary and Dispensary in Devonshire. E. B. P.

"And do not forget that if you want to please your Saviour, whatever else may or may not be necessary, one thing at least will be required: you must be kind to His poor. Without this, you cannot communicate worthily: you know that some alms, if you can afford it, and that cheerfully given, is part of the Christian Sacrifice. Neither without alms can you be prepared to meet Him at the last: you know the Judge's own word, 'Christ's Charity Sermon' as I have seen it called. "[m] Inasmuch as ye did it" or "did it not" "to one of the least of these My brethren, ye did it" or "did it not" "to Me." And this He

[m] S. Matt. xxv. 31—46.

will say not to the rich only. Now, my brethen, if this is so, here is something by which you may even now try yourselves whether you really wish to be getting ready to meet your Saviour. Here is a providential call on you in behalf of a Charity of which I doubt not you all know more than any one from a distance can tell you: an Infirmary and Dispensary at your very doors, now of more than twenty years standing; a good work, my brethren, who can doubt it, who believes that he will one day hear our Lord say to His blessed ones, "I was sick and ye visited Me;" and a good work, by God's blessing, well done, if we may judge by this among other facts, that in the past year two thousand out-patients were treated, of whom one thousand were cured, and seven hundred and forty relieved: there were one hundred and fifty five in-patients, sixty seven cured, and sixty two relieved: The proportion is encouraging: the work is growing in usefulness: there is every reason to hope for a blessing on what is given to it for Christ's sake.

In all these ways then, my brethren, as mortal men who must die and be judged—as Christians invited to prepare for meeting their Saviour both here in Holy Communion, and hereafter in the last Day;—and those who know that He will judge then especially by their charity to His little ones—we seem this day to have had a special call from Him.]

SERMON XXII.

THE VENTURES OF LOVE APPROVED OF BY OUR LORD.

BEFORE A CONFIRMATION.

S. Matt. xiv. 28, 29.

"*And Peter answered Him and said, Lord, if it be Thou, bid me come unto Thee on the water. And He said, Come.*"

That we may understand in some measure what were the great Apostle's feelings when he thus called on our Lord, we should consider what had gone before—what a course of wonderful sayings and doings had employed his thoughts for many hours. Our Saviour had retired from the many who came pressing upon Him, into a desert place, that He and His disciples might rest awhile. There had been leisure for S. Peter and the rest to commune with their own hearts, with Christ, and with one another, on the many astonishing events, which were daily going on before their eyes. But the leisure did not last long. Very soon the poor and afflicted people found out whither He had withdrawn Himself: and they came crowding to Him again. All day, for three days, He was teaching them, and healing those that had need of healing:

and on the evening of the third day, He fed them, five thousand at once, with five loaves and two small fishes. After this He sent them away and departed Himself into a mountain apart to pray, causing the disciples, and S. Peter among the rest, to get into the boat, and go without Him unto the other side. During all the night they were toiling in rowing, for the wind was contrary unto them: and no doubt, separated as they were from their Master, all seemed sadly against them. In the midst of their trouble and perplexity, when it was now the fourth watch of the night; i. e. towards three in the morning, they saw Him through the moonlight, walking towards them over the sea, and just about to overtake them. They did not at first know Him, but "supposed it had been a Spirit, and cried out for fear; for they all saw Him and were troubled:" as they afterwards were at first sight of His newly risen Body: but presently, amid the winds and waves, they heard the tones of His merciful and prevailing voice; "It is I, be not afraid:" and they knew Him by the sound, as S. Mary Magdalen afterwards, when He said unto her, "Mary." Now S. Peter was the one among them, who was always most eager to confess his Lord, both in deed and in word: and accordingly, that very day, he was the person to speak out before the rest, upon Christ's saying to His disciples, "ᵃWill ye also go away?" It was Simon Peter who spoke up and said, "Lord, to whom shall we go? Thou hast the words of eternal life: and we believe and are sure that Thou art the Christ, the Son of the living God." It was not that he knew or

---

ᵃ S. John vi. 67.

understood better than the rest the meaning of our Lord's wonderful sayings, or that he could give a clear account of it all in words: but this one thing he was sure of: he felt it in his very heart, and never forgot it: that Jesus his Master was the Son of the Living God: that He hath the words of eternal life; that if men go away from Him, there is no other for them to go to: this S. Peter knew, and therefore he stood fast by our Saviour, and could not be easy nor happy, whilst He was away. And therefore, when after that absence all through the long and dreary night, Jesus Christ came again in sight, it was as natural for S. Peter to hurry out to meet Him as for an infant to stretch out its arms towards its parent, appearing suddenly when he had been away for a time. And what was it to the loyal and affectionate Apostle, all overflowing with love and joy, if his Lord was coming to him on the water instead of the dry land? He was coming, that was enough: and water and dry land are all one, both to Him, and to His saints, where His miraculous mercies are. In this faith, and in eager desire to be with Christ, Simon Peter cried out, "Lord, if it be Thou, bid me come unto Thee on the water:" and Jesus, to reward his courageous love, said, "Come." It was little, to the holy and loving S. Peter, to believe and confess his Lord in words: he wanted to be *doing* something for Him, to be making some venture for His sake. Like David, he would not offer sacrifice to his God of that which cost him nothing. And did not our Saviour approve his dutiful zeal? It is true, He permitted him to sink for a moment, when seeing the wind boisterous he was afraid; but as

Peter still trusted in Christ only, and cried, saying, "Lord, save me;" so Christ immediately put forth His hand and took hold of him: and His words sounded indeed like a reproof, "O thou of little faith, wherefore didst thou doubt?" yet not for rashness does He reprove him, not for being too eager to come to Him on the water, but for permitting fear and doubt to get the better of him, when he was there. He had walked on the water a few steps, and why should he not trust the power which had brought him so far to carry him yet a few more steps onward, until he quite came to where Jesus was? In his Master's power, and by His invitation, he had so far got the better of the waves; and why should he tremble and begin to sink, because he saw the wind boisterous? For his doubt, then, and fear, he is reproved: no reason at all to suppose that he was blameable in his first wish, to go to Jesus on the water. That was indeed true faith, true affection, true thankfulness: the outpouring of a grateful heart, which greatly feared mere profession; which longed to prove itself truly loving by some work of pain, or toil, or danger; which was not to be contented, without at least putting itself out of its way for Christ's sake.

Well may such feelings as these be the feelings of any one of us, when we have been led in any manner to meditate more earnestly than usual on the great overpowering mercies of Almighty God, the wonderful things which He has wrought for us in Christ Jesus. When, for example, we have been preparing to celebrate the Holy Communion of Christ's Body and Blood, on any of His great festival days, and in order to do so, have tried to set before our hearts, more deeply and exactly than usual, the great things wrought by Christ Jesus; His Incarnation, Sufferings, Death, Resurrection, Ascension; surely we must sometimes experience some faint wish that we might be permitted to do some little, to deny ourselves in some real manner, by way of thankful acknowledgement of His gracious doings: surely we cannot grudge to have some scanty portion of that powerful cross laid upon ourselves. Or to take another example, and one which our present circumstances, my brethren, of themselves bring into our minds: you know what is promised us for next Wednesday: you know that he who stands to us in the place of the Apostles is to come here with a great blessing for those who are found worthy of it. Some of you have been preparing for that day, at least so we trust and hope, long, and often, and with no small earnestness. You have been led to consider, one by one, the great and aweful things of the gospel of God: step by step the Church has taught you to consider the broad and the narrow way, and where they both end: more especially has the Cross of Christ been lifted up in your sight, and you have been told its meaning, why He set it on you as His mark: you have been called on to think very seriously of your helpless condition through sin, of His great love, Who before you could know it took you up in His arms, blessed you and made you His own; of the infinite blessing of abiding in Him, the no less infinite ruin, if you fall from Him. All this is as it were Jesus Christ walking on the water, and coming in your sight: you see Him descending from heaven to the lowest depth of humility and poverty, in the Virgin's womb, in the manger at Bethlehem, in the carpenter's shop at Nazareth. You see Him going about to do you good, and suffer evil for you; reviled, rejected, agonizing, betrayed, bound, scourged, spit upon, crucified: and can you bear to go on quite at your ease, to deny yourself in nothing, to lead a life of gain or enjoyment? No: doubtless many a courageous young heart has before now whispered within itself, when it was told of these things, 'Bid me come unto Thee on the water: I am really ashamed to take mine ease, to eat, drink and be merry, while my Saviour and His saints are voluntarily enduring such things: I *must* deny myself, I *must* sacrifice something.' Thus, it may be, your heart is more or less moved, when you read or hear of the doings and sufferings of our Lord: and no doubt He approves of such feelings, if they are accompanied with modesty and humility. They are like the petition of S. Peter, "Bid me come unto Thee on the water:" He approves them and He will answer them: even now His coming invisibly with His servant the Bishop to confirm you is like His saying to S. Peter, "Come." 'Come away from the cold and dead ways of this selfish and heartless world, which would fain set you upon pleasing yourself, and practising a mere decent goodness: come away from all that, and walk on the water to go to Jesus: i. e. tread in His steps, take the path which you see will bring you nearer to Him, however hard and strange it may appear to the world. If you have in you higher and nobler thoughts than before; if you feel inclined to adopt a stricter rule, and to walk in more self-denying ways; if in the secret deeps of your heart you at all perceive the Blessed Redeemer drawing you to Him by the bands of that love which is stronger than death: fear not to give way to that impulse: begin at once to follow where it leads: be not too much troubled, though the path seem to you strait and narrow, and many things in it hard to flesh and blood. But be very much afraid of letting your present good notions and purposes die away, bearing no fruit. You are now, it may be, like that young ruler in the Gospel, disposed to come running unto Jesus: take care, lest when you find that He expects you in earnest to take up your cross, you be saddened, and go away sorrowful. Our Lord greatly approves of your good mind: doubt it not: even as we read that when He beheld that young earnest-minded ruler, "He loved him." He loves to have you so remember Him in the days of youth: but it is His merciful will that you should be aware, in some measure, of the hardness of the way. He will have you sit down and count the cost: whether you be able for His sake to give up this world and choose to have your treasure in heaven. He invites you to join Him and His Church, walking, by a heavenly strength, on the rude waves of this troublesome earth, but that you may not venture presumptuously, He shews you the chiefest of His Apostles, to whom He gave the keys of His kingdom, afraid for a moment, and beginning to sink. Not that He would have you turn back, and give up coming to Him in despair: God forbid: but that you may judge truly of your own frailty, and never for a moment let go your hold of Him. When loving and admiring thoughts, even towards Him and His saints, carry us away, there is danger of our depending too much on them, that is to say, on ourselves: there is danger of our forgetting to pray to Him, and watch for His coming. But when He shews us the wind boisterous, and we feel that we may at any moment begin to sink, then we naturally look to Him, and cry with S. Peter, "Lord, help me." Then He reaches out His gracious Hand, and supports us: be it our care never to let Him go.

Our safety is, not in being free from troubles and temptations: how dare we expect such favour to be shewed us while we are here on our trial? but in overcoming them by the help of that arm on which we are allowed to lean. It may be that when you are confirmed, nay even when you have become partakers of the Holy Communion you may be still more or less disquieted in mind. Our Lord and Saviour Himself had His great temptation in the wilderness just after the Spirit descended on Him at His Baptism: and His Agony came on Him just after He had appointed the Holy Eucharist. And when the Apostles had been first partakers of it, then Satan was permitted to have them and sift them as wheat, and they were preserved, S. Peter especially, only by the peculiar intercession of our Blessed Lord. Therefore ordinary Christians are not to be dismayed or cast down, if after seeking the grace of Christ in the manner He has ordained, they still feel as if greatly exposed to the crafts and assaults of the devil. They must make up their minds to it, as to something which God permits; as a call to more earnest prayer, more exact charity and humility, more entire watchfulness and self-denial, remembering always that the sharper the struggle, the brighter the crown of "him that overcometh."

Moreover we should consider that all public professions of faith, such as being confirmed and receiving the Holy Communion, put us in a different place with regard to our brethren, from what we should have been in had we never made such professions. We are more looked upon: more is expected from us. You may imagine how earnestly and anxiously the other disciples who remained in the ship must have watched S. Peter while he walked on the water: what a blow it would have been to their faith and love, had anything grievous then happened to him. Somewhat in the same way are we watched by our friends and neighbours, our kindred and companions, how we go on after devoting ourselves to Jesus Christ, and receiving His blessing. If we go on well, there is the better chance of their going on well: if we waver, they are discouraged: if we fall away, the Evil one obtains a great advantage against them.

For all these reasons—we dare not hide it from you—you do really take on yourselves a very great and serious burthen, when you make answer to the Bishop and say, "I do:" when you kneel before him to receive the Holy Ghost through the laying on of his hands. You take a great burthen upon you, but at the same moment your gracious Saviour gives you strength and power to bear it. He comes by His Almighty Spirit to make the yoke easy and the burthen light. His Presence, if you do not slight it, will be all in all to you. He will intercede for each one of you that your faith fail not: and let each one of you, having so turned, do his very best to strengthen his brethren.

SERMON XXIII.

THE WORLD'S THREE TEMPTATIONS.

BEFORE A CONFIRMATION.

1 S. John ii. 16.

"All that is in the world, the lust of the flesh, and the lust of the eyes, and the pride of life, is not of the Father, but is of the world."

HERE are two sorts of things, and two fountains or beginnings of them: the things which are of the Father, and the things which are of the world. On the one side we have Almighty God, the Father the Son and the Holy Ghost, with the angels in heaven and all pure and good souls, and all kinds of purity and goodness with the blessings provided for them. On the other side we have the world, i. e. the wicked world, such as we see it around us, and and such as we feel it, alas! within us: God's fallen and rebellious creatures, setting up themselves and their own ways against God and His ways: trying to do without God, and to be happy in a life which cannot have His blessing. And this wicked world, we are told, is made up of three sorts of things. There is the lust of the flesh, the lust of the eyes, and the pride of life. There is some difference in the three, compared one with another: but in this they quite agree, that they are all of one and the same evil beginning. They are not of the Father, but of the world: not of God but of His wicked and rebellious creatures. They are like three rivers of mortal poison, all flowing from one deadly fountain. They agree also in their latter end; they all lead to utter destruction: he only continues, and is safe, who keeps himself altogether from them. "The world passeth away, and the lusts thereof: but he that doeth the will of God abideth for ever [a]." The world with its evil desires and imaginations will soon come to an horrible end: the fire will lay hold on it, and all that belongs to it, whether it be the lust of the flesh or of the eye, or that which is called the pride of life; the world, I say, itself, and all these its evil belongings, will burn in that fire to all eternity. And we ourselves, my brethren, are in some sense within that world. It is around us on every side: we are constantly in danger of so giving ourselves up to it, that the last fire, when it breaks out, will lay hold on us, finding us meet fuel for itself: and then, as the Prophet asks, "[b] Who among us shall dwell with the devouring fire? Who among us shall dwell with everlasting burnings?" If we feel in some measure how dreadful that day will prove, let us look earnestly about us while there is time, and take care that we be not found even now in that evil world, which will pass away so fearfully. It seems that there are three ways in which it may approach us and wrap itself around us. There

[a] 1 S. John ii. 17.   [b] Isaiah xxxiii. 14.

is "the lust of the flesh, and the lust of the eyes, and the pride of life." To understand what these are, let us go back in our thoughts to the time when the world first began to be wicked. Remember our mother Eve in paradise: think of her standing by the tree of knowledge, the Evil one in the form of a serpent discoursing with her. He has praised the fruit to her, and has tried to persuade her that the Almighty did not mean what He said in forbidding it. She has not turned away, as she should have done, from his blasphemous words, but stands looking at the tree. That tree is to her what this evil world is to us: it tempts and draws her aside in three ways at once. She sees that it is "good for food and pleasant to the eye, and a tree to be desired to make one wise:" so she puts forth her hand, touches the fruit, takes it, eats of it, and gives to her husband that he may eat: and so "^c lust when it had conceived, brought forth" the first "sin." And in this sad history we find the very same things which S John says reign in this present evil world: the lust of the flesh, the lust of the eyes, and the pride of life. It was the lust, or evil desire, of the flesh or body, which made her think so much of the tree being good for food. There was also the lust of the eyes: we read especially that the tree was pleasant to the eye: she was attracted by its outward beauty and grace. There was also the pride of life: she wanted the satisfaction of knowing a great deal, and of being thought to know, and she supposed that eating of this tree would give her that pleasure: it was a tree to be desired to make one wise. Thus if we look back

^c S. James i. 15.

to the first beginning of sin, we find the very same bad principles at work which S. John warns us against in the latter days.

So again, if we turn our eyes to Him Who came to be the second Adam, to overcome and undo that original mischief: observe our Lord and Saviour, just entering on the work of His ministry: He too is in a manner alone with Satan, as Eve had been: alone in the wilderness, as Eve had been in the garden: and Satan tempts Him also in a threefold way: first, because of His hunger, he would have Him command these stones to be made bread; again he shews Him all the kingdoms of the world, and the glory of them; and thirdly he sets Him on a pinnacle of the temple, and dares Him to cast Himself down. Now the first of these temptations answers to the lust of the flesh; i.e. to satisfy His bodily cravings it was proposed to Him to take the devil's advice. The second answers to the lust of the eyes: the tempter sought to dazzle His mind's eye by shewing Him the glory and beauty of this present world. The third answers to the pride of life; to obtain glory and admiration among men, Satan would have Him throw Himself down: God, he said, would be sure to preserve Him, and then all the world would be astonished. This was no other than the pride of life: which moves people to take dangerous liberties for the sake of being admired by others, and shewing how much they can do.

Thus you see that both at the beginning, when men began to be wicked, and afterwards, when Christ came from heaven to undo that wickedness, the world had still the same ways and kinds of wickedness, wherewith to tempt those whom God had left on their trial. And even so it is now.

For consider, my brethren, as you look around: which of us all are most in the situation that Eve was in at the time of her temptation, or that our Lord seemed to the devil to be in, when he assaulted Him in the wilderness? Both of these to the outward eye appeared as untried persons, persons just setting out in the world, and having their course of life to choose: and so the devil thought there was a good chance of misleading them through their very inexperience. Now, who are most nearly in the like condition now? Who but young men and women, so far advancing towards full age, as to be entrusted with themselves, and free to make their own vows to God? Who so near as they are to that which Eve was, and which our Saviour seemed to be? I speak especially of those persons who are just of an age to be confirmed. They have their journey in a great measure to choose: the broad way and the narrow way are alike open before them: they are standing by the tree of knowledge, they may put forth their hand and take of the forbidden fruit, or they may refrain. I speak to such as these, and I say to them, 'Take heed what you do: it is a dangerous moment, a turning point in your life. Depend upon it, the Evil one, though you see him not, is at this time particularly busy about you. You perhaps have been brought up more or less in Christian goodness: you are in the habit of praying regularly: you trust that you have not yet fallen into any very serious sin: and for your soul's good you desire to be confirmed, that you may have more and more strength to keep the commandments. But at the same time the evil world, of which hitherto you have known little, is just coming closer to you than ever, and whatever good purposes you have, you must expect that they will be tried to the uttermost.'

To such as you the Apostle particularly speaks: the disciple whom Jesus loved, now in his old age, looking around him and seeing the dangers of the young, and having a very affectionate feeling towards them, as his Master had towards the young rich man, of whom we read that "Jesus beholding him loved him:" the Apostle S. John, I say, speaks to such as you who are preparing to be confirmed, especially to those who come to the work with an eager earnest heart, and says to them, "I have written unto you, young men, because ye are strong," i.e. vigorous and courageous in God's service, "and the word of God abideth in you, and ye have overcome the wicked one:" as yet you have the better of Satan, not having seriously broken your Baptismal vow: I am writing unto you particularly: and what I say to you is "Love not the world, neither the things that are in the world." You are just entering on the world: it looks gay and bright around you: you will be greatly tempted to love it, but I say to you, 'Love it not.' Why not? Because although God made it good, it is so fallen away by sin, that whatsoever is in it, may be truly said not to be of the Father: and to love it, is contrary to the love of the Father. S. John did not of course mean, that we are to hate all created things, the sun and the moon and the stars, our meat and drink, our friends and neighbours and our own bodies; but he meant that we are not to set our hearts on these things, so far as they are in the world: so far as they come to an end here in this short life: but we are to value them and employ them as helps towards the other world, which is far better, for it endureth for ever. For "all that is in the world," all that is pent up and confined within the narrow limits of this life, and can do us no good in the other life, "is not of the Father, but is of the world," and will come to an end with the world; therefore, my young brethren, set not your hearts upon it.

This is Christ's message by His beloved disciple to all young Christians who are just entering into life: and he accompanies it with that serious caution, which I beseech you to consider over and over, that you have the same three enemies, warring against your souls in the world, as your mother Eve had in paradise, and your Saviour Christ in His temptation in the wilderness. To you, as to them, the wicked world offers itself in three ways: the way of sensual pleasure, which is the lust of the flesh; the way of curiosity, which is the lust of the eyes; and the way of vanity, which is the pride of life. O beware of these evil counsellors: be on your guard against these fatal temptations. Beware of forbidden pleasures, how alluring soever they may appear. Think, when they come near, and seem temptingly within your reach, think of that fruit which Eve put forth her hand and took, because it seemed good for food and how it proved poison to her body and to her soul: and not to hers only, but to all mankind who were born of her. If it seem very hard to abstain, remember what our Lord said, "[d] Man shall not live

[d] S. Luke iv. 4.

by bread alone, but by every word of God." He can help you and bear you up, in foregoing this evil delight, whatever it cost you, though it seem like giving up your daily bread.

Again; Beware of curiosity: beware of the lust of the eyes; the restless fancy of acquainting yourself with new things; of knowing what sinners know, and doing what sinners do. This has ever been a most fatal snare to thousands, especially of the young and inexperienced. They are apt to imagine it a poor mean spiritless thing, if they are not as skilful in the ways of the world as others of their own age: they wonder, and are uneasy till they comprehend what it can be, of which others think so much: and they say to themselves, they will venture this once into the path which they know to be forbidden, just that they may know something about it: afterwards, they promise themselves to be very good. But the devil knows his advantage over them too well to part with them so easily: if they have once sinned he persuades them they may just as well sin once again: and then once again, and so on, till in an incredibly short time he have chained them down to a habit of sinning. Thus men are ruined by the lust of the eyes, by the mere wish to acquaint themselves with what is wrong. O watch and guard yourselves well in this respect: remember, our Lord has warned us that the most deadly sin may be committed, in the heart and before God, by merely allowing ourselves to look where we ought not. "Remember Lot's wife:" she did but look back from behind her husband, and the ruin of the burning city overtook her, and she became a pillar of salt. Never be curious to know what sinners are doing, how they order and contrive their sins. Look not that way: avoid it: pass not by it: more especially if it be a sin to which your conscience tells you you are yourself inclined. If Eve had looked away from the tree, instead of feasting her eyes on it, what a world of sin and misery might have been avoided by that simple action.

Lastly, Beware of the pride of life: of praising yourself in your heart, or of seeking to be praised by others. This again, is a fatal snare to the young and unwary. They desire to shew themselves bold and spirited, therefore they take liberties which they know to be wrong, expecting to be admired and praised by their foolish companions. They are afraid of being scorned and pointed at, therefore they do wrong, or refrain from doing right, at first perhaps with a heavy heart, but soon their scruples wear off, and they come to love the sin for its own sake. Poor vanity! miserable cowardice! that we should be ashamed of Christ more than we are of sin: yet, alas! how common! Be on your guard against it, I beseech you: and be quite as much on your guard against that deeper and more subtle pride, which is the devil's last hope. When he finds a young person proof against the lust of the flesh and the lust of the eyes, and also against that outward pride of delighting in the praise of the foolish world, his way is to set that person on praising himself in his own heart, and thinking how good he is, how much better than many others: and so the fruit of God's merciful gift is lost, and the unhappy soul is after all cast away. Therefore, my brethren, take heed, not only of outward boasting, and shewing off before men, but also of this inward boasting in your own hearts. Consider with yourselves, what a thing it is, that sinful dust and ashes should be proud of not being more sinful; that a man should be proud of not being yet a devil.

And in respect both of this inward satisfaction of praising one's self in one's heart, and also of those outward satisfactions of worldly pleasure, curiosity, and vanity, never forget that they are but for a very short time. "The world passeth away, and the lusts thereof." Even now whilst you are enjoying them they are vanishing into thin air: a moment more, and they will be gone for ever: all but the miserable, bitter, guilty remembrance of them: all but the dark stain which they will leave upon our souls. Already, what seemed fair in prospect, how sad and shameful does it appear, when we have to look back upon it! What will it be when you are old, twenty, thirty, forty years hence! (should any of you live so long): and how much more in the other world! "But he that doeth the will of God shall abide for ever." As he thinks of things now, so he will think of them in his old age, and in paradise, and in heaven itself: only with infinitely clearer and more perfect thoughts. What he loves now, he will love then: it shall never be taken away from him. Now is your time to choose that good part; to leave off sin before it be meddled with. One humble, hearty, devout endeavour now may obtain such grace from God, as to set you above the world for ever.

SERMON XXIV.

GOD OR THE WORLD.

BEFORE A CONFIRMATION.

S. Matt. vi. 24.

"*Ye cannot serve God and mammon.*"

OBSERVE, our Lord does not say, Ye *must* not, or Ye *ought* not, or Ye *will* not, but Ye *cannot*. It is quite entirely out of the question, a thing impossible, you cannot manage it, though you try ever so much. You may go on for a long time, nay all your lives long, thinking to serve both God and mammon; to please your Maker, and yet to have all your own way in this world, but all your labour will be in vain: Jesus Christ Himself tells you so.

Now why is this? It is not what we should ourselves have imagined: the world would not tell us the same. People who are left to themselves, or who merely watch the outside of other men's lives, not going deeply into their own consciences, nor into the Scriptures of God, such people certainly think it strange, when they are told that there is no middle way, that they cannot serve God and mammon both. They perhaps have gone on for a long time, fondly endeavouring to make the two agree: to please themselves, and get the best of everything, here, and at the same time to please God and secure a happy place in heaven. They give, as they imagine, their right hand to God: why then may they not give their left hand to the world? To let it go altogether seems to them foolish, extravagant, impossible. Whatever else the Bible means, surely, they think, it cannot mean this.

Well: but consider, Christian brethren, what it really does mean: for a meaning it must have, and that a very deep and serious one, and one which nearly concerns us all; why else did our Saviour impress it so earnestly upon us, in that Sermon, which we all know is the very rule of our Christian life? If breaking one of those least commandments, and teaching men so, will cause us to be least in the kingdom of heaven, how will it be, should we stand guilty of despising this great warning, which runs through our whole life and behaviour. Whatever we do, let us look earnestly to this.

"Ye cannot serve God and mammon." Why not? Because the word 'serve' means such an entire giving up of one's self, as cannot in the nature of things be practised towards two persons or things at once. To serve God, in the New Testament, means something more than being His servant, as we commonly use the word. Rather it means being His slave: absolutely and entirely His, both in body and soul: given wholly up to do His will and pleasure in all things. Slaves, such as we read of in old time, such as we hear of in some places at a distance, even now, are not like ordinary hired servants: for a hired servant may go away when his time of hiring is over, and seek another master or not as he pleases: but a slave is not free to go. Again, a master accounts a slave to be absolutely his own property, just as a horse or an ox is: but towards other servants or apprentices of course there is no feeling of that sort. But even a hired servant, as we know, could not serve two masters: two separate masters, I mean, each having a right to his whole time. For suppose they both wanted him at once, and were calling him different ways: how impossible it would be for him to obey and satisfy both! And if this be so in service like what we are used to, wherein a person is hired but for a time, and under certain conditions, how much more in actual slavery: when a man wholly belongs to one person, one perceives at once that he cannot belong wholly to another and an opposite person, any more than he can be in two places at once. "Either he will hate the one and love the other, or else he will hold to the one and despise the other."

And if this be so in respect of all service, much more in respect of what Christ meant, when He spoke of serving God and mammon. Consider first what it is, truly and in earnest to serve God, i. e. to be God's slave, His absolute property, always at His bidding. Imagine just for one day, how such a person will go on: and then imagine how a slave of mammon will conduct himself that same day, and you will see how entirely out of question it is, that the two should ever agree. The servant and slave of Jesus Christ as soon as he opens his eyes in the morning, recollects Whose he is, and Whom he serves: he loses no time, but presently lifts up his heart to the Holy Trinity by fervent prayer, and begs to have his task set him for that day, and to have God's help to do it as it ought to be done. In his dressing, his meals, his conversation, he still remembers his Master and Owner, and in a quiet way, gives everything, little and great, a turn towards God's honour and service, as far as he can. More especially in the proper work of his calling, whatever that be; in his trade, his labour, his profession, his care of his property or of his family, he will bear it in mind all along that it is God's work which he is doing, God's creatures which he is handling: and that all, quite all, must be accounted for to God. If he is at a loss, or in any kind of sore distress, he will turn to his Master in humble and secret prayer, beseeching Him to make known His will: and will also make use of Holy Scripture, and of all the best helps that he can get. He will take care to do his Master's bidding, not only in what he sets about, but also in the manner in which he sets about it. He will in no wise set up his own judgement against that of his employer. As the evening comes on, he will not think that he need not go on minding his Master; that now he has been obedient enough, he has been hard at work so long, and it is high time for him to enjoy himself, without thinking of his Master at all. The true slave and servant of our Lord Jesus Christ indulges no such childish or unworthy thought: in the evening when he is tired, as in the morning when he is fresh, he still thinks of his Master Who is always holding him by his right hand: his rest as well as his labour, his weariness as well as his strength, are part of the sacrifice which he is constantly offering to his great Owner and Benefactor.

All his joys and comforts he takes thankfully as from the Master's hand: all his chastisements patiently at least, feeling sure that He sends them, Who knows and wills the best for him: and he is kind and friendly to all, because all as well as himself belong to the same great Proprietor, Whose will it is to have peace and order in His household.

This, and a great deal more than this, is being a servant or slave to God: now let us see what it is to be a servant or slave to mammon. Mammon is "riches," or "money:" the wealth, honour, consequence, and other good things, as they are called, of this present world: and a man serves it, and is a slave to it, when he makes it his chief care. When he wakes in the morning, instead of lifting up his heart to God, some way of getting money, some plan of prospering in business presently comes into his mind. If he says his prayers, yet he suffers them to be grievously interrupted by wandering thoughts about money. All day-long, money and goods, gaining and saving, are what his mind is employed about. By that he measures everything: just as the good man measures all by the favour of God. At night, instead of examining his conscience, and asking pardon for the sins and negligences which he has that day been guilty of, he is haunted with anxious vexing meditations about profit and loss; he wanders after them in his evening prayers: he is so full of them that he cannot give himself to God when he lies down on his bed: and if he lies awake, these are what occupy his mind. Thus he goes on from day to day, from week to week, from month to month, and from year to year; till the very light that is in him is darkness: the reason and understanding which God gave him to refuse the evil and choose the good, is quite entirely taken up with contriving how he may make himself a little richer, and have more money in his coffers, and more consequence in the world, than he now has.

You see what the two kinds of life are, the service of God and the service of mammon. Do you not see how utterly unsuitable the two are one to the other; so that, although a person endeavour with all his might to make them agree, it never was nor will be possible to do so? Yet how common is it to imagine that we may go on very well, leading a mixed and divided life, serving God and mammon both. Look at the many who live decently, and keep up a tolerable reputation among their neighbours, while yet they secretly indulge in practices and habits which they know to be displeasing to God. Many things they do well, and fancy themselves, and are generally fancied by others, high in their Creator's favour: but the Angels who watch them in secret may discern, and still more may the All-seeing Eye of the Lord discern, that in their hearts they are going after their covetousness. They are slaves to money, although they little suspect it, as long as they allow themselves, for money's sake, to take any dishonest liberties: they are slaves to money as long as they go on in a fretful discontented way for want of it: they are slaves to money as long as they look enviously on those who have more of it than they have: as long as they admire it, and think a great deal of having it, without thinking at the same time of its proper use, for the service of God and the good of their neighbour. In a word, our Saviour has said distinctly, how hard it is for them that trust in riches to enter into the kingdom of God. Yet we see that people of all ranks go on without scruple trying night and day to be a little richer than they are, and have no scruple, no fear for their souls, no notion that in what they are doing there is any special danger to be guarded against. They think to serve two masters; to have one eye for God, another for the world. But this the Almighty will not allow: the jealous, pure, Holy One, will not suffer us to halt between two opinions. We must be evermore striving to be all His: otherwise, wish and dream as we may, we shall be all His enemy's. If we serve God, we shall despise mammon: if we serve mammon, we shall be neglectful and weary of God.

Beware then, all of you, and beware especially all you of the younger sort, who are hoping to take soon the holy Confirmation vow upon you, beware of loving and honouring money: beware of imagining it a fine thing to be rich. And for the same reason beware of worldly pleasure. If you are not on your guard, it will soon steal your heart from Christ. It is very subtle, very bewitching, and to young persons it seems to have a great deal to say for itself. But listen not to it, until you have tried it by the standard which our Saviour set. You cannot be a slave both to it and to God at one and the same time. You cannot serve God and Belial, the evil spirit of luxury and sloth, any more than you can serve God and mammon, the evil spirit of covetousness and envy. S. Paul teaches as much, when he asks, "ᵃWhat communion hath Christ with Belial?" You

ᵃ 2 Cor. vi. 15.

cannot, if you would, hold with both: if Jesus Christ is heartily welcomed and received, these earthly enjoyments appear in comparison as nothing: if on the other hand, forgetting our baptismal vow, we return wilfully to the lusts of the flesh which we had promised to renounce, we must give up our God and Saviour: we cannot have Him in our hearts along with such impure visitors. Do you not see, even among us, sinful and imperfect as we are, how persons are apt to draw back and wish themselves away, when any man of notorious abandoned character comes into the room and offers to sit by them? And how then, think you, will the good Spirit of God endure to have the spirit of uncleanness or drunkenness abiding in the same soul and body with Himself? O turn your minds earnestly to this, and as you are going to renounce with your lips both mammon and Belial, both the world and the flesh, take care that you really renounce them in your hearts also. The words we utter in Confirmation are most plain and distinct: "I DO." They cannot have two meanings: there is but one way of fulfilling them. O may the Giver of all goodness in His fatherly bounty grant you this grace, that your lives may henceforth speak out as plainly as your lips will have to speak now: that without speech or language your very behaviour may say to Angels and to men looking on, 'We serve but one Master: we would not halt, if we could, between two opinions: we know that we cannot, but even if it were possible, God forbid we should think of such a thing. We know that we have vowed to be entirely His, and that He expects us to be so: and we thank Him with all our hearts that He hath chosen us out of the world for so great a favour; hath chosen us to be Christians; while so many of our brethren, naturally no worse than **we, are heathens** sitting in the shadow of death.'

Christian brethren, is it not so, that all **of you in** your hearts acknowledge, when you hear such sayings as these, that they are no more than what is good and true, and what each one of us ought to feel? **See to it, then,** lest hereafter these inward acknowledgements of yours rise up **in** judgement against **you.** You that have now your way of life to choose, take care **that** you choose **God with** your whole heart: pray most earnestly for grace to do so: else, though to you it may seem otherwise, you will in reality **be** choosing mammon.

You, on the other hand, **who have chosen** long ago, but have unhappily swerved from your choice, **now at least make up your minds to** be more sincere **in** your penitence than you **were in your first vows.** God be thanked, you are yet **in time: only make** use of your time. Begin **at** once, and never cease from your penitence, until mammon and Belial, the world and the flesh, are quite turned out of your hearts **and** lives, and *Christ* **is** become to you All in all.

SERMON XXV.

THERE IS NO DISAPPOINTMENT AT LAST IN THE SERVICE OF GOD.

BEFORE A CONFIRMATION.

Joel ii. 26.

"*My people shall never be ashamed.*"

LAST Sunday God shewed us an awful vision: children of God, His faithful people, walking in the fires unhurt, because one was with them in form "ᵃlike the Son of God." This was a lesson sent from Him to shew us how all His faithful people may walk unharmed through the fires of evil desire, and may come out safe at the last, and by the help of Him Who hath declared, "ᵇ I will never leave thee nor forsake thee." The Son of God is with them, and they can have no hurt. The tyrant, the Evil one, the king of pride, may make the temptation ever so strong, he may heat the furnace seven times more than it was wont to be heated, but it shall not touch them: no smell of fire shall pass on them. This was the promise of last Sunday, and to-day the good Spirit comes

ᵃ Dan. iii. 25.   ᵇ Heb. xiii. 5.

to us with another no less gracious promise, "My people shall never be ashamed." Did you observe, my brethren, in the first lesson, how remarkably those words were repeated? Locusts had come over the land, and there was a dreadful famine, and the Lord by the prophet had been telling them how to obtain relief. "ᵉTurn," he saith, " unto the Lord your God: ... who knoweth if He will return and repent, and leave a blessing behind Him:" i.e. though He is come in anger, spoiling your crops, He may even now, if you truly repent, prepare and dispose your land to bring forth abundantly in a short time. Repent, "ᵈ and the floors shall be full of wheat, and the fats shall overflow with wine and oil, ... and ye shall eat in plenty, and be satisfied, and praise the name of the Lord your God that hath dealt wondrously with you:" and then it goes on "My people shall never be ashamed." And in the next verse again, because He delighteth in comforting men's poor dejected hearts, and is never tired of shewing mercy, He repeats the same words again, "My people shall never be ashamed." But this second time the promise comes after a greater blessing than the former. The first time, God's people were not to be ashamed, because there should be such abundance in their harvests. This second time the words are, "Ye shall know that I am in the midst of Israel, and that I am the Lord your God, and none else : and My people shall never be ashamed." Before it was a bountiful crop; now it is the special Presence of God, whereby they are assured that they are His people and shall never be ashamed. What is this, but a most loving

ᵉ Joel ii. 13, 14.   ᵈ Ib. 24, 26.

declaration from Him **Who cannot lie** nor repent, that neither in this world nor in the next shall they who truly serve Him be subject to disappointment and confusion of heart, in the same sense as they are who will not be His faithful servants. For this is the meaning of the word "ashamed," in the text and other like places of the prophets. It means the uncomfortable, humbling trouble of heart, which people experience when something fails them on which they had depended: as in the drought which the prophet Jeremiah describes: they "ᵉhave sent their little ones to the waters; they came to the pits and found no water; they returned with their vessels empty; they were *ashamed* and confounded, and covered their heads." And to the same purpose in the book of Job. In his great distress, Job had depended on his friends for relief, and they had scorned instead of comforting him: and he says it was as if people in the waste burning wilderness should come where a brook ought to be, and find none: "ᶠ'They were confounded' he says 'because they had hoped; they came thither, and were ashamed.'" Such in the end will be the case of all who depend on anything but the Lord, the Fountain of living waters: " But Israel," i. e. the true and faithful Israel, the Lord's own people, the assembly of good Christians, "ᵍshall be saved in the Lord with an everlasting salvation: ye shall not be ashamed nor confounded world without end."

And this promise has two parts. They shall neither be finally disappointed, nor shall they want present support. Whatever trials, inward or outward,

ᵉ Jer. xiv. 3.   ᶠ Job vi. 20.   ᵍ Isa. xlv. 17.

they may meet with, God will be with them to uphold them sufficiently whilst they are here on their journey, and when their journey is over, and they come to their true home, He will provide for them exceeding abundantly, above all that they can ask or think. Not one of them will be for one moment disconcerted or disappointed there : it will not be at all as it is so often, not to say always, here on earth, that when people come to any good thing which they have been long waiting for, still it is not *so* good, such *entire* joy, as they had pictured to themselves; in some way or other there is sure to be a falling off, and people are ashamed and humbled in heart to find it so. Thus it is here, but thus it will not be in the heavenly and eternal world. "[h] In His presence is the fulness of joy, and when we awake up after His likeness, we shall be for ever satisfied with it." For then we shall see Him no more by glimpses, in times of refreshment, fruitful seasons coming and going : but we shall *know* that He is in the midst of Israel. God Himself shall dwell among us and be our God : we shall see His face, His Name shall be written in our foreheads: how then should we ever be ashamed?

And now see, my brethren, what God promises to be the pledge and earnest and foretaste of all these blessings. "[i] I will pour out My Spirit upon all flesh; and your sons and your daughters shall prophesy .... And also upon the servants and upon the handmaids in those days will I pour out My Spirit." This came to pass on the first Whitsunday, when our Saviour *confirmed* His Apostles and those who believed on Him through their word by pouring out

[h] Ps. xvi. 12.   [i] Joel ii. 28, 29.

His Spirit upon them. But it is also fulfilled; doubt it not, my brethren, as often as our Bishops and Pastors come among us and lay hands on those who are baptised, according to the Apostles' ordinance. Then He pours out of His Spirit on all who do not make themselves unworthy: on servants and handmaids, male and female, the poorest as well as the wealthiest, all alike humbly kneeling before the Altar of our common Lord, all alike invited to partake of Him, all alike sealed by the Holy Ghost with His true oil of gladness, His heart-cheering, strengthening grace. And is not that other word in a manner fulfilled also, "your sons and your daughters shall prophesy?" When Christian youths and maidens stand up and make their solemn profession, "I do" 'I do believe all the articles of the Christian faith,' is not this very truly prophesying? For they are handing on Christ's message, repeating the truths which He taught them. They are foretelling things to come, His coming to judge, the resurrection of the body &c. And who can doubt, if they come with a good mind, that the Lord Who hath taught them all this will at that very time, by the laying on of His servant's hands, give them, according to His promise, His Holy Spirit, for a sure token, that if they be not wilfully wanting to themselves, they shall never be ashamed, never forsaken, never finally disappointed? He will be their Strength and Guide in this world, as they may from time to time require: and in the last dreadful day He will be their Comforter, helping them to stand upright, and will thereafter abide with them for ever. For He is the Water of Life, and it is written, "[k] They shall drink of the fountain of the water of life freely."

So it has been ever since Pentecost. They who have worthily received Confirmation have had the Lord's seal set in their foreheads, according to S. Paul's saying, "[1] He which establisheth us with you in Christ, and hath anointed us, is God; Who hath also sealed us, and given the earnest of the Spirit in our hearts." Now we know what the uses are of a *seal:* it keeps things safe, and it marks things as belonging to the person whose seal it is: so Confirmation makes, as it were, a mark on the soul of him who receives it, which can never wear out: there it is, my brethren, and there it will be for ever: to your glory and joy if you walk worthily of it, to your shame and everlasting misery, if you break your vow. But God forbid it should be so. Rather we will hope that having the Lord's seal in your foreheads, even the mark of His saving Cross, first set there at the font of your regeneration, and now renewed and as it were brightened up by the fresh gift of the Holy Ghost, you will go out into the world as valiant soldiers of Jesus Christ, making up your minds not to swerve, not to draw back from any service which your great Commander lays upon you, for any thing that the tempting spirit may whisper in your ear, for any scorn of the world, or frailty of the flesh. Why should this be too much to hope and expect from you, from each one of you, my children, who are to come kneeling to God's Altar on Friday next? By His mercy, it has not been too much to be performed by hundreds and thousands and millions of Christian

---

[k] Rev. xxi. 6.   [1] 2 Cor. i. 21, 22.

men women and children, who from time to time have drawn near, since that first Comfirmation at **Pentecost, and** have received this seal of the Lord. Knowing that they would not be ashamed in the end, they made up their minds once for all, **not to be ashamed** on the way. They considered beforehand that if they set themselves to **serve God with all their heart,** they must of course expect to find many who would scorn them in their hearts, and some who would shew their scorn, **and try to keep them from going on in the** right way. Sinners, they knew, would entice them, and would **be angry and contemptuous** if they did not consent, therefore they armed **themselves** beforehand with earnest prayer and good resolutions, **they** took care never to go long without the Body and Blood of their Saviour, and so their hearts being strengthened and refreshed, they were not ashamed when the trial came, they minded neither laughter nor anything else when their Lord's work was to be done. They had set their " face like a flint, **and they knew they** should not be ashamed." And so God preserved them in temptation, **they were kept from walking in the** way of the scornful, from casting in their lot among those " **whose steps go down to hell."** Among many sad drawbacks, they yet won their way on the whole. Often **and** often they were downcast and dejected, often and often they stumbled, and **not seldom they** fell, but their word in the evil day was, " [m]Rejoice not against me, O my enemy: when I fall, I shall arise; when I sit in darkness, the Lord shall be a light unto me." And now they are safe and at rest; they have departed **and** are with Christ, they wait in sure and

[m] Mic. vii. 8.

certain hope for the resurrection to eternal life : and when that day comes, they will appear all glorious; no mark of shame will be in their foreheads; they will have confidence and will not be ashamed before Him at His coming: and all because they were not ashamed of Him here. He will confess them, He will call them His own, He will say, "ᵃCome, ye blessed of My Father;" and they will be out of reach of all shame and disappointment for ever.

And we all shall meet them, my brethren, we shall be there, both you and I, to see Christ's faithful soldiers receive their crowns: in their persons, if not in our own, we shall then at least understand how great things the Holy Spirit doeth for those, who come worthily to receive the grace of Confirmation. God grant that we may not have to cry out in unutterable anguish, 'All this joy and glory might have been mine, but I wilfully (madman that I was) cast it from me.' Many, we know, who were once as you are now, set by God's providence in the path of life, the way to heaven open before them; many who have kneeled as you are about to do, under the Bishop's confirming hand; many who meant well at the time, whose hearts seemed overflowing with holy and good desires, will be on the wrong side in the great Day, from want of steadiness. What if any of you should be among them? You will not at least be able to say that God left you without warning. But if such should be your miserable case, I will tell you beforehand what the reason will be. It will be for want of rightly considering, and turning your thoughts, to God's immediate Presence, and to

---

ᵃ S. Matt. xxv. 34.

the Day of Judgement. Confirmed persons fall away like others, because they do not say to themselves, daily and hourly, in their hearts, 'God seeth us; we shall have to give account to Him.' Force yourselves to think more on these two things, not to talk but to think; and it hardly can be, that you should fail as often as you do. How could you help trying to please God, if with your mind's eye you even *felt* His All-seeing Eye fixed upon you: if you thought on His awful Countenance, gazing right downward upon you, as you know it will at the last Day, full of love or full of anger. O, that one Look of Jesus come to be our Judge! How can we ever think enough of it? How can we ever watch and pray, pray and strive earnestly enough that it may be to us an approving Look? Do you believe that you *shall* then see Him? I know you believe it: then try and fix your belief. If you have good serious thoughts on this day, or on the day of Confirmation, wish, pray, contrive to keep them strong in your heart. What is true one day is true another day also: if you feel it to-day, why not try and feel it to-morrow? Remember, there is such a thing as grieving and even quenching the Spirit. Who are in danger of that sin, if not they, who trifle at all with their Confirmation or the remembrance of it? I say, the remembrance of it, because what I am now speaking of concerns the old as well as the young: it concerns all who have ever been confirmed as nearly as those who are preparing to be confirmed. I say to them all, I say to myself, 'The mark of our Confirmation is or will be on our soul, as surely as the mark of the cross was once made on our forehead.' There

s

it is, for a sure token that if you are not ashamed of Christ, Christ will never be ashamed of you. Settle it in your hearts to think of this, whenever you are tempted to please men rather than God. Remember God's Eye fixed upon you: remember His holy Angels waiting to help you: more, far more on your side, than ever those against you can be. Think on the books which will be opened at the judgement of the great Day: think on your account in particular; in which it is even how being set down, how you are spending this Sunday, the last, please God, before your Confirmation. Think, and pray for a serious heart: for these are times which if trifled away can never never be recalled.

SERMON XXVI.

THE BREAD OF LIFE.

BEFORE A CONFIRMATION.

S. JOHN vi. 22.

" My Father giveth you the true Bread from heaven."

THIS time of Lent may be likened to a time of recovery from dangerous sickness. For sin, as we have been trying to consider at large, is the very sickness of the soul, and a person keeping Lent as he ought is in a way of recovery from that sickness. Our Lord is the Physician, coming to him day by day, attending him regularly all the time; the Church is the nurse, giving him with religious care the very remedies which Christ the Physician has appointed, in the way which He has appointed. The remedies and means of recovery are such as we have been speaking of during these former Sundays in Lent: first, fasting and other self-denial: for you know that when a sick person is mending he must by no means have his own way: he must not please himself, but must go by rule in eating and drinking, in exerting himself in body or mind, in seeing people and talking with them. He must take disagreeable medicines, and sometimes undergo even painful operations: he must punish himself for a time in many ways, if he would have a fair chance of returning to perfect health. All this answers to what S. Paul calls, "[a] keeping under the body and bringing it into subjection:" it is the Christian rule of living more hardly, that you may do penance, and be less tempted to sin.

Lent also is a time of *prayer*, and when people are weak through sickness, they are made to feel that they cannot depend upon themselves, and are forced to call on others for aid continually. If they are too proud and stubborn for this, they will much hinder their own recovery: just as persons not diligent in prayer, thinking that they can do well enough without so much calling upon God, will never get the better of their sins.

Thirdly, Lent should be a time of holy *hearing*, dutiful listening after God's Word: and those who are rising from the bed of sickness know how careful they had need be to mark, learn, and remember in due season all that their physician would have them do.

Once more: when you are recovering from any serious illness, one great point is, to come back entirely to your natural appetite; to be again in a condition in which you can without harm to yourself feed on the food which suited you best in health. And do you not see that this answers exactly to the care which we sinners should take in Lent to prepare ourselves for Holy Communion at Easter? For the Holy Communion is the regular spiritual food of the

[a] 1 Cor. ix. 27.

living and true members of Christ, and the healthful soul longs after it, as the healthful body for its common, wholesome food. But when the soul is diseased with wilful unrepented sin, we know that this best of food becomes poison to it. And on the other hand, the best token of amendment, and the best help to complete recovery, is when the Holy Sacrament agrees with men, when it makes them better and stronger each time they receive it.

In the mean time, while men are desiring and endeavouring to improve, but feel unable, perhaps with reason, to make up their minds as yet to seek Christ in His Holy Sacrament, such a time as that ought to be a time of very frequent [b] *spiritual* communion. That is to say, persons feeling themselves too unworthy, or otherwise unable to come to the holy Table ought to be continually endeavouring to become worthy, to be communicating with their Lord in the way of prayer, confession of sins, thanksgiving, interceding for others; they should give the Master of the Feast no rest until they have obtained His leave to come to it again, and have made the wedding garment again clean and white, which He put on them long ago, only they have since defiled it with sin.

[b] See third rubric after the Service for Communion of the Sick in the Book of Common Prayer.

"But if a man".... "by any just impediment, do not receive the Sacrament of Christ's Body and Blood, the Curate shall instruct him, that if he do truly repent him of his sins, and stedfastly believe that Jesus Christ hath suffered death upon the Cross for him, and shed His Blood for his redemption, earnestly remembering the benefits he hath thereby, and giving Him hearty thanks therefore, he doth eat and drink the Body and Blood of our Saviour Christ profitably to his soul's health, although he do not receive the Sacrament with his mouth."

Every Sunday, by God's mercy, there are some, however few, who come together in this Church of ours for real Sacramental Communion: and in Lent especially, those who do not communicate ought to be constantly getting ready to do so. It should be one of the main exercises of the holy and blessed time.

Of this exercise we are particularly reminded by the Church in her Gospel for this day, the day on which we get half through Lent: we are as it were on the top of the hill, and see Easter, the end of our penitential journey, and the Easter Communion, our refreshment, plainly before us: and accordingly the Gospel for the day is the relation of our Lord's great miracle, in itself a prophecy and type of what He would do hereafter in His Sacrament. The Gospel coming three weeks before Easter, as it will come again a month before Christmas, sets before us our Blessed Lord taking bread and blessing and breaking it, and causing His disciples to distribute it to the multitude which had come to Him from all parts, while by His Almighty power He made it sufficient for them all. What was this taking bread and blessing and breaking and distributing in such a marvellous and miraculous way, but a clear token and pledge of His blessing breaking and distributing in a far more wonderful way that Living Bread from heaven, His Spiritual Body, to be the food of the whole Church? What was it but a figure and type of the Real Sacramental Communion to which He invites all His elect in His own mysterious Feast?

Why do I call the worthy partaking of that Sacrament Real Communion, Real participation of

Christ? Because our Saviour has taught me to do so, declaring that He, i. e. His Flesh, is the "true Bread;" "ᶜ Meat indeed," more truly and perfectly meat than anything which we are used to call meat on earth; "the true Bread from heaven," as compared with that which in old time was called by that name, that which Moses gave to the Israelites, and of which the Psalmist wrote, "ᵈ He gave them bread from heaven to eat." For the word "true" very often means that the thing in the New Testament so called was meant to be the fulfilment of some other thing like unto it in the Old. It points out the substance answering to some shadow well known of old but never before understood. What was the shadow, the old bread from heaven, typical of our Saviour's Flesh, the true Gospel Bread? It was the manna, that which God gave of old to the Israelites, for them to feed on through all the forty years of their trial in the wilderness. Observe in how many respects this gift of manna was so ordered, as to be an image of the greater gift, the Body of our Lord. First, it was to them for bread, the very support and staff of life, without which in an ordinary way the greater part of mankind would hardly know how to live at all. The manna was to be to the Israelites for bread, forty years and no longer: even as the blessed Eucharist is to be our spiritual Bread during the years that we are to spend in our journey through the wilderness of this world. It is our daily, i. e. our regular Bread: we cannot do without it: for what says our blessed Lord the Giver of it? "ᵉ Except ye eat the Flesh of the Son

ᶜ S. John vi. 55.   ᵈ Ib. 31.   ᵉ Ib. 53.

of Man, and drink His Blood, ye have no life in you." We shall always need our Lord's Body and Blood: even as the Israelites depended on the manna till they came to the very borders of Canaan: so we, eating that bread and drinking of that cup, are to "[f] shew our Lord's death till He come." The manna ceased when they were in Canaan, because they had no need of it, there being plenty of corn. So, it would seem, there will be an end of Sacramental feeding on Christ's Body, when we come to heaven itself: but until then, I say again, we cannot do without it: it is even necessary to our salvation. I wish those who neglect Holy Communion would well consider this: Where would they have been, had they refused to eat manna, being Israelites, in those forty years—must they not have perished then from among the congregation? And who would have pitied them, their destruction being so entirely their own fault?

Christ's Body then is like manna in being so very necessary to us: and again, the two things are alike in being both so very mysterious: appearing to men in ways and means quite beyond the understanding of any of us. As to the manna, we know that the children of Israel, when they first saw it, "[g] wist not what it was," therefore "they said one to another, It is manna," as if they should say, 'It is'— 'What is it? I am sure I know not.' 'Manna,' amongst the Jews at that time was altogether a mystery, one of God's secrets: and Moses did not explain to them, nor attempt to do so: he simply said "[g] This is the bread which the Lord hath given

[f] 1 Cor. xi. 26.   [g] Exod. xvi. 15.

you to eat." If any of the people then had refused to eat of it, wanting to know more of it, to receive a fuller account of it, you see plainly how very foolish as well as presumptuous that person would have shewn himself; and you see what would have become of him, had he gone on refusing to eat. My brethren, such an one would have been very like those people at Capernaum, who "[h] went back and walked no more" with Jesus, because they said, "[i] How can this Man give us His Flesh to eat." And I do suppose there are many such persons who say or think, 'Why is it not enough if we really try to be good moral men, living quietly, hurting no man, ready to do good and encourage goodness? Why should so much be said of outward things, such as Baptism and the Supper of the Lord? I do not see but that I am as good as many whom I could name who come regularly to the Feast. I will not therefore let my heart be troubled, nor go out of my way, for Holy Communion, which in part is but an outward thing.' Alas! for those who so encourage themselves to make void the dying request of our Lord, "[k] This do in remembrance of Me."

Observe, thirdly, in how many ways the manna was used by Almighty God to prove the faith and obedience of His people: how it put them on their trial. For instance, it came with the dew in the early morning, and departed soon after the dew: for we read that "[l] when the dew fell upon the camp in the night, the manna fell upon it;"... "[m] and when the dew that lay was gone up," the manna lay round

---

[b] S. John vi. 66. [i] Ib. 52. [k] S. Luke xxii. 19.
[l] Num. xi. 9. [m] Ex. xvi. 14.

about the host, and then was the time for them to gather it, for "ⁿ when the sun waxed hot, it melted." Thus it came early, and lay on the ground but for a few hours, perhaps one might say but for a few minutes. Why was this, but to shew us, in the first place, that God's grace must be sought early? "º We must prevent the sun to give Thee thanks, and at the dayspring pray unto Thee." If the children of Israel, were not up and gathering before the sun waxed hot (which in those regions is very early), they lost their manna for that day. If you, the "ᵖ children of God by faith in Christ Jesus" neglect the spiritual treasure which lies all around you, all around His camp the Church, in the morning of your lives, the time of your youth, it is not only so much time, so much grace lost, but there is also an extreme danger of your missing God's gift entirely. The sun, the burning fire of temptation, will soon wax hot, and the grace which you might have gathered and would not, will too likely be withdrawn for good and all: and in *whose* power will you then be?

Again, the people were to come *daily* for their Manna; there was no gathering enough in one morning, to last them for one or two mornings more. So we are bidden to pray and labour for our *daily* bread; the bread of the day: trusting God for the morrow, and then coming to Him again, and so on for the next day, and the next, until all the days of our life here are over. So also, for God's special grace we must learn *at all times* to call by diligent prayer; not depending upon one or two good times and godly motions; one moment, one hour, or one day of effec-

ⁿ Ex. xvi. 21.   º Wisd. xvi. 28.   ᵖ Gal. iii. 2.

tual conversion: but seeking His help regularly, as we look after our daily meals.

And as the people might learn of the manna to seek God early, and to seek Him again every day, so they were also warned how necessary it was to believe Him and to keep all His rules as to the *manner* of receiving His grace. He told them, "⁹ Let no man leave of it until the morning." Some of them did so, I suppose to save themselves trouble; and "it bred worms, and stank:" and Moses was obliged to reprove them. On the other hand, the Lord had said, "ʳ Ye shall not find it in the field" on the Sabbath, but some were unbelieving, and went out and lost their labour, beside drawing on themselves a severe reproof. My brethren, shall we not learn from this to keep God's times and seasons, and the holy rules of our mother the Church, and not to be choosing for ourselves when and how and where we will seek His grace?

But if such dutiful care be necessary in our ordinary prayers, much more in our use of that which is the true manna, the Real "Bread from heaven," the Body and Blood of our Lord Jesus Christ, 'verily and indeed' given and taken and received in the Holy Sacrament of the Lord's Supper. The Israelites had to come early, or they forfeited their allowance of manna. How many Christian men and women forfeit "ˢ the Bread which cometh down from heaven:" forfeit it, alas! for ever and ever; for want of coming early to it; i.e. for want of coming in their young days; coming when Christ especially invites them, i.e. at the time of their Confirmation, or as soon after

⁹ Ex. xvi. 19, 20.   ʳ Ib. 25, 26.   ˢ S. John vi. 50.

as they can be duly prepared! One of the first lessons you learn as very little children indeed is to come when you are called: and can you, when your Saviour calls, when you all but see Him looking lovingly upon you, when He has just laid His fatherly hand upon your head, and has interceded for you, that you may not only "continue His for ever," but also "increase in" His "Holy Spirit more and more," till you "come to" His "everlasting kingdom:" and when He at the same time plainly tells you, '*This* is the way to abide in Me: this is the way to grow in My grace:' can you find it in your hearts at such a time coldly to draw back, and unthankfully to refuse to come? That be far from you, dear children: your hearts are young and loving hearts: you cannot be so unbelieving, so hard and cold to your best Friend and only Saviour. If your pastors and Christian friends think it better, of course you will wait until you can come better perpared: but you will not put off your preparation, no not for an hour. To-morrow by this time, if it please God, you will have solemnly promised your Saviour that you will keep all His commandments, and amongst them surely this His dying commandment, "Do This in remembrance of Me." If you say the words, "I do," without meaning to be a communicant, you will be telling a lie to God and it will be the very sin of Ananias and Sapphira, the sin of taking His Name in vain: and then, when you kneel to be confirmed, the mark set upon you will be a curse and not a blessing. Rather than it should be so, rather than that you should stand and kneel before God to-morrow with an unbelieving heart, I earnestly beg of you to draw back from Confirmation and not use the permission which has been given you. But I hope better things. I hope that there is none of you in wilful sin, none of you who does not distinctly intend to come in good time and with a good mind to his Lord's holy Sacrifice and Sacrament. I particularly beg of you all to think of that Sacrament at the very moment that you say, "I do;" and again at that other yet more solemn moment, when you will feel the Bishop's hand (which is Christ's Hand) upon your head. May God give you His special grace tomorrow, to mean what you say, and afterwards to practise what you mean: to look betimes, and in earnest, after the manna from heaven: worthily and speedily to come to His holy Altar table; having once begun, to go on coming regularly; and never in any way to trifle with so great a blessing.

It is God's bread: why should you starve?

It is the medicine of life: why turn it into poison?

SERMON XXVII.

OUR LORD'S PROVIDENTIAL DEALINGS ARE AS WARNING LOOKS, TO REMIND US OF HIS WORD.

BEFORE A CONFIRMATION.

S. Luke xxii. 61.

"The Lord turned, and looked upon Peter, and Peter remembered the word of the Lord."

The great, and wonderful, and Holy God, Who is above all, and through all, and in us all, has infinite ways of speaking to the hearts of men, of warning sinners, and encouraging the penitent, more than we can possibly know of: but according to that little, which in His mercy He allows us to see, there are two principal outward ways, in which from time to time He so calls upon us: His Word read or taught, and the dealings of His Divine providence, and there is an amazing, a most gracious yet aweful correspondence between them, comparing them one with another. The Lord first gives us His Word, and then when it has failed to enter into our hearts, as it should do, He turns and looks upon us, as He did upon S. Peter; gives us by His doings some token of the true meaning of that word, and of the sense in which He would have us receive it. Something happens which causes us to understand the true practical intent of sayings which we had been used to all our lives long: and again those sayings, being brought to mind, cause us to think very deeply of the astonishing Presence, and goodness and wisdom of Him Who so prepares beforehand all even the slightest things for His own glory and the good of them that love Him.

Sometimes, it may be, verses of Holy Scripture which we have heard or read over and over, and with the sound of which our ears may be quite familiar, nay, and we may have thought on them, and imagined that we had a fair understanding of them, may be brought to our minds in a moment, by some turns of God's providence, and shew themselves to be meant for us in a way which we never dreamed of. As when Nathan said to David, "Thou art the man," it flashed upon his mind suddenly what the parable meant which he had just heard from him, of the rich man who had taken the poor man's ewe lamb: so oftentimes after many years such and such portions of God's holy Word come before us with quite a new aspect, far more directly bearing on ourselves than we had ever imagined. We discern more in them than we ever did before of the fearful Presence of the Almighty: the Son of Man reveals Himself in them as the lightning which cometh out of the East and shineth even unto the West: we feel and are astonished at the thought, that it is He Who has been so long standing at the door and knocking, as often as we have heard those words, and we have taken no notice: they seemed to us meant for some one else. We feel in some sort as the disciples did, when future events made known to them the right understanding of certain sayings and doings of their Lord: which kind of thing S. John frequently notices: as when he says, "[a] These things understood not His disciples at the first, but when Jesus was glorified, then remembered they that these things were written of Him, and that they had done those things unto Him." And again, "[b] When He was raised from the dead, His disciples remembered that He had said this unto them: and they believed the Scripture, and the word which Jesus had said." So it is, from time to time, with all who are not altogether thoughtless. They are continually coming on views and deep meanings of this or that place in the Bible, which make it seem as if it was meant for them in particular, in such a way as they never before had imagined.

And it is the same in regard of the other methods, by which the word and will of God has been made known to each of us: the early lessons, for example, and warnings of our parents, and friends who were to us as parents. I suppose we might all of us remember sayings of theirs, which at the time made in comparison very little impression on us, and which bye and bye have been somehow called to our remembrance: we have laid awake in the night, and thought of them, and they have come over our memories fresh and distinct, and we have felt that we could understand them better than when they were first spoken in our hearing. These also were words of God for our good: not words in the same sense that the Holy Scriptures are, yet still His words, to be greatly regarded by us, and when things happen

[a] S. John xii. 16.   [b] Ib. ii. 22.

to recall them to our minds, it is truly the Lord turning and looking upon us, as in the text He looked on S. Peter, and we remembering the word of the Lord, which He spake to us years ago.

Much more is this true as concerning the lessons of the Church, our spiritual mother, and the guardian of the written word: her catechisms for example, and her Creeds, and the other instructions which from time to time we have received from her in our childhood and youth:—it happens I believe not seldom, that expressions in them to which we have been long used, come into our memories after many years, perhaps when we are lying on a sick bed, or when anything has happened to make us more thoughtful than usual: and we feel in our hearts that those words were intended for us. And if catechisms and exhortations have this effect, much more surely may prayers be expected to have it. The words which from our youth up we have been accustomed to use when we were speaking to our God, too often with little attention and regard, how deeply do they sometimes affect us, when altered health, or change of times, or disappointment, or loss of friends, or fear of coming evil, bring them freshly into our minds. The light cast on them is altogether new, while the words themselves sound more familiar than ever. We wonder that we should have heard and used them so often, and never before discovered, as we now do, the voice of Almighty God in them.

The most frequent occasion, perhaps, of men's coming to have such deep thoughts of their prayers and of texts and verses and lessons heard long ago, is when they have been carried away into some grievous sin, which in the better days of their childhood and youth they had thought themselves incapable of committing. Imagine any, the wickedest sort of person, a murderer, an adulterer or a false swearer; do you suppose that in his youth, when he first learned the ten commandments, he thought that he was not only the sort of person, but even one of the very persons who were in His mind, Who spoke those commandments from heaven. But bye and bye, when the crime is committed, then men feel that the Book of God, in condemning it, spoke beforehand of them. Few, if any, of us, it may be hoped, have such crimes as these upon our consciences: but most, surely, have enough to cause them to shrink from certain sentences of the holy law of God, which at one time they little thought would ever apply to them.

Or if we are so happy as to have escaped grievous sin, yet temptations and trials are continually coming near, and as they come on, to a thoughtful spirit they bring with them the remembrance of some warning of past years, which we had heard and recollect, but never till now fully learned and understood its use. We may have gone on peaceably, without being wronged by any one, many many years of our life, and then on a sudden, enemies and slanderers or at least disturbers of our peace, may seem to be gathering round us: what an unthought-of meaning and interest will this cast on those many portions of Scripture, which dwell on the duty and blessing of Christian forgiveness. How strange must it seem, to find that rules of perfection, which we, till now had but humbly to admire, are brought home to our own bosom, that examples such as those of David or S. Stephen (or of Him Who is above all, praying for His enemies on the Cross), must be followed in our own life, if we would have our many sins forgiven. Or to take a different kind of example, there are sins, we know, which as children we are taught to abhor, while yet we are through our very age far enough from all temptation to commit them: but in process of time, when the temptation comes on, the Divine sentences against such sins, being laid up in our memories, are a treasure of strength for us to meet them with. Then the temptation itself, drawing near to us, is an instance of the Lord's turning to look on us, and putting us in mind of His word spoken in our ears to condemn that sin before we could know what it was. Or we may be charged perhaps falsely, and suspected of wickedness which never came into our hearts: yet even this may be considered as a warning, as the Lord casting His eye upon us, to remind us of some word or other of His, which we have slighted, For what if we are not guilty of the very thing which our accusers lay to our charge? Yet surely we know of much real evil in ourselves, many things which we should be most unwilling for an evilspeaker to lay hold of and bring forward against us, and if we feel so much pain and confusion at the thought of these imputations which we know to be false, how will it be with us when the books are opened, and the true charges which are there written against us, are read before men and Angels to condemn us in the last Day? These are the thoughts which a truly humble spirit will accustom itself to, should it be tried, as is commonly the lot of God's saints, with false accusations. Instead of nourishing unkind thoughts of his slanderers, such an one will be rather led to think very penitently on those matters, in which he might be truly censured, if his detractors did but know it. And thus the slander will do him the greatest good: it will lead him to prepare by true repentance and amendment, for the fearful time when all shall be made manifest.

Thus we have seen how every man's own experience may supply him with instances of the remarkable way in which God's providences answer to the lessons of His Word, in that the true meaning of those lessons is brought out long after by the events of our own lives and the changes of our natural feelings; so that one after another, in one respect or another, we have each in turn to make the confession of Job, "[a] I have heard of Thee by the hearing of the ear, but now mine eye seeth Thee."

The case therefore of S. Peter in the text is no rare or miraculous event, but it is just an instance of our Saviour's ordinary way of dealing with His frail and imperfect servants in order to give them a chance of repentance and salvation. S. Peter, it seems, had forgotten for the moment our Lord's earnest warning so lately given, "Before the cock crow thou shalt deny Me thrice." We may wonder how this should be, considering that our Lord spoke the words but a very few hours before S. Peter's denial, and spoke them not once, but repeatedly, and very earnestly, so that Peter's own attention, and that of the other Apostles, had been thoroughly drawn to it, and they had one and all made the declaration,

[a] Job xlii. 5.

"Though I should die with Thee, yet will I not deny Thee in any wise." One would have thought that at least the cock's first crowing after his first or second denial, would have startled him and put him on his guard. But it was not so: possibly he might not have heard that sound, and if he did hear it, it failed to convey to him any very particular meaning. It was a call from his Lord, but he did not hear it: whether it was the hurry and confusion of that moment, dread of what might next happen to our Lord, grief and fear and shame at not being able to help Him, wonder that he did not interfere by His mighty power, fear also of the cruel death which he saw close at hand, and of the shame, which was gathering round: these and perhaps other feelings with them were quite too much for the Apostle's remembrance even of what he had heard so lately: and so he went on and committed the very sin which he had thought himself most secure against. Dare any man be severe on him? Let us only consider how it is with too many of ourselves on the like occasion: how far too easily we allow the words and warnings of our Lord, by our parents and teachers, or by His own Divine Book, to pass away out of our minds: in how short a time we quite part with our best resolutions and promises made to ourselves and to Him: how many cockcrowings, i. e. warnings and special hints from His providence, it commonly takes to recall us to ourselves: let us think fairly on all this, and we shall see good reason to leave off blaming the Apostle, as if he did worse than others, and shall rather be set on looking earnestly to ourselves, lest our repentance fall too far short of his.

Well indeed would it be for most of us, were we willing to turn, as S. Peter did, on the first look of his offended yet most merciful Saviour. He waited not for a word, much less for a judgement which he might feel. A look was enough to turn him. "The Lord turned and looked on Peter, and Peter remembered the word of the Lord how He had said unto him, Before the cock crow, thou shalt deny Me thrice. And he went out and wept bitterly:" not only wept bitterly for the time, but continued in earnest dutiful repentance all the days of his life after; and though he had all the consolation that true obedience and mighty works could give him, and especial promises of God besides, yet it is said of him that so bitter was his sense of this one short falling away, that he never after could hear the cock crow without bursting into tears. So entire was this chiefest Apostle's repentance in both parts of it: I mean, both in his thorough amendment and in his lasting contrition of heart. Well will it be for us, if we turn as he did, when the Lord turns and looks upon us. He perceived in a moment how far he had been from realizing our Lord's warning, and making it his own. The words indeed had fallen on his ear, but he had not seriously considered and applied them to himself; he had not kept in heart that he was the very person declared to be in so great danger; consequently, when the danger came, it found him more or less unprepared, and of course he sank for a time under it. But the Eye of his Lord turned towards him in the midst of His Sufferings (for at that very moment, as it should seem, they were mocking and smiting Him) was enough to make him understand his sin and danger, and to bring him back to the right way, once and for ever.

My Christian brethren, dare we deny that we too in many ways have the Eye of our God and Saviour from time to time turned upon us? Are not we too able to discern many distinct calls of His wonderful and gracious providence, many things in life so exactly answering to warnings and instructions long ago received, that if we have any faith at all, we must believe, "Here is the Lord turning and looking upon us. He would have us remember such and such a word?" Surely the regular services of the Church are full of instances of this kind. If we attend to them, we must be continually meeting with verses and sentences which we have passed over hundreds of times, but which now go straight to the very deep of our hearts, and prove themselves especially suited to us in particular. The written devotions of good men which by God's providence have been preserved to us (those of Bishop Wilson in particular) have many instances of this kind. And we shall find more and more of them, as we are more constant and obedient to the Church in our own devotions, and more watchful of the ways of God's good providence over us.

And if the regular services of the Church, her daily and weekly prayers, are abundant in such tokens of the All-seeing Eye turned towards us, very evidently the same may be said of her occasional services also. For example: this very day the Lord has turned and looked upon us all, upon every one of us here present who is able to hear and understand what is said in Church, in the notice of Confirmation which our Bishop has directed to be given. It is a distinct call upon every one who hears it, whether as yet confirmed or no, to remember the word of the Lord spoken to them in times past, His warnings of their sin and danger: and wherein they have swerved from that word, to weep bitterly. But I must endeavour to say more of this another time. For the present, I beseech you only to consider whether the fact be not so. Is not the Bishop's notice of Confirmation a call from the same gracious Lord Who looked on S. Peter, to set us elder ones on considering how we have kept our Confirmation vows, as well as the younger, how they are preparing for them? And if this be so, with what sort of mind should we depart out of Church to-day? And if we neglect such warning, will it not be with us as if S. Peter had slighted his Lord's reproving eye? And shall we not have more and more cause to fear the word spoken to the unbelieving Jews: "I said therefore unto you that ye shall die in your sins: for if ye believe not that I am He," that My Voice is in these solemn messages of My Church, ye slight the appointed way of true penitence and amendment, and what then remains, but that ye must die in your sins?

SERMON XXVIII.

A CONFIRMATION A SPECIAL REMINDER OF THE WORD OF CHRIST.

BEFORE A CONFIRMATION.

S. Luke xxii. 61.

" The Lord turned, and looked upon Peter, and Peter remembered the word of the Lord."

IF we believe and consider what the Creed teaches of the One Catholic and Apostolic Church, we cannot but feel that our Bishop and pastor coming among us to confirm is a very special instance of the Lord turning and looking upon us and causing us to remember His Word. For the Bishop is as one of Christ's Apostles, a visible image of Him, speaking in His Name, and by His authority. As the Holy Sacraments are the means and tokens whereby it pleases Him to come inwardly and dwell in our hearts, so the presence and control of the Bishop is the token that He is with us, so to speak, outwardly as our King. The Bishops, as being the Apostles' successors, are those to whom the word was spoken, "As My Father hath sent Me, even so send I you." As S. Paul says, they are "ambassadors for Christ." As therefore if a king's ambassador were to come into a place, with a message to the people, all who honoured and reverenced the king would naturally not only be on the watch to hear what message he had sent, but would be moved by the very presence of the messenger to think of their king as regarding them, so the mere coming of a Bishop into a place in discharge of any of these duties which belong to him as a Bishop cannot but prove to a thoughtful person a very serious and awakening circumstance. It is a sign of our Lord's special Presence, a token from Him that we are in His kingdom, an earnest that He is watching us, and will soon come visibly to call us to the great account. It is a call upon us, then, to tremble and fear before Him, and consider what account we are able to give. All this may be said of the simple circumstance of a Bishop coming as a Bishop among his flock, apart from the particular occasion, whatever it may be, on which he comes. It is the Lord turning and looking upon us, that we may remember His word.

As to the particular thoughts we should have, the particular words of His we should remember, when His messenger comes for the particular purpose of confirming, they are such as every thoughtful Christian will at once acknowledge, when they are mentioned. First, we see plainly that it is a call from heaven to remind us of our baptismal vows: those among us more especially, who have already been confirmed. It may have been a great many years ago, so long that we may not distinctly remember the time: as indeed we can none of us remember the time of our Baptism: but the vows notwithstanding remain just the same: they are in God's sight as fresh, and as deeply and truly binding upon our consciences, as if they had been made only yesterday. This should be thought of: for this is a matter in which I fear many of us are apt to deceive ourselves. As men forget their old sins, and then imagine that God forgets and forgives them, so they are apt to think lightly of promises and vows made a very long time ago; as if the very time did in a manner wear them out of God's Book, and they were not so accountable for keeping or breaking them. We see this not seldom in respect of the marriage vow. Persons who would be ashamed of ill-using a wife or a husband, very soon after they had taken that solemn vow on them, appear to think very little of doing so, after many years have passed. And there seems reason to fear the like in regard of the vows which we have all of us made in Baptism and Confirmation immediately to God Almighty. The Bishop's coming among us to confirm the young people is as if the Lord Jesus Christ Himself turned and looked earnestly upon us, to revive in us the thought of our own vows and promises. It is somewhat as if an Angel came and said to us, 'Do you see that holy Altar table, and the young persons kneeling before it? Did you attend to the question put to them in the Name of Jesus Christ by His own chosen minister? Did you hear them answer aloud, I *do:* I do promise and vow to renounce, believe and do as was promised and vowed for me in my Baptism? Did you hear the solemn prayer which the Bishop offered up for them, that God would "strengthen them with the Holy Ghost the Comforter, and daily increase in them His manifold gifts of grace?" Do you see him now, how one after another he lays his hands upon each one of them kneeling in order, in token of God's sealing him with His holy and gracious Spirit? Do you see all this?' the Angel might go on and say 'and does it not put you in mind of the day and hour when you yourself answered in the words of the same vow, knelt to hear the same prayers said over you, bowed your heads to receive the same blessing at the hands of your bountiful Saviour? And can it fail also to put you in mind of the manner in which you have kept those vows, the treatment which that good Spirit has experienced at your hands, Who then vouchsafed to enter in and dwell in your hearts more and more. You' (he might add) 'have perhaps forgotten these things, but we, the Angels who were waiting by at the time, we have not at all forgotten them; they are registered in heaven, both the vows themselves, and the manner in which you have kept or broken them. You were cared for by the Angels of God when you made those vows, there was joy in heaven for you, so far as you sincerely kept them: and will you not now care for yourselves so far, as to consider and examine your own ways accordingly? Will you not bethink yourselves what a sin and shame must be on you, if all those holy prayers were offered up in vain for you: if you have cast away the remembrance both of them and of your own promises made at the same time, for any thing this world could give? Will you not, though late, endeavour so truly to repent, that we, the Angels, may have joy in heaven over you?'

Such thoughts as these, we may well imagine, those ministering spirits may love to encourage in the minds of us who have been confirmed long ago, when God sends His earthly angel to remind us of our baptismal vows. They would wish us to think, not only of the vows themselves (though no thought one would suppose could well be more serious than that) but even more of the grace that was then given to keep them. We must consider that Confirmation is not only a solemn engagement on our part, but also on God's part a real and most holy Gift, the Spirit of counsel and ghostly strength, actually poured into our hearts, to make us, if we cast it not away, perfect, full grown men in Christ Jesus. This Gift, if we were confirmed worthily, we received at that time: and now the Bishop comes with the same gift to offer to those who have grown up after us. Can we help asking ourselves how we have ourselves employed it? Have we grieved or vexed that gracious Visitor, offering Himself to enter more and more into the very deep of our hearts? or have we made much of the unspeakable Gift, beseeching Him to abide with us, and watching ourselves that we might do nothing to drive Him out of the place which He had chosen for His abode? Have we suffered the unclean spirit to return? or have we tried to keep our bodies and souls in chastity, fit to be the temples of the living God for ever? He is the Spirit of Wisdom and Understanding. Have we sought to grow in the knowledge of Him, such knowledge as would help us to keep His commandments? or have we suffered our minds to run after ordinary matters, not giving a thought to real spiritual improvement, except in time of sickness and trouble, and then quickly forgetting it? He is the Spirit of Counsel and Might:

Have we been wise and strong by His aid to fight His battles against the world, the flesh, and the devil? Or have we been unstable as water, afraid to follow His plain leadings, and permitting every childish and vain excuse to lead us into sin or encourage us in neglect of duty? He is the Spirit of true Godliness: Have we by His help, kept God always before us? He is the Spirit of the Fear of the Lord: Have we even so far entered on the beginning of wisdom, as to fear God for His sake, Who dwelleth with us and is ever in us?

Again; over and above the grace which God actually gave us in Confirmation, we were admitted to a still higher and more sacred privilege. The laying on of the Bishop's hands prepared us for the receiving of His own Body and Blood. Here is another great talent to be accounted for, another exceeding grave question which Almighty God seems to ask of our conscience, when He causes us to hear warning of a Confirmation, or to be present at one. 'What have you done,' He may be understood to enquire, 'in respect of that aweful invitation, which the Almighty Saviour gave you to His holy Table, when you were confirmed? Did you ever pay any attention to it at all? Did you not treat it as mere words of course, appointed to be spoken to all who came to the Bishop, but not really to be acted on, except by those few who by chance might feel a disposition that way? Or if you thought of it for a while, did you seriously follow up the thought, by seeking instruction from your pastor, which you knew you might have at any time? Or if you began attending to the subject, did you not very soon leave off, like a child attracted away from his task by any little accident? If you went on, and were sufficiently instructed, did you actually come to the Sacred Communion or did you not rather take up with any excuse that occurred, and so indulge yourself as before, in neglect of holy things from indolence and love of the world? If you ever came there, did you keep on with it? or did you too easily allow your good beginnings to pass away, and sink back into your old indifference? Or if you still come occasionally, are you endeavouring in earnest to come more and more worthily, and to honour Him Who has brought you so near to Himself, by a holy and obedient life?' In particular, the occasion calls on you to consider, Have you since communicating, by any deadly and wilful sin provoked your God, endangered your souls, and brought reproach upon Christ and His Altar? If such is your sad case, have you truly turned from that sin, both in thought, word, and deed, and are you continually humbling yourself for it, with real shame and fear to have so behaved towards Him Who not only died for you, but also gives Himself to be your spiritual food and sustenance in this holy Sacrament?

These are the sort of questions which we even seem to hear Almighty God asking of us when we hear notice of a Confirmation, or are present at that holy Service: we, I say, who have been ourselves confirmed long ago. As for the young, who are as yet only preparing for this sacred ordinance, they too according to their age and understanding must consider how they have served God hitherto: how dutiful they have been to their parents, how attentive to their prayers, how true in their words, how honest and kind in their actions, how obedient to their betters, how thoughtful of God Who ever watches them. They are warned too not to lose the opportunity which perhaps may never return, of receiving God's grace and blessing: nor again to profane that blessing, and turn it into a curse, by coming carelessly, without any heart to be instructed, without any serious desire to improve. There are however two dangers, more especially, which such warnings of course bring with them, whether to the old who should be reminded of their past Confirmation, or to the young who are drawing near to be confirmed: on each of which I desire to say a few words. One is the danger of neglect, the other, of promising without performance. S. Peter's case, before and after the gracious look which recalled him to himself, may help us to understand and guard against both.

"The Lord turned, and looked upon Peter, and Peter remembered the word of the Lord." He remembered it, not only for the time, but during his whole future life. In short, he attended to his Master's eye. The warning was not, as we say, thrown away on him. That is the first and great point, when occasions like this befal us. There is an Evil one always at hand, who is but too eager to withdraw us, he cares not how, from serious thought of the holy things which only can save our souls. If he could, he would hinder Christ's warnings from coming at all to our ears. He would turn our minds another way, as perhaps he did S. Peter's, when the cock crew the first time. If we permit him to do so, we throw away for that time God's mercy and our own hope: and what reason have we to expect that another time will ever come? If when our Lord really turned and looked on S. Peter, he had refused to remember the word of the Lord, if he had made haste to turn his attention to other things, which were going on around him: if he had said to himself, 'This is not the right time, I will think on this seriously bye and bye, but not as yet:' who can say what his end might have been, or whether, instead of becoming chief among saints, he would not have been shut out from repentance altogether. And which of us can tell, whether any given warning and notice of Christ's Presence, which at any time is graciously vouchsafed him, may not be the last that he will ever receive: so that if he slight it, he may be finally cast off? especially when we consider that the least favoured of us is by special grace brought nearer to Jesus Christ than even S. Peter was at that time. For he had not yet received the Holy Spirit to make him a member of Christ, as we all have received Him in Baptism. Therefore of all things let us beware how we slight this, or any other notice of eternal things, which Almighty God puts in our way. However many do so, however amiable and good they may seem in some respects, it cannot be safe for us to follow them. When the Lord turns and looks, what shall become of His erring Apostle, if he will not " remember the word of the Lord ? "

But there is another way, besides open defiance and neglect, in which it is but too possible, and too common for Christians to slight Christ's warnings: to put aside from them, for example, the notice of Confirmation, without receiving the benefit God intended from it. That is, when they get into a way, too common among us, of promising without performance. It is a sorrowful thing to say, but I much fear that this word, 'promising without performance,' will be found too true an account of the whole conduct of many of us in this whole matter of Confirmation. First, young people promise, and their parents or masters promise for them, that they shall come to be instructed, and come diligently: but presently they begin to break this promise with all manner of foolish excuses. Then they promise to be attentive and diligent in preparing themselves for so great a matter: but it is too plain, often, that they are only seeking to get over it with as little trouble as possible. Sometimes they promise, that after Confirmation they will come again to be taught concerning the Holy Communion, but when the time comes, they draw back without shame or scruple. All these things going wrong, so many promises broken all the way along, give but a sorrowful earnest of what one may expect in regard of the great promise and vow of all: the baptismal promise and vow, renewed in Confirmation. If we use ourselves lightly to forfeit our engagements in the several particulars of so serious a work, how can we well be in earnest in the sum of all, or expect the blessing of Almighty God upon it? It is a serious thought, too, that no one of these our promises which we are so ready to trifle with and forget can be altogether forgotten. All is laid up and registered in a book which will assuredly one day be opened before our eyes. "[a] The sin of Judah is written with

[a] Jer. xvii. 1.

a pen of iron and with the point of a diamond:" i. e. an account is kept indeed of the transgressions of all mankind, but as for those who like Judah of old are brought especially near to God, their sins and negligences are written in such a way that it is unusually hard to blot them out: they are treasured in a peculiar manner against the great Day of wrath. I wish we bore this in mind more than we do; especially at solemn times like these, when the Lord seems in a manner to turn and look upon us, calling some to draw nearer to Him, and reminding the rest how near they are already.

Some of us perhaps may think in their hearts, 'We know that we mean well at present; we really mean to keep our promises; why need we hear so much of unfaithfulness and trifling with God?' But here again the remembrance of S. Peter may come in. As his constant repentance, after Christ had looked on him, may encourage us, hopefully to obey Christ's warning now addressed to ourselves, so the remembrance of what had happened to him just before may make us greatly afraid to trust our good resolutions, how strong soever we may for the present feel them. He had most undoubtingly declared that he never would deny his Lord, but we know how he was led to do so when temptation came very near him. Why? Because he did not watch and pray so steadily as he might have done.

Let us fear how it may be with us. If we hear a warning from God; if Christ turn and look on us, and we for the time remember His Word, and make good resolutions, let us beware of trusting in those resolutions. But let us give all diligence to add to our good meaning, obedience, and to obedience, perseverance, and to perseverance, humility: lest, as our backslidings have commonly been more fearful than the Apostle's: so our repentance prove far more imperfect, and we have to recollect hereafter our Lord's gracious and chiding looks with the sad thought, that they were turned towards us in vain.

SERMON XXIX.

OUR LORD'S SPECIAL LOVE FOR THE YOUNG
AND EAGER.

BEFORE A CONFIRMATION.

S. MARK x. 21.

" Then Jesus beholding him, loved him."

WE know that our Saviour beholds and loves all men continually. He is God Almighty, ever present in all places, and to Him all hearts are open. "ᵃ The Eyes of the Lord are in every place, beholding the evil and the good." "ᵇ All things are naked and opened unto the Eyes of Him with Whom we have to do."

We know also that He loves all men. The whole world, wicked and fallen as it is, is so dear to Him, that for its sake He came from His glory and His Father's glory in heaven, and took to Him a frail and mortal body like our's, and a soul capable of pain and anguish, and offered up that Body and Soul, whole and entire, keeping back nothing, to bear the punishment which we had deserved. And as it was then with Him, so it is now and for ever. His Eye is not waxed dim, that He cannot see us, nor

ᵃ Prov. xv. 3.   ᵇ Heb. iv. 13.

His Heart cold, that He cannot love us. We must take it for a most certain truth, that He beholds and loves all, as perfectly as He did at the very moment of His death.

Yet here we are told of one particular person, whom at one particular moment He beheld and loved. There came one running, a young man who was very rich, and kneeling down to Him, besought Him saying, "Good Master, what good thing shall I do that I may inherit eternal life? And Jesus said unto him, If thou wilt enter into life, keep the commandments. He saith unto Him, which? And Jesus said, Thou shalt not kill, Thou shalt not commit adultery, Thou shall not steal, Thou shalt not bear false witness, Thou shalt not covet, Honour thy father and thy mother, and Thou shalt love thy neighbour as thyself. The young man saith unto Him, all these things have I kept from my youth up: what lack I yet?" Then it goes on, "And Jesus beholding him loved him." That Eye which sees all things, was fixed on that young man with a look of especial, intense affection: and that Heart which comprehends all men in Its infinite, unspeakable love, yearned at that moment with overflowing and most fatherly kindness towards him, kneeling at His Feet.

We know by every minute's experience what astonishing power God has given to the eyes of men, to reveal as it were our hearts one to another; to encourage, to alarm, to soothe, to vex, at our will; how in one moment the eye of a tender mother speaks comfort to an afflicted child, or the grave, reproving eye of a father will check a son or daughter in wild or foolish talk: and we may partly understand the power of His **All-seeing Eye,** when earnestly fixed on the countenance of any of us His creatures. We may imagine in some sort His look of grave and sorrowful indignation, when He looked about on the hypocritical Pharisees "in anger, being grieved at the hardness of their heart:" or of compassionate reproof, when He turned and looked on S. Peter, at the very moment of cock-crowing: or of warning, when He turned and looked on His disciples, before rebuking S. Peter, who could not bear what He said about the Cross. In all these instances we may imagine a little how the Eye of Jesus Christ, fixed on the eyes of those to whom He was speaking, would enter into their hearts as it were, and subdue and win them to a deep and holy fear: but no one of these instances is quite like that which we read of in the text: "Jesus, beholding him, loved him:" that is, looking stedfastly on him, He was moved with a deep overflowing affection towards him: He looked at him ten thousand times more lovingly than the fondest parent looks at the best beloved child: and yet surely among them are continually passing looks of unutterable love. "Jesus beholding him, loved him." Who would not wish to know the secret of that most merciful love—what it was that drew and won the heart of the condescending Redeemer towards that young man? in the humble yet transporting thought, 'Who knows but I too may prove in some respect or other so far like that favoured young man, as that Jesus Christ, earnestly beholding me, may yearn in love towards me also?'

Observe then what we are told of him. First of all, he was young. He had about him that freshness of early life, which is so engaging to all hearts, as is the freshness of early morning to our bodily feelings. He came to our Lord as yet uncorrupted by the world, in comparison at least with those Pharisees, who were continually besetting Him with their hypocritical questions. So that as He looked on him, He might feel something of the same tender care, as He expressed towards the little babes, when He took them up in His arms and blessed them, and said, "ᶜOf such is the kingdom of God."

Secondly, the young man was rich: and our Saviour therefore looked on him with a deep compassionate anxiety, knowing how hard it is for them that have riches to enter into the kingdom of God. His unerring Eye knew beforehand all the dangers and temptations to which a person in that condition, a rich young man, would be exposed in his journey through life: and He pitied him and cared for him accordingly, as the true shepherd pities and cares for the sheep which he fears is going astray.

Thirdly, this young man came running to Christ. With the natural eagerness of his time of life, he quickened his pace, and was impatient of any delay: the time seemed long to him until he had seen the Face of the holy Jesus, and offered Him his homage. He was not contented with walking, but came running to Him. Now our Lord's own rule is, "ᵈThem that honour Me, I will honour." "ᵉHim that cometh to Me, I will in no wise cast out." Therefore we need not doubt that this zeal of the young rich man had something to do with our Saviour's loving look. Even such as we are, the coldest and hardest of us

---

ᶜ S. Mark x. 14. ᵈ 1 Sam. ii. 30. ᵉ S. John vi. 37.

all, are pleased when the young and simple come eagerly towards us, in affectionate trust: how much more might the blessed Jesus, Who is the fountain of all love, welcome the young person who was making such haste to come to Him with all the desire of his soul.

But fourthly, **the young man kneeled down to our Lord.** In all his eagerness he did not forget the reverence due to so great and holy a Teacher, but cast himself **down on the ground to receive His instruction.** Here surely is something to be considered by those, who thinking to be true lovers of Jesus Christ, neglect or disdain the outward marks of reverence to Him. When He saw the young man on his knees, He loved him. Is there not some reason to apprehend, that we may lose some portion of His love, if when we come to hear from Him about the way of eternal life, we think much to fall on our knees before Him, and to shew Him such other outward tokens of reverence, as the law and rule of His holy Church requires?

But lastly and **principally, this young man was anxious about his soul.** His earnest enquiry of our Lord was, "Good Master, what good thing shall I do to inherit eternal life?" He had great riches, a good name, and no doubt many friends; means more than enough for ample enjoyment in this life: but he wishes and intends to set them all apart, not to think of them at all as of any thing of his own, while he offers himself, heart and soul, to his Saviour. 'What,' he asks, 'shall I do?' This and that I have already done: I have kept all the commandments of the second table; have tried to do all my duty to my neighbour: What lack I yet? What more wouldest Thou have me to do, Thus he spake: and although his love was sadly imperfect, and could not at the time stand the trial to which it was put, yet our Lord looked on him with love. His gracious endearing Eye was turned towards him, and the very words which seemed too severe a trial to him, were unquestionably uttered as a token of distinguishing love: as when a commander invites a young soldier to some particularly hazardous and painful service, we know that he does it as loving and delighting to honour him.

There are some among you, my brethren, to whom at this time I will venture to apply, I trust without presumption, that gracious saying, "And Jesus beholding him, loved him." You will guess that I mean those especially, who are now preparing, with earnest hearts to present themselves before their Lord for the blessing of His confirming Spirit, to strengthen them for the courageous fulfilment of their whole baptismal vow, which they are about to take on themselves anew in His immediate Presence. I love to think that in them we may see many of those qualities which drew our Lord's gracious Eye towards the petitioner of whom we have been speaking; and therefore we may well hope, that Jesus beholding loveth them also: that His looks of most unspeakable loving-kindness, which are better than the life itself, are at this time turned upon them and their humble endeavours.

Yes, you, my brethren, now to be confirmed, are as he who came, as you have heard, to our Saviour; for in the first place, you are most of you young, as he was. You are going to offer to God the flower of your days, the top and crown of your life. You are professing to remember your Creator in the days of your youth: to begin courageously warring on His side against the world, the flesh, and the devil. We trust that you all come with a sincere and simple mind: but you do not, you cannot yet know half the dangers which encompass your path. Your elders, by sad experience, know something more of them: but no one knows them as your Saviour does Himself: no one therefore can feel for you as He does, or look on you with such anxious love, as one by one you come forward and kneel down at His Altar. Parents perhaps are there, and elder friends, and dutiful godfathers and godmothers, and pastors who tremble, or who ought to tremble in their very hearts, for the account they may one day have to give of you: but what are all their looks to the compassionate, loving look of your Saviour Himself, knowing as He does beforehand all your wanderings, all the temptations and trials you will have to go through, which of you will sink, and which prevail against them? O, depend on it, your very youth, your simple, innocent, confiding time of life is a reason why you may trust His fatherly affection. He will not bear to see you wronged and oppressed. He will not let the congregations of evil spirits rob you: only do you trust Him entirely. Some of you are apt to think, that your being young is a reason why you should draw back from the Communion of His Body and Blood: whereas in truth it is a great reason why you should lose no time in coming. For the younger you are when you come, the more you attract that special love of of our Lord's, which He shewed by His sweet and gracious aspect towards that young man in the text.

Next, whereas he was rich as well as young; you are not indeed, the greater part of you, rich in the gold and silver of this world: yet as compared with many of your brethren elsewhere, you have certain worldly advantages and comforts, quite sufficient, if not carefully watched, to draw you away from your God as riches draw the rich man away: and on this account also, we may well believe, the Eye of your God and Saviour looks anxiously towards you. He knows beforehand which of you all will be led astray, by the notion that an easy quiet decent life is enough, without any particular attempts to be religious: He knows, and He grieves beforehand for them all. Which of you would not earnestly desire to spare your Saviour this grief? Resolve then, and with all your hearts keep your resolution, never to be content with a mere decent ordinary religion: to beware of the world's shew of godliness: to fear greatly the sentence of those whom our Lord rejected as being neither cold nor hot [c].

Thirdly: as that rich young man came running to our Saviour, so I trust there are some of you, who knowing that your hearts are set at liberty by holy Baptism, are endeavouring, and purposing to endeavour still more, not merely to walk but to run the way of His commandments. He comes out to meet you by His minister and messenger, the Bishop: I trust there are some of you who will go not languidly but heartily forth to meet Him, as to a most high

[c] Rev. iii. 16.

and glad festival: some who will indeed pour out their hearts before Him, acknowledging Him as their only Hope, and giving up themselves entirely to Him, now and for ever, when His overshadowing Hand shall be visibly spread over them. Who can express the love of our gracious Master towards all whom He shall behold so minded? how entirely He will receive them for His own: with what high and heavenly guardianship He will protect their way through life: what a treasure of humble and contrite thoughts, holy desires and wise and good purposes, He will open in answer to their prayers.

Again, I trust that you will, none of you so come running into His Presence as to forget to kneel to Him when you are there: that is, as the Church directs you to kneel when you receive the Bishop's blessing, so I trust that you will both then and always endeavour to kneel in heart before Him: to pass through life in a serious unfeigned sense of His most awful Presence. Never allow yourselves in any sense to trifle with God. Never be ashamed to be serious, thoughtful, and considerate, in what you do for Him. Endeavour so to feel in your hearts, and be not ashamed to shew it in your outward conversation, whether your companions look strangely or kindly on you: be not cast down, though they should even jeer at you, or teaze you. What signify their disapproving or scornful looks, so long as you may reasonably hope that Jesus Himself beholding you loveth you?

But last and chiefest of all, remember always, that this young man, for the time at least, was truly anxious about his soul. He did not come to our

Lord out of custom, or because others did, or that he might be well looked upon; for indeed very few came to Him at that time. He came, no doubt, from real care for his soul: real, though for the time imperfect and unstable; and Jesus, seeing this, loved him accordingly. We will trust and hope that so it is with you; and be sure that if it is, the loving and approving Eye of your Lord rests upon you. You may be as sure of it, as if with that young man you were kneeling before His visible bodily Presence, and could look up and see something of the gracious expression of His countenance. Be sure that He loves you: but take good heed of the way in which He confirms His love toward you. As then He put the young man on a very severe trial, requiring him to sell all that he had and give it away, and follow Him, taking up the cross: so He requires of you, as soon as ever you are confirmed, that which is to all a real trial, and to many, no doubt, a severe one: that you should *immediately* turn your minds and heart towards the blessed Communion of His Body and Blood: either coming to it at once, if duly prepared, or at least beginning to prepare yourself seriously for it. Some of you may think this too great and hard a thing; but be it great or little, hard or easy, it is what the Lord your God requires of you. In His tender fatherly love He puts it upon you, as the very first instance in which you may prove that you are in earnest in the promise and vow you are making. Consider it well, and beware of trifling with the Almighty. May He guard you from that great sin, and bless you with His Holy Spirit, now and for ever.

SERMON XXX.

HARD TRIALS, OUR LORD'S LOVE-TOKENS.

AFTER A CONFIRMATION.

S. Mark x. 21.

"Then Jesus, beholding him, loved him, and said unto him, One thing thou lackest: go thy way, sell all that thou hast and give to the poor, and thou shalt have treasure in heaven, and come, take up the cross, and follow Me."

We considered last Sunday our Saviour's loving look, when He turned His All-seeing eyes in pity and fatherly care towards the rich young man, who came running to Him in anxiety about his own soul. We left him as it were wistfully gazing on the Divine and merciful Countenance; hearkening what the Lord God should say unto him. Now we have to consider His answer, how He began to shew that great and distinguishing love. And as we found last Sunday, that His look of love to the young ruler answered well to the welcome which He gives to sincere young persons coming to Him in Confirmation, it may be we shall find to-day something which answers no less exactly to His dealings with them presently after Confirmation.

Observe then first of all, how very unlike was the token of our Saviour's love to those which men ordinarily bestow on such as are dear to them. An earthly father, beholding his son, loves him; and how does he shew his love? He gathers together all he can for his son: as much credit, power, riches, and consequence, as ever he can manage to get together: and encourages the child to go on doing as much as he can for himself in the same way. Again, an earthly mother, beholding her daughter, loves her: and how does she manifest her love? She desires to make her as perfect as she can in all that the world admires and approves in such young persons; a happy and comfortable home in this world is what she chiefly seeks for her. But here, when Jesus, beholding a person, loves him, His love-token, His fatherly wish and bidding, is, "Go thy way, sell all that thou hast, and give to the poor, and thou shalt have treasure in heaven, and come, take up the cross and follow Me."

See, my brethren, how unlike the love of our Lord for us is to our earthly love for one another: and since there are some here, on whom, this very week, He has graciously turned His loving and life-giving Countenance, laying His Hands upon them, and blessing them: I call upon each one of them especially to consider for himself, that he too must expect to be tried in something of the same way; to have something put upon him, very different from what we, in our ignorant earthly love, should naturally choose for such as are most near and dear to us. We are not indeed charged as the young man was, to forsake outwardly friends, home, and comforts, and to become Martyrs and Confessors to Him Who died for us. God Who knows our weak and frail hearts, spares us such a severe trial as that; still He has prepared a real trial for each of us, more or less of the same kind: and for you, my young brethren, as I have already repeatedly told you, He has prepared at least this trial, that immediately on your being confirmed, He bids you make yourselves ready, and come to His sacred Altar table. Nothing can be plainer than our duty in this respect, nothing sweeter or more encouraging than the invitations and promises of our gracious Shepherd and Saviour: yet so it is, that for several reasons, communicating immediately is to many of those amongst us, rather a hard and severe trial. In itself it is a simple and most blessed duty, common to all Christians alike: but such as we unhappily are, I do not wonder that many draw back from what is said to them about the Communion, somewhat in the same way, as if it was said to them, 'Sell all that thou hast, and give to the poor, and take up thy cross.' Communicating is, as the catechism says, a plain duty, generally necessary to salvation; yet it strikes many people's minds as a thing extraordinary, a rule fit for a few perfect souls only. Why should this be? Why should so many of the young draw back from it in the manner they do?

One reason no doubt is, a feeling that it requires real self-denial and holiness, real and watchful amendment of the whole life and heart in a greater degree than persons are yet willing to practise. People say to themselves, and very truly, 'Though I am not called on outwardly to give up all that I possess and delight in of an earthly kind, yet I am told to wean myself from all in heart, not to make an idol of anything, by loving it and caring for it more than I love God: I am told to put away from me, not only all wilful sin, but all unnecessary occasions and temptations to sin: and all this is more than I like to pledge myself to at present: I will wait till I am steadier, and then I hope to come.' Something like this, I fear, lies at the root of many young persons' unwillingness to do this, as Christ bade them, in remembrance of Him. But of their case I will say no more at present than what I have said over and over, that such an objection ought equally to have prevented them from coming to Confirmation: it is an objection, in fact, to their being Christians at all: for all that they shrink from in the Communion, they are already bound to by their baptismal vow; and as they cannot unbaptize themselves, they must answer for it in the last Day.

But there is another very sad reason why so many of those who have been confirmed find the doctrine of the Communion a hard saying: I mean that after they are convinced of their duty, and really and honestly wish to do it, and would fain go on and love God above all things, they are damped, and checked, and often finally turn back, by the opposition they meet with among others, who ought to know better. Is it not so, that in many families, I might say in whole villages, a blind notion has prevailed, that the Sacrament of Christ's Body and Blood is not for ordinary Christians, especially not for the young: and so many of those who otherwise would, and ought to have come to it, have been hindered by fear of what others would say of them: have felt as if they were doing a thing which all the neighbourhood, perhaps their own parents, thought they had better let alone? It cannot be denied, this heathenish way of thinking has too much hindered Christ's little ones from coming to His Altar: but let us hope that by God's blessing we shall find less and less of it, and that if people have not the heart to come themselves (as perhaps they ought not, being impenitent sinners) at least they will not, by deed or word or even look, scorn and hinder the devout purposes of simple and loving young people, who wish to come.

So it is, however, that from one or other of these reasons, a large proportion of those on whom the Bishops lay their hands, when they are told, 'Prepare yourselves and come to the Communion,' go away sorrowful, like that rich young man: and some, alas! never return. Death cuts them off, before they have had will or opportunity to partake of Christ in that way, without which, He Himself said, they can have no life in them. Some, alas! never return: some repent after a time, as we may hope that young man did: and although they cannot but be losers of so much grace, as our Lord had prepared for them in the Communions which they have missed, yet no doubt, as soon as ever they come sincerely, they are freely forgiven, and received into the fulness of Christ's favour: only let them strive and pray to have their amendment sincere and lasting, and not the mere passing effect of sickness or other worldly trouble.

But most blessed and happy will the day of Confirmation prove to all those who so understand the vow which they then make, as to set their faces without any delay towards the holy Altar of their God: and who so value the grace which they receive, as to employ it, with earnest and humble prayer, in making the preparation which Christ and His Apostle require of them. Some such, I trust, are now here among us: may Almighty God increase their number, and cause holy desires to bring forth abundantly the fruit which He loves, of good counsels and just works. Our Lord's look of especial love, which He turned towards them in their Confirmation, is doubtless now turned again towards them, and will be so as often as they come hither, faithfully prepared, for the same holy purpose. We read that immediately on the departure of the young man in the text, Jesus *looked about Him*, and spake to His disciples about the difficulty of a rich man entering into the kingdom of God: and when they cried out, "Who then can be saved?" *looking stedfastly upon them* He saith, "With men this is impossible, but not with God, for with God all things are possible." Thus our Lord repeated His gracious and loving look to those who stedfastly abode by Him: and you are not to doubt, but earnestly to believe, that in like manner He looks on you, newly confirmed and coming humbly to His Altar, with the same Eye of mercy which fell on you when you were confirmed. He still beholds and loves you; and His love is an everlasting love. Only, I beseech you, take notice that your Saviour's look of fatherly love, with which He regarded His disciples and that young man, was in some sense a look also of fatherly anxiety and care. He beheld them earnestly, willing them to attend to Him, and treasure up in their hearts the cautions which He was giving them. Even so, now that this awful Sacrament has in a manner drawn your attention towards Him, and fixed the eyes of your whole heart upon Him, mark well how gravely He warns you. In His deep tender affection He warns you, *first*, that now you are His more than ever, you really must renounce the world. Whatever He trusts you with here, you must withdraw your heart and affection from it, so far as to be ready to part with it, whenever He shall require, for His sake. In particular, you must not have riches, that is, you must not have them for yourselves, but account yourselves His stewards, to use them for His service: and whether you have them or no, you must not depend on them, nor desire them. Moreover, Christ calls upon each one of you, as it were by name, to renounce his own will in that particular respect, in which he is most tempted to go wrong. If, as we trust, you have been searching deeply into your own hearts and consciences, to prepare yourselves for Holy Communion, you must be aware, each among you, of some one or more things, in which you are especially inclined to go wrong: tempting things, from which to refrain will be especially hard and painful to you. Here is your trial, and here, by God's grace, shall be your victory. It matters not much what it is: to some it will be the government of the temper, to some, driving away bad and shameful thoughts, to others, perhaps, overcoming discontent, to very many, putting down self-conceit: but whatever it is, now is the time for you to set yourselves resolutely against it: now in the solemn hour of your first Communion, while the gracious Eye of your Divine Saviour is specially fixed upon you in love, now is the time for you to beg most earnestly of Him grace to overcome this your too powerful enemy: now is the time to declare such war against him, as shall never end until he is put down for ever. This is our Saviour's first caution to you who now communicate for the first time: see to it, that in respect of your prevailing temptation you leave all and follow Christ.

Now perhaps some one may be ready to say in his heart as S. Peter did, 'Lo, we have already left all, we have already taken these vows, and have come before Thee, determined by Thy grace to keep them.' To such our Lord speaks again a word of caution: He warns them not to think they are doing great things, in coming while they are young to the Holy Communion. 'So far,' He seems to say, 'it is well: you have made a good beginning: you have overcome certain hindrances, and have obeyed Me in spite of certain difficulties: but beware of self-satisfied thoughts; beware how you begin to praise yourself in your heart; if you do, that is at once going back, and losing all the ground you have gained.' Remember that awful saying, "Many that are first shall be last, and the last shall be first." Though we were first on earth, we are not safe; and we alas! how far are we as yet from the very least of God's saints! Depend not therefore on yourselves for a single moment. Begin at once in trifling every day matters to give up your own will, preparing so for great trials: but do it always in dependence on a better strength than your own. If you think to deny yourselves without constant and earnest acts of devotion, your strength will soon fail you: you may seem to go right for a while, but perhaps Satan spares you now in order to take his advantage of you more surely bye and bye. If on the other hand you expect that prayer and Communion, earnest though it seem and punctual, will save you without constantly denying yourself, you will find this, sooner or later, a mere shadow of religion, which will end in the ruin of your souls.

In a word, your Saviour bids you at this time be full of fear, yet of trust also: fear yourselves, that you may be diligent in prayer, and may never pass any long time without coming to Christ's Altar for strength: yet never cease trusting in Him Who now lays His Cross on you and bids you follow Him; promising thereby that He will be always at hand to help: trust in Him always, and in His strength overcome your own will in great matters and in small. By this course your crown in heaven will be safe, whether God send on you great visible trials or no. Fear the effect which the world may have on you: fear how your doings may look after a time in sight of God and His Angels. Fear above all things all trifling with God Almighty. But trust to His aid to keep the good rules which His Holy Spirit puts into your heart. Trust to Him to keep you in countenance in professing His Name openly before men; in performing religious duties, such as going to Church and Communion, whether others encourage you or not; in saying No with a stedfast heart, when things are proposed which you know to be wrong. Trust to Him to help you in denying yourself, when the choice lies between yourself, and your God. And since there are several of you whom God's providence is now calling to fight the good fight together, why should you not resolve to help one another, and keep one another in countenance in doing right, like Christian brethren and fellow-soldiers, like the holy Apostles themselves, to whom next to their Saviour's Presence it was the greatest encouragement to see one another forsake all and follow Christ? Resolve yourselves, and help one another, to remember this day and also the day of your Confirmation, as long as you live in the world, and may the remembrance be still happier and happier to you. One word more. Do not allow yourself to feel, when you have communicated, as if you had done a work, and need take no more pains. Rather make up your minds to be tried in some respects more than ever; for Satan generally attacks those whom he sees endeavouring to grow in grace. Assuredly you will be tried, only you will have greater strength to bear the trial. One trial at any rate will very soon come upon you, if you live: I mean when you are invited to the holy Table again. In some respects, and to some persons, the second Communion is a harder step than the first. Think of it beforehand: pray that you may be guided to do right when it comes. The safe way is, to begin preparing for it as soon as the first Communion is over; and that will be best done by taking care not soon to let your Lord go when you have once happily received Him. This evening at least, and to morrow, from time to time, remember Who has come to visit you, and what a glorious Guest you have received. God means it to be a great and good day for you: strive and pray by His grace to make the most of it.

SERMON XXXI.

HOW WE SHOULD DEAL WITH RELIGIOUS DISAPPOINTMENTS.

Jer. xiv. 8.

"O the Hope of Israel, the Saviour thereof in time of trouble, Why shouldest Thou be as a stranger in the land, and as a way-faring man that turneth aside to tarry but a night?"

THERE never, I suppose, was an eager affectionate person, but he had in his young days, more or less, to undergo this kind of disappointment: that when he had set his heart upon being intimate with some one or other among his companions, who seemed to him very amiable, he found not the return of affection, which he expected, on the other person's part: a damp, a chill, a blight came over him, such as the great Apostle complains of, or seems to fear, in his Corinthian converts. "[a] O ye Corinthians, our mouth is opened unto you, our heart is enlarged:" he had spoken freely and cordially to them, had poured himself out, as one who felt sure of a return: but they had checked him by their cold heartless ways: "Ye are not straitened," saith he, "in us, but ye are straitened in your own bowels:" 'it is no lack of love

[a] 2 Cor. vi. 11.

on my part, but you seem as if you had no love in you to meet it with.'

Thus the Apostle complains, not meeting with the kindness he looked for from his brethren: and all thoughtful persons, who have lived any time in the world, have come to know and understand his feeling: but there is another disappointment, not uncommon, yet more trying and painful: I mean when persons fail to find even in God's own service, and in the Sacraments of Jesus Christ, the inward contentment and satisfaction they had looked for. Where the Father, the Son, and the Holy Ghost are: God all whole in infinite Power, Wisdom, and Goodness, there who would doubt to find full and lasting joy and peace? But, generally speaking, it is not so in this world: it is not always clear sunshine even in the purest and best prepared soul. God sometimes hides the light of His countenance, sometimes lets it beam gloriously out: as flowers in some sorts of weather give out their fragrance, so that you cannot walk near them without perceiving it; in other weather you do not discern them at all. We are warned of it by the Scriptures of God, and by the experience of all saints: therefore when it comes we ought not to be greatly disappointed: yet the truly affectionate heart can for the time but hardly bear it, and many and grievous are the complaints uttered by faithful servants of God in the Old Testament, on feeling this banishment of the heart. "[b] Lord, why abhorrest Thou my soul, and hidest Thou Thy Face from me? Hide not Thy Face from me, lest I be like unto them that go down into the pit." Thus prays the psalmist

[b] Ps. lxxxviii. 14.

in many places: and so does the prophet Isaiah, "[c]Verily Thou art a God that hidest Thyself, O God of Israel, the Saviour:" and again, "[d]Why hast Thou made us to err from Thy ways, and hardened our heart from Thy fear?" So Job very often: "[e]He goeth by me, and I see Him not: He passeth me also, but I perceive Him not. He hath set darkness in my paths." "[f]My days are past, my purposes are broken off, even the thoughts of my heart: they change the night into day: the light is short because of darkness." So especially the mourning prophet Jeremiah, in such passages as that from which the text is taken, "O the Hope of Israel, the Saviour thereof in time of trouble, Why shouldest Thou be as a stranger in the land, and as a way-faring man that turneth aside to tarry but a night?" It is as if he had said, 'Thou didst come very near us, we felt the joy and gladness of Thy Presence, we knew it was great comfort, and hoped it would be endless: but in how short a time is it departed. We hoped that Thou wert come to dwell with us, why art Thou so soon gone? like one who wert but a stranger and sojourner. We hoped never to lose the sight, the happy thought of Thee and of Thine abode within us: why is it passed from us, as the remembrance of a guest that tarrieth but a day?' This I believe to have been at times the experience of all, even the greatest saints. "[g]By night on my bed I sought Him Whom my soul loveth: I sought Him, but I found Him not." God has tried His most faithful and beloved ones by withdrawing for a while, not His

[c] Isa. xlv. 15.   [d] Ib. lxiii. 17.   [e] Job ix. 11.
[f] Ib. xvii. 11.   [g] Song of Solomon iii. 1.

Presence, but—the cheering and comfortable sense of His Presence. But more especially may some such inward trial be expected after certain solemn moments, and turning points (so to call them) in the heavenly life of a Christian: moments which have been long looked forward to; which have been prepared for with great earnestness, which have mingled for many days, weeks, months, sometimes perhaps for many years, with our prayers and meditations and serious discourses: moments to which a great blessing is promised, and from which therefore great comfort is naturally expected: such moments, I mean, as the Confirmation of a young person, or his first Communion, or, when any one has fallen away, his being admitted after penitence to the Holy Communion again. I say, such times as these are very apt to be accompanied or followed by a certain sense of languor and disappointment: to a person's feelings they seldom, perhaps, bring the expected comfort in its fulness: or if it seem to come (and certainly now and then the God of all Pardon makes His cup of joy overflow in an unspeakable manner to some who know themselves most unworthy) I say, if the comfort of our solemn times do seem to come, yet it seems in general to pass too quickly away, and when in thought we dwell on it afterwards, there is more or less of disappointment and dissatisfaction: sometimes men come to doubt whether God has indeed been with them, and very often they are tempted to think it hard, and to complain with the prophet, that He Whom they looked for to be their constant Hope and Saviour, proves on trial to be but a visitor and sojourner in the land: "a wayfaring man that tarrieth but a night." Such feelings must be dealt with meekly and wisely, else there will be danger of their settling down into something like cold and sullen unbelief: the world and the devil will whisper to us, 'you have tried religion and it would not do: you had best enjoy yourself while you can.' Such miserable consequences have sometimes followed on good and hopeful beginnings, in consequence of people's depending too much on the present consolations and delights of devotion, and feeling too much disappointed when the Lord seemed to hide His Face.

I suppose there may be some among us, to whom such a warning as this may prove not unseasonable just at present. For it is only four days, as you know, since more than fifty of those who should come to worship in this Church drew near to God's Altar and bowed down their heads meekly to receive His servant's blessing: that blessing, which worthily received is the sure pledge of God's strengthening Spirit, entering more and more into our hearts, to enable us to keep our holy baptismal vow. Most of you, who so came, had been preparing yourselves for a long time; we hope and trust, preparing yourselves in earnest; it was a moment then long looked forward to; prayers, and readings, and catechisms, and self-examinations, your thoughts and plans both on Sundays and on working days have been more or less mixed up with it: like a birth or a marriage, it has been long waited for. And now it has come, how has it proved to you? I mean, in respect of what we are talking of: the feelings and impressions of the time, and for these few days, which have since passed over? I speak not now to the careless and profane ones, if such unhappily there were, to whom it may not have seemed much one way or the other; but to those who had really set their hearts upon it, as on a way of drawing near to our Lord, as something to do their souls good: and I think it very likely that a good many even of these have felt in some degree vexed and surprised at the reality of that which they had been so long imagining to themselves. I think it likely that either they found themselves at the time far less moved and carried away with the holy ordinance than they expected to be, or what still more commonly happens, that the remembrance and effect of it appears to be fading away far too quickly out of their minds; they are settling down sooner than they wished and hoped into the cares and pleasures of ordinary life: on the whole, it seems to them rather unreal, and they are tempted at times to ask themselves, 'Is this all? have I really been confirmed? am I indeed partaker of a great additional blessing? is it not rather an edifying kind of dream, which I may use for good among other things, but which has left me on the whole nearly where I was before?' People are the rather tempted to such thoughts, as the Service itself, the most solemn part of it, the blessing, is so very soon over: it takes a very few minutes to walk up to the front of God's Altar, to kneel and receive the benediction, and return to your place; as before, the renewal of your serious promise and vow had been transacted in one moment, and in two very short words, "I do." The very scantiness of the time, the little that seems to be said and done in it, makes something of a trial for our faith: those who are naturally slow and cold, have hardly time to be moved: those who are more eager, yet find themselves very soon at leisure to mind other things. And as in all outward duties, there are innumerable little cares and circumstances of dress, posture, behaviour, whatever is around us, which in greater or less degree are apt to disturb our attention at the time, and to make the memory of our Confirmation less blessed afterwards. So that probably scarcely any young person, however serious he might strive to be, both during the holy service and afterwards, will have recollections of pure and unmixed comfort when he calls the day to mind in his after life. As the devoutest worshippers may confess at the end of their prayers, 'We have need to say them over again, and to say them better,' so might the best of us well wish, if it might be possible, that he could be confirmed again. And such disappointment tempts on the one hand (as I said before) to a hard and sullen mind: on the other hand, it will dispose many lightly to look out for something to satisfy them better, some form of worship, or kind of doctrine, which may engage the mind more entirely, and so they may become quite unsettled, and wander from the Church's teaching, no one knows where. Indeed this seems to have been in old times one of the greatest temptations to Christians to fall back into heathen idolatry: there was a sort of eager excitement kept up in the feasts and sacrifices of the false gods, which quickly drew away unstable minds, from the calm, sober, majestic Sacraments of the Church.

It must of course be a good thing for you to be aware of this danger; and to be not too much disheartened: it is part of your trial: and you have great helps to meet it with. Consider, in the first place, that the same kind of disappointment belongs more or less to the very condition of Christians in this imperfect world. Our Lord and Saviour was the "Desire of all nations:" the world waited for Him more than four thousand years: the whole creation groaned and travailed in pain together until that aweful blessed moment: and when it came, how disappointing it was! The Babe was found wrapt in swaddling clothes, lying in a manger: for thirty years He lay hid in a lowly village, working at His trade and seemed to do nothing to fulfil His high calling, and He did fulfil it at last upon the Cross. Those who had watched for Him, when they saw Him, found no beauty that they should desire Him, such as they had before imagined. Now as it was so in Christ's coming once for all to the whole world, so in some measure it is when He comes by His sacramental visitations to each several soul. It is far unlike what men expected, and at first almost always disappointing. Doubtless, what we now experience of this sort in Confirmation would be experienced still more remarkably in Holy Baptism, if Providence kept us waiting for that until we were grown up. The work of Baptism, so great and aweful, so long looked forward to, yet over in so very short a moment, must greatly try the faith of such as are brought to it in riper years: only that generally in heathen countries it has brought men into a state of persecution and danger, which would drive them continually to the thought of Christ, and force them to live by faith in His Presence, if they would still be Christians at all. As we are in this country, it does seem one of the greatest mercies that we are brought to the holy Font before we can know of it: our temptation would else be so very sore, in many cases, to think even more unfaithfully of it, than we now too often do of Confirmation.

Be not then too much cast down if you have found the *sensible* effect of your Confirmation, the glowing thoughts which belong to it, either too much interrupted at the time or too soon appearing to fade and pass away from you. Be not too much cast down, yet be not satisfied with yourself that so it should be. But take the remedy which the Holy Spirit has provided for you in the law of the Church: which is, not to rest, not even to pause, as though contented with what has been done for you at Confirmation, but immediately to begin looking forward to, and preparing for, that far greater thing, to which as you know the Bishop's blessing is but the preparation and entrance. Begin without delay to prepare yourselves in good earnest for the Holy Communion. Let that take up in your minds the same place which Confirmation has for some time taken up. So looking on to a yet more heavenly blessing, though you will be humbled, you will not be hardened or disheartened by the feeling how your imperfections blemished your Confirmation. You will strive and pray with all your might to make up as far as may be for those blemishes, by your exact zeal and humility in the yet more solemn moment of your first Communion. And although this also will no doubt

Y

bring its measure of disappointment along with it, yet in all likelihood you will have sufficient tokens of God's blessing on your endeavours: and at any rate there will be no question as to the next thing you have to do: after that first Communion, you will have presently to begin preparing to communicate a second time still more worthily; and then again a third time: and so on: till at last, doubtless after many disappointments, and with constant matter of self-humiliation, yet on the whole, with constant improvement, you will come to your last Communion, and from that to Paradise.

Much then as we may regret our own many failures, yet let us not fail to admire and adore God's mercy, in gently leading us on so far. Let us thankfully accept and use all His gracious invitations for the time to come: never let Him knock at the door of our hearts in vain: that so His saving visits may gradually grow more frequent, and in the end He may cease to come and go like a wayfaring man, but finding us constantly, though imperfectly, prepared, may make His home with us, and depart no more.

SERMON XXXII.

THE NEED OF STIRRING UP THE GIFT OF GOD.

AFTER CONFIRMATION.

2 Tim. i. 6.

"*Wherefore I put thee in remembrance, that thou stir up the gift of God which is in thee by the putting on of my hands.*"

Some persons might imagine that the gifts of God would have no need of stirring up: that what He does, He does perfectly and at once: that we frail mortals can neither add anything nor take away anything from it. We might imagine so, but it would be mere imagination. Look around you, my brethren, look at things as they really are, and you perceive that it has pleased our Almighty Maker and Ruler so to dispense His gifts and mercies to us, as though without man's doing his part they could bear no fruit worth speaking of, nor ever come to perfection. E.g. God gives us life: being born into the world, we live: but how long should we live, if no one gave us food? Life is the gift of God; of God only: but it requires to be stirred up, as it were, and rekindled from time to time, by proper nourishment. Again: all bodily skill and strength, dexterity in any art or trade, the power of speaking eloquently, of talking any language, of keeping accounts; every thing in short which men call a gift or a talent, requires more or less of stirring up: it needs exercise; it fails if left to itself. Though you can now read ever so well, yet if you quite gave up reading, if you never looked into a book for ten years, do you think that you should not entirely forget how to read? One meets continually with persons who tell us it was their own case. If a smith laid aside his hammer, or a gardener his spade, if a physician saw no patients, for a great many years together, what would become of their skill in their several ways? Nay even the most ordinary powers of the body, as it is well known, fail, if they are not exercised. If a man gets any how into a way of never using any particular limb or muscle, that limb or muscle becomes in a manner benumbed: he quite loses the use of it. If he never sings, he loses the power of singing; the management of his voice. All these that I have mentioned, and many more, are the gifts of God, and yet they have need to be stirred up. And it is just the same in regard of His spiritual and heavenly gifts. He does not merely bestow them, He entrusts us with them. They are free gifts, perfectly undeserved, pure bounty on His part: but it rests with us to use, to neglect, or to abuse them. Thus in Holy Baptism, He gives us spiritual life, makes us members of Jesus Christ, partakers of His Divine nature, children of God, inheritors of heaven. All this is His free gift: but it is such a gift as may be forfeited and lost. We are truly and really alive, by His mercy; our souls are alive, but they will die if they are not nourished. We are alive by Baptism, that is God's original gift, but we must keep ourselves alive, by resorting to His other Sacrament, to receive from Him that other gift, the gift of nourishment by the Body and Blood of Christ.

As it is in these first and greatest gifts, so it is in the other spiritual favours which our Lord grants unto His people; they are in themselves unspeakable gifts, precious beyond all reckoning, but they may and will be lost, if they are not attended to: they require cherishing, feeding, stirring up, on our part. Hear how the Apostle speaks to Timothy, one of the first Christian bishops. "Remember," says he, "that thou stir up the gift of God which is in thee by the laying on of my hands." He means of course the laying on of his hands in Ordination, when Timothy, as the manner was and is, knelt down before S. Paul, who had also a council of priests with him, and was solemnly consecrated by the great Apostle, and bidden to receive the Holy Ghost for the office and work of a Bishop in the Church of God. Then there was given to Timothy a very great gift indeed—the grace of God's Holy Spirit to make him a true Bishop, a true successor of the Apostles and of Jesus Christ Himself, in governing the Church, and in giving the Holy Ghost. It was such a power as no man, understanding it, could ever dream of winning for himself. But S. Paul plainly enough intimates, that it was too possible he might lose it for himself. He says, "I put thee in remembrance, to stir up the gift of God which is in thee by the laying on of my hands." As much as to say that if he did not stir it up, he would sooner or later lose it, freely as it was given of God, and altogether beyond anything which man could ever obtain of himself. Do you not think that such a warning as this must have made the holy S. Timothy very anxious, very full of care, lest by his own fault he should lose so great and unmerited a blessing?

But now, as there is in the Church other laying on of hands, besides what is used in ordaining ministers, and as there are other gifts of God bestowed upon the Christian people by such laying on of hands, so we cannot doubt S. Paul's words spoken of Ordination may be rightly applied to Confirmation. The Bishop who confirmed some of you last Friday did in effect say to those whom he confirmed, and might very well have said it in so many words, "Remember that ye stir up the gift of God which is in you by the laying on of my hands." For you know what our Lord does by His servant the Bishop, when he confirms any person. He gives to that person, coming to Him sincerely, a portion of His strengthening Spirit, to help him in keeping his vow made in Holy Baptism. The Holy Ghost, so given, is as a fresh spark of fire, kindled in the heart of God's full-grown child, who is now endeavouring and purposing to draw nearer to God than ever. For as the Holy Ghost is likened to fire, and as He came down in tongues of fire, so each new gift of the Holy Ghost is as a spark of that saving and purifying fire, which our Lord came to send upon earth: and which it is His Will to have kindled in all hearts, far and near. The strengthening Spirit given in Confirmation is indeed a spark of fire from heaven. We by our solemn renewal of our Baptismal vow offer to our God ourselves, our souls and bodies, as the Israelites of old time were wont to offer their whole burned sacrifices, casting all at once on the altar; and as then the fire came down and consumed the whole offering, so now cometh down the Holy confirming Spirit, and kindleth that fire within us, which in time will happily change our whole being after its own Divine nature. But for the present it is within us as a spark: and therefore it requires stirring up. The very word which S. Paul uses contains in itself all this meaning. For whereas he says, *Stir up* God's gift, the word properly and exactly taken means not any kind of stirring up, but only the rekindling of embers, the stirring up of a fire which would otherwise be in danger of going out.

You know that when a fire is lighted it still needs to be looked after. It may be quenched and put out on purpose, it may be neglected and go out of itself. So it is with that Divine fire, the Holy Ghost given in Confirmation by laying on of Apostolic hands. It may be overlaid and quenched by sin and the world. Woe be to those who do so: but as sad experience shews us daily that it is but too possible, so we need not be startled at the thought, seeing that we are expressly warned, "[a] Quench not the Spirit." It is then in our power to quench It, if we will be so perverse. Or, what is yet more common, this heavenly spark may be neglected, and go out as it were of itself: which is the case when people allow themselves to lead a quiet and easy, and, it may be, a de-

[a] 1 Thess. v. 19.

cent life, without any special thought of God and their souls; or to be swallowed up inwardly in the world's business, or in some overwhelming passion, even while outwardly they do not leave off religious exercises. In either of these cases, I say, the heavenly spark will die down, its light and heat and life will quite pass away, and the soul will be left altogether cold, dead and earthly, like the souls of the heathen, or worse. Is not this a fearful thought? Do you not shrink from it with all your heart? I trust you do: I trust that none of you, who have so lately tasted of the heavenly gift, being made partakers of the Holy Ghost, can think without horror of quenching that gift by wilful and known indulgence in grievous sin: by lying, stealing, profaneness, impurity, malice. I trust you are also aware and deeply afraid of that other more subtle snare of the devil, whereby he would tempt you to let the spark go out. I hope you think very much of the danger of spiritual sloth, of lukewarmness, of giving yourselves up to pastime, of taking things easily. To you and to all who have been confirmed, the Church and the Bible say plainly, 'This fire has been kindled within you: if you quench it, or let it go out, you are lost.' The warning is brought home to us all at such times as these: to the newly confirmed, by the Confirmation itself: to all the rest of us, by our being witnesses of the same: for you may depend upon it, that as often as we are told of the Bishop coming for that purpose into our neighbourhood, or hear the Church bells giving notice of his presence, or see any young persons preparing for Confirmation, going to or returning from the service, or are put in mind of it in Church, so often our Lord and Saviour speaks to our souls, distinctly though inwardly. Though it may be scores of years since we ourselves were confirmed, yet He speaks to us as if it were yesterday: and what saith He? "I put thee in remembrance, that thou stir up the gift of God, which is in thee by the laying on of those hands which are as Mine own Hands." Stir it up: revive it if ready to die: feed, cherish, rekindle it into a blaze: for if, when you die, it be gone out, there will be no reviving of it again.

'But what must we do to stir up the heavenly spark?' Why, what is it men and women do, when they come in and find the fire nearly gone out, and would fain light it up again? First, they gently rake out what is dead and useless, and so make a way for the draught of air to blow upon what sparks remain, and fan them up into a glow: so must we do, morning by morning, and evening by evening, if we would keep up the heavenly fire upon the altar of our souls: we must rake out the dead ashes; i. e. we must examine ourselves, and by humble confession and good purposes clear away the noisome and encumbering dust, the worldly and sensual thoughts and ways, which we have allowed to defile our conscience. And then the pure air, i. e. the Holy Spirit, will be free to blow upon us, and encourage and revive His own good and gracious gift, the spark which He kindled in us so long ago.

But you know that when a fire is nearly gone out, it is not enough to let the air breathe upon it: we must blow with the bellows, and fan the spark into a flame: so it is by no means enough to examine ourselves and confess our faults; we must use earnest and constant prayer, inviting the good Spirit to help us. We must feed and nourish the fire with new fuel; else it will go out of itself: so must all Christian people feed and nourish their Baptismal life with the Holy Communion of our Lord's Body and Blood. If you thus cherish the heavenly spark, the confirming Spirit freely given you of God, it will by degrees warm and kindle you into all kinds of good and holy works: as a fire when well lighted and carefully tended lays hold of dry and prepared fuel, and changes it all into its own nature, all is pure light, and warm and comfortable glow. "[b] For the path of the just is as a shining light, which shineth more and more unto the perfect day." And more than this: it is the quality of fire to spread: one torch kindles another, and that another, and so on continually: and thus it may come to pass, that that one silent invisible spark of God's grace, which He mercifully kindled in any of you at the moment of your Confirmation, may break out into an unknown number of holy fires, which shall brighten for ever and ever. O rich reward of a dutiful and loving heart! to be acknowledged at the Great Day by the Saviour of all with some such word as this, 'The lamp which I lit for thee, thou didst not wickedly quench it, nor yet unthankfully and carelessly permit it to go out: rather thou didst so feed and cherish it, that others without thy knowing it have drawn light from thee. Well done, good and faithful servant: well done, wise virgin: enter thou into the joy of thy Lord.'

[b] Prov. iv. 18.

Who could have dared hope that such words might ever be spoken to him, were it not that our Lord Himself, He Who will come to be our Judge, has invited us to have such hope: and has told us moreover, that either those words, or others as fearful as they are gracious, must be one day spoken to every one of us. We cannot help ourselves: we must hear one or the other. He most earnestly desires to speak to us the good and merciful words: and for a sure token of that His mercy, He hath laid His Hands on you, by His servant the Bishop, and hath given you His Holy Spirit. You are now under the shadow of His wing: why should you ever wander from it? Why should you not even now make up your mind to some such rules as these, —plain and simple rules enough, yet sufficient, if sincerely kept, to bring you by God's help to the joyful sight of your Saviour.

First, remember this solemn time, remember your Confirmation day; let it never slip out of your memory. Remember it in your thanksgivings, for it is one of the greatest of God's mercies: remember it in your self-examinations, for it exceedingly aggravates the guilt of your sin and carelessness. Whatever good thoughts and purposes you had, when you were drawing near to the rails of God's holy Altar: whatever love and fear you had in your heart, when Christ by His servant laid His Hands upon you and blessed you: let it not all pass away as in a dream, but recall it from time to time: make much of it: examine yourself, whether or no you are still trying to become what you then wished to be.

Next, as the Church would have you lose no time

in coming to Holy Communion, so when you have been once there, she requires you presently to think of coming again. For it is our daily bread: we cannot go on long without it. If you will obey the Church, you will do well to lay down this law for yourself, that at each Communion, before the congregation departs, you will form a settled purpose in your heart, at what time you will by God's permission, present yourself again. And having so purposed, and prayed God to bless your purpose, you will not lose sight of it: day by day you will say to yourself, I am to communicate at such a time: it is drawing nearer: I must prepare myself for it. In this way, keeping as it were short accounts with our Great Master, and stirring up the grace which He hath given us, we may hope to be always going on: never stopping, much less turning back: until we come to that last and happiest Communion, which will be our seal and passport, not to another sacrament, but to the open and blissful sight of Jesus Christ. What joy will it be in that day to the faithful, to remember their Confirmation and first Communion! What misery to those who shall have suffered their lamps to go out!

SERMON XXXIII.

THE MYSTERIOUS WORKING OF GOD THE HOLY GHOST.

AFTER CONFIRMATION.

S. John iii. 8.

"*The wind bloweth where it listeth, and thou hearest the sound thereof, but canst not tell whence it cometh nor whither it goeth; so is every one that is born of the Spirit.*"

IN the Hebrew language, which our Saviour spoke, the same word signifies both spirit and wind: He therefore, having occasion to speak of the Spirit, naturally sets forth the power and working thereof by that which all men know concerning the wind, which being in some respects like the Spirit was called by the same name. The circumstances which led to His so explaining Himself were these. He had been doing many miracles in Jerusalem: much attention had been called to Him: many persons were thinking about Him. Many indeed had come in a way to believe on Him: not however with that kind of faith, that our Lord could accept them as friends, and trust Himself to them. They believed on Him, as sensible and thoughtful heathens, in India or any other country, hearing the Gospel preached for the first time, might say to one another, 'Really there is a great deal in this: we must enquire more about it;' and yet might be very far from understanding the full truth, and feeling it in their hearts.

Among those who believed with this imperfect faith was a rich man, a councillor, a ruler of the Jews, called Nicodemus. He came to our Lord by night: unwilling, as persons of that rank often are, to seem to declare himself either for Christ or against Him: yet earnestly desiring to know more of Him than he did. Yet one cannot think that Nicodemus had anything like a proper notion of what our Lord came to do, or of His real nature and being, as both God and Man. Only by the miracle he was convinced that Jesus was a Teacher come from God: and so much he avows to Jesus: and in saying it, perhaps he thought he was saying a great deal, judging very favourably of our Lord and His doctrine: after the manner of the world, which will go a great way with you in praise of Christianity and the Gospel, as long as you keep yourself from *strictness*, and from requiring *any kind of self-denial*. Our Lord will not let him rest in so light and superficial a notion of His Church and Gospel. He explains to him, that without an entire change, so great a change that it may well be called a new birth: so entire that this our natural birth is but a figure and shadow of it: I say, without such a change as this, no man can even *see* the kingdom of God, much less can he enter into it. Without a new birth, one cannot understand, one can have no real idea of, the wonders of God in the salvation of souls by the setting up of His kingdom. A heathen, an unbaptized person, may see enough, and more than enough, to draw him towards the Church and the true faith; but he cannot possibly understand it as a Christian may. This, no doubt, was at least part of our Lord's meaning, when He said, a man must be born again, before he could even see His kingdom.

Nicodemus, you know, could not understand it. He made what sounds like a perverse sort of answer, "How can a man be born when he is old? can he enter the second time into his mother's womb, and be born?" The words sound very much as if he was determined to argue with our Saviour, and said the first thing that came into his head. And our Saviour replies to him much as He did afterwards to the obstinate Jews who disputed with Him at Capernaum. He seems as if He were at no pains to satisfy Nicodemus at the time, but were rather taking the opportunity to say something which should be of greatest use to true believers in all times. "Verily, Verily I say unto thee, Except a man be born again, he cannot see the kingdom of God." As much as to say, There must be a new birth: the man must be made new, and all things about him must become as it were a new creation: and this birth must be by Baptism: so our Lord teaches, as the whole Church has always believed: and because He saw that Nicodemus could not at all understand Him, He went on and said further, that people must not expect to understand this new birth, the signs and effects of it, as they seem to themselves to understand about ordinary things: thus much however they might understand, that the offspring must be more or less of the same sort and nature, as the parent. "That which is born of the flesh is flesh, and that which is born of the Spirit is Spirit:" as therefore the natural man is of the same nature with Adam, so the spiritual man is of the same nature with Christ, and with the Spirit of Christ which has entered into him, to give him the benefit of this new birth. But the natural man cannot understand the things of the Spirit of God. That which the Spirit works, can only be understood by the instruction of the Spirit, by the power which He gives to the inward sense to discern His own working. The natural man therefore, the unbaptized, unconverted world, cannot understand the thoughts and doings, the purposes and ways, the whole condition, of the Christian as he is a Christian. This our Lord sets before us by the image of the wind. It blows, He saith, where it listeth; it is free and unfettered in its motion; no chains nor bars that we can contrive may restrain it: and in this respect it is like the Mighty Spirit Whose Name it bears; the wind freely blowing where it will is like the Holy Ghost dividing to every man severally as He will. We know that when He descended upon the Apostles it pleased Him to do so not without the sound of a rushing mighty wind, which filled all the house and was the token of His saving entrance into each one of them: just as the wind which is the type of Him, when it comes vehemently blowing upon a deep thick wood, fills the whole of it, rushes in wherever it can find an entrance, moves every bough of every tree, and yet does not move any two exactly alike. We see its effects, we hear the sound of it, we know how near, how real, how powerful it is: but as it is altogether out of sight, so we cannot at all measure or discern the manner of its approach and departure: "thou hearest the sound thereof, but canst not tell whence it cometh and whither it goeth." So is the Holy Spirit, in His mighty working for us men and for our salvation, and so, says our Lord, "is every one who is born of the Spirit."

There must be some great and merciful reason, we may be sure, why our Master and only Saviour should have taught us such a lesson so very earnestly in this, His earliest discourse as far as we know, on Sacramental grace: and part of the reason probably is this: that as our Lord had before Him at that moment in the person of Nicodemus an example of the ignorance even of wise men, when without the guidance of the Spirit they try to judge of spiritual things, so He knew that even those who from time to time should receive the Spirit, and be true Christians, truly united to Him, would yet be unable to discern and understand the ways and doings of that blessed Comforter, either in themselves or in others; and would at times be perplexed and unsettled thereby. Therefore He gives us all notice beforehand, that the Holy Ghost works in a mysterious way: as we see Him not, so neither can we discern the measure and manner of what He does: we recognize His Presence by the sound of His Gospel and the Word of His Sacraments which are gone out into all lands; but we cannot tell whence He cometh nor whither He goeth. We know that He comes in the Sacraments, but why He comes to one and not to another: who will profit by Him, and who will receive Him in vain: all this no man can tell: nor yet the manner of His operations, how He works upon our souls in His several ordinances, what means He may even now be using to bring us to any particular grace, or to what especial step in faith or holiness He may be secretly urging us on: of these things we are quite ignorant. We may ask, and dream, and guess, but we can no more tell one another for certain, than we can say exactly at what particular point the wind which is even now blowing began, and where it will leave off.

To take that instance which of course must be freshest in all our minds—That Holy and most gracious Spirit, which "bloweth where it listeth," because It is God, God the Holy Ghost, the Third Person in the Blessed Trinity, was pleased to blow or breathe upon us, in His great mercy, on Wednesday last, in the holy Sacramental ordinance of Confirmation. We heard the sound thereof, but we knew not whence He came, nor whither He went. We heard the sound: i. e. we were not ignorant of the assurance given in the holy Gospel, that the Apostles and their successors, being sent as Christ was sent by the Father, have power to give the Holy Ghost by imposition of hands. That we knew well: the sound of the Bishop's voice, when he spread his hands over our young people and blessed them, was the rushing mighty wind which certified the Church of the Presence of the Comforter. We heard the sound, but we knew not whence He came nor whither He went: how the several persons, who, kneeling in order had the blessing, were prepared in heart and conscience to receive it: from which of them He went away grieved (God forbid it should be so with any) and who obtained the fulness of His blessing: nor among those who worthily received Him do we know the difference between one and another: from what beginnings He set out in His work of confirming each, and to what height of grace He raised and is raising them: that it was a great day's work, we humbly believe and know; but of the beginning, the ending, the degrees of it, we are quite ignorant. We know not those things concerning others, nor yet do we know them perfectly concerning ourselves. I do not of course mean that each one of those who was confirmed on Wednesday may not in his heart and conscience form some probable judgement whether or no he received Confirmation worthily. No one can well help knowing, to-day, whether or no he was on the whole seriously inclined on Wednesday last: whether he said the weighty words, "I do," with full purpose of heart or no; whether his eyes and thoughts were suffered to go astray, or whether he kept himself in order, and minded the aweful work which was going on. He must know how he himself behaved, or tried to behave: but how the Spirit of the Lord dealt with him he cannot certainly know, except that he may be sure He dealt most righteously, most graciously. I desire to make this very clear to you, on account of two sorts of persons especially: for as we are all too apt to walk by sight, not by faith, and like the Jews of old, to demand a sign, to make us comfortable, and save us trouble, as concerning the things of God: so it is in regard of this holy ordinance of Confirmation, and still more, perhaps, in regard of that other and yet more holy and aweful Sacrament of the Lord's Body and Blood, which comes after Confirmation: we are apt to depend rather in a wrong way on our feelings at the time, instead of going altogether by such sober self-examination as the Church, taught by S. Paul, enjoins. As I said before, there are two sorts of persons, likely to be the worse for this, to whom I would wish to speak particularly.

First, I should not wonder if there were some who having endeavoured, according to human infirmity, to come worthily to Confirmation and Holy Communion, have been greatly disappointed both during the service and afterwards at finding their thoughts inclined to wander, and their hearts, as it seems to them, dull and dry and hard as ever. They do not appear to themselves to have entered at all really into the holy service: [a] they had neither tears of sorrow for the confession of their sins, nor of thankfulness for Christ's comfortable words and assurances of mercy, nor of joy and heavenly transport at finding themselves united to the choirs of Angels, praising with them the most Holy Trinity: neither have they at all felt as they expected to feel at the very near and most aweful Presence of our Lord's Body and Blood, and in the act of receiving Him into their souls and bodies: it has all seemed to them more or less of a dream, they were quite unable to deal with it as with something quite true and real: and it may be, they are now in trouble about it, and are saying in their hearts, What if should I have received unworthily? and are half ready to wish they had not ven-

[a] [Something here of Confirmation]—probably extempore, Ed.

tured. On the other hand, there may be some who seemed to themselves at the time quite different from all this: their hearts seemed full, the service was very moving to them, perhaps they were ready with their tears: and so now on looking back they conclude that God was with them of a truth as He is with the children in whom He delighteth, and they say to themselves undoubtedly, "all is right." Now it is plain enough that neither of these feel exactly as one could wish, but of the two, I should suppose the first feeling would be safer for most of us than the second, because it tends more to humility. However, without making comparisons, I should say to each of these two sorts, that they would do well to keep in mind what our Lord tells us of the Holy Spirit hiding Himself, how that we cannot tell whence He cometh and whither He goeth: we are not judges of the good He is doing us, by any feelings of our own at the time, *unless those feelings bring forth afterwards* the fruit of good and holy works. Therefore to those who are disturbing themselves because the holy service did not seem to touch them as it ought when they were present, I say, Be not too much cast down: go your ways and serve God faithfully in your proper calling whatever it be: and pray to Him to give you a tender conscience, and keep your thoughts and all your senses from going after sin, little and great, and He will give you a tender heart, and overflowing eyes, when it pleases Him: only serve Him not the less faithfully because it seems dull and dry at the time, and trust Him for a blessing. On the other hand, to those who are lifted up by the consciousness of seeming holy tears, and of something like a touch of heaven, I say, For God's sake, "be not highminded, but fear." If you trust to these good and tender feelings, the Evil one will know too well how to deceive you by them. Remember how he persuaded the Jews to go on seeking for a sign from heaven, while they neglected their plain duties on earth, judgement, mercy, faith, the love of God and their neighbour. No, my brethren, the only way is to trust God in His Sacraments, and not our own feelings: and never to flatter ourselves that when we do wrong, it is owing to His refusing us grace, or that it is any one's fault but our own.

SERMON XXXIV.

THE HIDDEN PRESENCE OF CHRIST OUR LORD.

AFTER A CONFIRMATION.

S. John viii. 59.

"Jesus hid Himself."

"ᵃ Verily Thou art a God that hidest Thyself, O God of Israel, the Saviour," so spoke the prophet Isaiah seven hundred years before our Lord appeared. It was ever a mark of the only true God, as distinguished from the idols of the Gentiles, that He hid Himself. They, as their worshippers fondly believed, really appeared from time to time and shewed themselves to men as they are, so that images carved or molten could be made of iron, brass, wood or stone, which should be really like them, and through which, as ways of worthily knowing them, they delighted to be worshipped. But the God of Israel, our God, He is not like any of these: nor like the sun nor moon nor any of His own creatures, nor like all of them put together. He, the Lord, the Holy One of Israel, beside Whom there is no other, He from the beginning has been a God that hideth Himself:

ᵃ Isa. xlv. 15.

"ᵇ dwelling in the light which no man can approach unto;" a God " Whom no man hath seen, nor can see." So that even to His own ancient people it was said, by our Lord, "ᶜ Ye have neither heard His voice at any time nor seen His shape." Yea, and to His new Israel, after He had revealed and declared Himself by Jesus Christ " the Only-begotten Son Who is in the Bosom of the Father," even to them it had to be repeated, "ᵈ No man hath seen God at any time."

And yet all the while He was close at hand: near us, around us, within us. "ᵉ He was in the world" which was " made by Him;" He was, He is, always in it, else it could not continue in being, for He is Preserver as well as Creator of all things. He was and is in the world, and will be so long as the world standeth, even although the world knoweth Him not: though none of His creatures were aware of His Presence, it is not the less true that He is present, and that from Him only we "ᶠhave our being." Holy Job was most deeply impressed with this. As far as we are told, Job knew not the law of Moses, was not at all aware what great things God had done for His people. To such as Job especially God was as though He hid Himself: but who ever had a deeper sense of His awful Presence than Job had? Hear how he owns God, and at the same time his own ignorance of God. "ᵍ Lo, He goeth by me, and I see Him not." You might fancy him one of the two on the road to Emmaus, when our Lord " made as though He would have gone fur-

---

ᵇ 1 Tim. vi. 16.   ᶜ S. John v. 37.   ᵈ Ib. i. 18.
ᵉ ib. 10.   ᶠ Acts xvii. 28.   ᵍ Job ix. 11.

ther," and they by the wonderful breaking of of bread began to discern Who He was. And in another place, more at large, the holy man in his *very* low estate wishes that he could find the Lord, but owns himself unable: "[h] Oh that I knew where I might find Him! that I might come even to His seat!" but as it is, "Behold, I go forward, but He is not there; and backward, but I cannot perceive Him: on the left hand, where He doth work, but I cannot behold Him: He hideth Himself on the right hand, that I cannot see Him." Job looked every way, and could not see God, could not find Him; could not by any sense, any understanding of his own, make himself certain of God's Presence. What then? did it make him an unbeliever? did he at all begin to doubt whether the great God was with him? No: quite the contrary: he is troubled the more at God's Presence, by how much the more he finds it more awful and unsearchable by man. "[i] Therefore am I troubled at His Presence: when I consider, I am afraid of Him."

So it was always, the God of Abraham, Isaac and Jacob, the God of Israel was always a God to hide Himself, and so from time to time He caused it to be, even when He was here in the Flesh. He made Himself, as it seems, invisible; He disappeared now and then, and as suddenly re-appeared: that those among whom He came in and went out might know for a certainty that He is the Most High God, still near us, still among us, quite as much so now, to us who see Him not, as He was to those who looked upon His Blessed Face, and might feel the touch of

[h] Job xxiii. 3—8. [i] v. 15.

His life-giving Hands. His messenger had told us so from the beginning: "[k] I indeed baptize you with water: but there standeth One among you, Whom ye know not." As if he should say, 'Here you are, so many of you, but whatever your number there is One more than appears, one more than you can count: if two are in a room together, He is there as a third: and if a thousand, He is there too, and His Presence is infinitely more than that of all the rest.'

This great truth, which S. John preached in words at the beginning of our Lord's ministry, He Himself made good in deeds, and drew people's attention to it, by the manner in which, when He thought fit, He vanished out of their sight, and shewed Himself again, sometimes quite suddenly and when He was least expected. Thus it was at Nazareth in the very beginning of His ministry, when His unbelieving countrymen were filled with wrath and were going to cast Him down headlong, "[l] He passing through the midst of them went His way:" i. e. (seemingly) He made Himself invisible, and when they looked angrily round for Him, their eyes perhaps being directed towards the very spot which He was passing along at the moment, they saw nothing but empty air. Again, when He had healed the impotent man at the pool of Bethesda, and the Pharisees were wanting to seize Him and persecute Him to death on pretence of His breaking the sabbath; then again we read, "[m] Jesus had conveyed Himself away," glided secretly away and disappeared, even though there was a multitude in the place. This is in S. John's Gospel, and it contains three other in-

[k] S. John i. 26.   [l] S. Luke iv. 30.   [m] S. John v. 13.

stances of the same kind—the most remarkable, perhaps, that in the Gospel for this week. Our Lord was in the temple whither the Jews always resorted: there He was publicly teaching, at the time of the feast of tabernacles, when they came into Jerusalem from all the world; and He said words in His teaching whereby He declared Himself to be the most High God: they in their blind madness took up stones to stone Him: "but Jesus hid Himself and went out of the temple, going through the midst of them, and so passed by." You see, brethren, how it was: He wrought then and there a great miracle in direct proof that He is indeed Eternal and Equal with the Father, as He had just affirmed Himself to be. Those who saw Him so vanish out of their sight, when next He vouchsafed to shew Himself to them, how could they choose but cry out with S. Thomas, "My Lord and my God?" And if we believe what they saw, as surely we must, or we are no Christians, how can we help feeling in the bottom of our hearts, that wherever we are, there He is; when men are most unmindful of Him, perhaps taking part with His enemies and doing their worst against Him, there He is in the midst of them: and what if He should be passing through them, on His way to leave them for ever?

The same thing occurred again, if I mistake not, a few months afterwards, at the feast of the Dedication, when they wanted to stone Him again for saying, "[n] I and My Father are One." "They sought again to take Him: but He escaped out of their hand." And lastly, within the last, the holy week

[n] S. John x. 30.

of His Death and Passion a wonderful witness having been borne to Him from heaven, the Voice of the Father answering the Son's call, and promising, "º I have both glorified it, and will glorify it again:" then when they had as usual their perverse words to say, our Lord having warned them how short their time was ᵖ, "departed;" glided gently away; "and did hide Himself from them;" it is the very same word, "hid Himself," which we heard in the Gospel just now.

After His Resurrection as you well know, I hope, most of you, our Lord's appearances were all of this occasional kind: like the coming and going of an Angel or of the spirit of some just and good man. Where they least looked for Him, there He was. Mary Magdalene turns herself suddenly, to see who is coming near to her, and behold it is the Saviour Whom she had been so much longing to set eyes on. The two disciples as they walk, are discoursing lovingly of Jesus, and behold Jesus Himself, a third in their conversation: and when they are dealing kindly with Him as a stranger He proves to be their best and only Friend. The fishermen on the sea of Galilee look wearily towards the shore in the morning light, and see Jesus standing, and know not that it is Jesus, until He has a second time wrought a wonder of His mercy for them. Were these three exceptions to the general rule, so as to be nothing to us? or are we rather to understand that they are just samples and specimens of our Lord's dealing, our Lord's love, towards His faithful servants, all of them.

But how, if men's talk and behaviour in regard

º S. John xii. 28.   ᵖ Ib. 36.

of Christ be altogether of an opposite sort? How if S. Mary Magdalene had been seeking opportunity to destroy Him, or the two disciples laying their heads together "ᵠ to catch Him," as the Pharisees and Herodians wanted, "in His words?" Would Jesus have *then* been present in their hearts? Might persons have been quite sure *then* that that Lord against Whom they were talking, Whose will they were contriving to make void, was just at hand, listening to every evil word and plan? Yes, they might be all quite sure of it: our Lord was as truly one of the company when Caiaphas and Judas were bargaining about His price, as when the disciples were discoursing at Emmaus; only He hides from those wretched ones, so putting them more entirely on their trial.

Now, brethren this is an awful thought. For if it was so then, surely it is so always. If Christ was present and watching the wicked Pharisees quite as exactly when He had vanished from their sight, as while they were still able to set eyes upon Him, depend upon it, He is equally present with the sinners of this time also; with us who never set eyes on Him at all. He hides Himself from us, but we cannot hide ourselves from Him. How do you like this thought, you who have gone on sinning and tempting others to sin, as you thought in secret? Is it pleasant to you, when you look back, to reflect that at such and such a time you committed an act of disobedience or spitefulness, or uncleanness, or theft, or profaneness, and that all the while Jesus Christ was standing by and looking on? If you had

ᵠ S. Mark xii. 13.

found at the time that somebody was watching you, you would not have put forth your hand to steal: if a little child had come into the room, it would have stopped you in your uncleanness: if any person likely to tell of you had been there, you would not have openly disobeyed your parent or your master, or any one on whom you depended for the good things of this world. But because it was only Jesus Christ Who was watching you, only He Who made and redeemed you and will soon come to be your Judge, therefore you went on sinning, and your conscience did not smite you: but What do you think of it now? What will you think of it when you come to die? What, when you look back upon it from the place where God keeps the souls of the dead? What, when you rise from your grave to give account of it?

The hidden Presence of our Lord is surely then a most aweful thing to think of: and for this very reason it is a most necessary thought for most of us. Aweful, alarming thoughts, are just what the greater part of Christians have need of: for we are sad triflers, nine out of ten of the best of us; mere children in respect of our duties to the Almighty. "ʳThe fear of the Lord," which "is the beginning of wisdom," *that* is what we need to be taught. Use yourselves then, I beseech you, brethren, to think steadily at all times of Jesus Christ looking on you, for that is the only way to have the true Christian fear of God.

Now for example, in this time of Lent, you know that for these five weeks past the Church has been

---

ʳ Prov. ix. 10.

putting you in mind of the ways in which Lent might do you good if you were willing, how our Lord would have you deny yourselves, and pray, and read and hear His Word, and prepare yourselves, for the Blessed Communion. Now then bethink you. He was close to you all the time: you did not hear His Voice, yet the words came from Him: you did not see His Shape, yet He met you in this place, if you came here, and if you staid away, He accompanied you wherever you were for evil or for good. How does it seem now, looking back?

And He was also in an especial way present with those among you, whom by His providence He had called at this holy time to prepare for Confirmation. His servant the Bishop invited you to it: other servants, His priests, ministered to Him in preparing you for it: and the Bishop again, as you know, blessed you and prayed over you, in His Name, having first, also in His Name, received from you the promise to be good and true to Him. I say, it was Christ all the time, although He was hiding Himself, for He is pledged to be with us "[a]alway, even unto the end of the world." Christ it was, Who received you from time to time to instruct you privately in the Catechism: Christ, Who accompanied you to the place of Confirmation; Christ, Who asked you the question, and listened to you saying, "I do," or noticed you, if any pretended to say it and did not; Christ, Who laid His hands upon you, for an unspeakable blessing if you were in earnest, for a very sore judgement if you were not.

[a] S. Matt. xxviii. 20.

SERMON XXXV.

ON THE LITANY. I.

INTRODUCTORY, AND ON THE INVOCATION OF THE HOLY TRINITY.

JOEL ii. 17.

" Let the priests, the ministers of the Lord, weep between the porch and the Altar, and let them say, Spare Thy people, O Lord."

I HAVE thought it might be good for us, my brethren, during this Epiphany season, to go over the Prayer book, by catechizing the children in it as we did with the Baptism service last year. And I have chosen the Litany; a portion of the service which I am sure must be very dear to us all, if we really are used to attend to the solemn service of God: and concerning which it was said by one of the best and wisest of our forefathers, that it is "a work, the absolute perfection whereof upbraideth with error or something worse those whom in all parts it doth not satisfy."

How the Litany differs from the ordinary sort of prayers, is easy enough for us to understand. It is a *general* supplication: i. e. a form of prayer in which all the people join, not by saying it all after the minister, as we do the Lord's prayer, and certain confessions of sin: nor yet by only saying Amen at the end of each short wish; as we do in most of the collects: but by a short verse, repeated at certain intervals, and breaking into a number of short portions what would otherwise be a very long prayer to be said all at once. The rule and beginning of such a service may be found in the Old Testament, especially in that very aweful and serious chapter of the prophet Joel, from which the text is taken. The prophet is speaking of a host of terrible enemies, who might soon be looked for to overspread and ruin the land: which prophecy seems to have been fulfilled partly in a frightful swarm of locusts, who should come upon the sinful land, partly in an invasion from some unpitying enemy; such as the Assyrian at that time, the Roman long after, and it may be, in the Last Day, some other power worse and more wicked than both these. At such a time the Spirit of God directed the old Church of the Jews to seek mercy and help of God by special and very solemn services in which the whole people should join. First, the people were to repent, each one inwardly in his heart, each family in its quiet home. "Therefore also now, saith the Lord, turn ye even to Me with all your heart, and with fasting, and with weeping, and with mourning: and rend your heart and not your garments, and turn unto the Lord your God." That was to be each man's preparation of heart in those evil times: unfeigned sorrow for his sin, self-denial, and punishing the flesh, and true conversion to God, as to an offended but loving Father. But not only was each one so to be prepared inwardly in his heart, and in his devotions privately and at home, but publickly also the whole Church was to join in solemn acknowledgment of sin, and in beseeching God to turn away His judgements from the land. "Blow the trumpet, he says, in Zion, sanctify a fast, call a solemn assembly; gather the people, sanctify the congregation, assemble the elders, gather the children and those that suck the breasts: let the bridegroom go forth of his chamber, and the bride out of her closet." You see, even those who might be best excused from attending public services, little children, and those who waited on them, and also new married people, were expected to attend the particular service of which the prophet was speaking. And what was that service? It was a Litany. The priests, the Lord's ministers, were to take their places in the temple, between the porch and the Altar, i. e. in some such place as the entrance of our chancel, where, as you know, we kneel to say the Litany. There the priests were to kneel and weep, i. e. they were both outwardly in voice and behaviour, and inwardly in heart and soul, to shew how grieved they were, and how deeply they felt God's anger and their own sinfulness. And what was their prayer to be? God Himself put a word in their mouth, in that He taught them to say, "Spare Thy people, O Lord, and give not Thine heritage to reproach, that the heathen should rule over them: wherefore should they say among the people, Where is their God?" This was the service prescribed by the Almighty to His ancient people in time of trouble: and see what encouragement He gave them to perform it religiously. "Then" (so He expresssly promises), "Then will the Lord be jealous for His land, and pity His people." He will, as in former times, interfere to prevent their being ill-used (for that is what it means when He says He will be jealous for them): and for all their sins, He will pity them in their sad distresses. So great was the benefit to be hoped for of old from such a service as our Litany, provided only it were earnestly attended by the people in general with a true penitent heart.

And is the Lord's hand waxed short? May we not hope for the same blessing now? We Christians as well as those, Jews—the members of Christ, as well as the children of Israel? Surely we may: the Christian Litany will not be less favoured than the Jewish. I say, the Christian Litany: for this is one of those Services which the Church of Christ from very early times has taken to be its own, out of the Old Testament. For thus it was, brethren. More than thirteen hundred years ago, when the old Roman Empire was in a most miserable condition, the wild savages attacking it on every side, and God's dreadful judgements coming upon it in sword, in famine and in pestilence: it came into the mind of a holy Bishop to gather the people of his flock together, and make a solemn procession with prayers after the manner of our Litany, and according to there commendation of the prophet Joel. The people readily came into it, and the custom spread from one place to another: and though at first it belonged especially to the three days which come next before Ascension Day (which we therefore call Rogation days, or days of special prayer), it was by no means confined to those days, but was generally practised in times of trouble, to the great comfort of God's people, and often with a manifest blessing from Him. This then being a very ancient and godly custom of the Church, when our English Prayer book was put in order about three hundred years ago, order was taken that it should be kept up among us, by the saying of the Litany in the Church three times a week, i. e. on Sundays, Wednesdays and Fridays, and at such other times as the Bishop shall direct. And this, for the obtaining pardon of our manifold sins, and turning away God's heavy judgements, too likely to fall upon us. And Wednesday and Friday were fixed upon, I suppose, because from the beginning they have been the penitential days of the Church: Wednesday, as being that day of the week in which Judas made his bargain to betray our Saviour; Friday, as being the day of our Saviour's death. And Sunday was added afterwards, as we may suppose, because it is the day when most people come to Church: and seeing that the Church is altogether in a fallen state, compared with its first days, it seems well that even her Sundays, her glad and good times, should be marked with this exercise of penitence: even as she begins her daily services with the most humble confession of sins. But indeed since the world at all times is full enough of sin and misery; God dishonoured everywhere, and man afflicted; there is always reason enough for saying of Litanies. However, it has seemed to me especially seasonable just now. For we seem to be, in some sort, in the midst or on the edge of many troubles, both spiritual and temporal. It is a season, not so much of sharp sickness, and such as is known to be dangerous, but of lowness, and weakness, and helplessness: as if many persons, though not quite ill, were on the verge of being so. And in fact, on counting our burials of the past year, I find more of us have passed out of this world than in any one year, the accounts of which I have had occasion to examine. We may therefore, in a manner, apply to ourselves S. Paul's saying to his Corinthian children: "ᵃ Many are weak and sickly among us, and many sleep." Death, my brethren, is and has been knocking at our doors: very gently and mercifully it is true, yet very distinctly. And then we hear of a good deal of distress among many of our brethren: and I doubt not we hear truly. The poverty and misery may not, by God's mercy, be so great here as in many other places. But who can doubt that there is in the land poverty and misery enough to make it the duty of all charitable people to pray for their brethren who are so tried? Even for our temporal and worldly condition, therefore, there seems great reason why we should be quite in earnest in saying our Litanies at this time. But for the spiritual condition of our English Church, believe me, my brethren, when I tell you that it is indeed very distressing. We are hard beset on both sides: and why? Because people have not the faith which they ought to have in the blessed Sacraments of Christ, whereby He both received us at first, and hath fed us all our lives long unto this day. Some persons do not like to believe that holy Baptism saves us at all, although the Prayer-book teaches it so plainly: and these unhappily have so great power at present, that there is

ᵃ 1 Cor. xi. 30.

great danger of their altering the words of the Prayer-book, as they have already perverted its doctrine. These, it is plain, have no faith in the Sacraments of Christ. Others are so disgusted at seeing such liberties taken with such very holy things that they begin to think the Body which allows them can be no part of the true Church of Christ, and so they wander away to the Roman Catholics; not considering, that in so doing they are giving up all faith in the holy Sacraments which have been their soul's health hitherto. These two sorts, unlike as they appear to each other, agree in this, that neither of them has faith in what Christ has done for them: and between these two, as I said, our mother the Church is even now hard beset; and if her hope and strength were of this world only, I cannot say how it would be with her. But, my brethren, "[b] God is our Hope and Strength." Only we must call upon God, for He loves to be called upon: His Title is, "[c] Thou that hearest the prayer." This is why we have endeavoured of late to have more Litanies in the parish: to give those who fear God and believe His Sacraments and love His Church a chance of calling upon Him in the early morning, while they are on their way to their day's work. We have said to ourselves, 'What if God in answer even to such weak prayers should begin to be gracious to His land, and to pity His people? and to restore to us the blessings which our own sins, and Evil powers, seem to be depriving us of?' And so, for several months past, twice a week, in the early morning, sometimes in light, and sometimes in dark-

[b] Ps. xlvii. 1.   [c] Ps. lxv. 2.

ness, the sound has gone up here, "Spare us, good Lord; spare Thy people, whom Thou hast redeemed with Thy most precious Blood: and be not angry with us." The words have gone up, and even if it were, as far as man could see, from a very few, yet may we hope that it has not been all in vain. We may hope that some have thought of that early Litany, and may have been the better for it, though other duties prevented their coming near it. They may have profited in ways that we know not of. The very sound of the bells may have done them good, as they were preparing for their day's work, or resting on their bed of infirmity. And our Lord's promise does not require a large congregation. It is given to two or three, gathered together in His Name. The Angels, we trust, keep watch in this house: and "[d]there is joy in the presence of the Angels of God over one sinner that repenteth." Therefore, if it please God, we hope to go on with that early Litany, at least during the present distress of the Church: and *that*, in all probability, will last more years than we shall in this world. And may God increase the number of those who delight in such holy and regular services, whether they can attend them or no.

There is one reason why our Litany is particularly fit to begin the services of the day: which is, the way in which it begins: we begin it with commending ourselves to the most Holy Trinity in Whose Name we were sealed in Baptism. As we began our whole Christian life, so it is well to begin each separate day, under the shadow and protection of that saving

[d] S. Luke xv. 10.

Name: it comes into our Litany, as the Name Jehovah into the Litany of the Jews: "Spare Thy people, good LORD, spare them." But we first acknowledge and seal the Church's full doctrine, how that They are three real Persons, distinguished as in the Creed of S. Athanasius: The First, God the Father of heaven; The Second, God the Son, Redeemer of the world; The Third, God the Holy Ghost, proceeding from the Father and the Son: yet one only God, All-Holy, Blessed, and Glorious: and how that before each of the Three Persons, as also before the Holy Blessed and Glorious Trinity which is the Three taken together, we, one and all, are miserable sinners, and can only approach Him as such, humbly pleading for His mercy.

Such is the great Invocation, as you may call it, with which our Litany begins: even as it ends with a blessing in the Name of the same Divine Persons: " The grace of our Lord Jesus Christ, the love of God, and the fellowship of the Holy Ghost." For such as is the kingdom of God itself, such are all the services which we are permitted to do for Him in His kingdom: they all begin and end in the same Holy Name; the Name of the most Blessed and Glorious Trinity. Let us by His grace bear the remembrance of that Name always with us about the world. The Name itself we cannot but carry with us: it was stamped on us at our Baptism, never to be worn out: we may neglect, disgrace, insult it, but never can we be as the heathen who never had part in it. Miserable sinners indeed we are, and shall be to our lives' end: our birth from Adam makes that certain, to say nothing of our own backslidings: but that need not keep us from Him: only may we always take care to mean what we say when we call ourselves by that title: for many, I fear, are in the way of kneeling before God and saying the Litany regularly, who in the bottom of their hearts neither count themselves miserable nor sinners, but think they are as good as other people, and have a right to all the enjoyment they can get in this world. May God deliver us from so trifling with His blessed yet aweful invitation, since He invites us thrice a week to come to Him, miserable sinners as we are; to come to the Holy, Blessed and Glorious Three Persons and One God, and to call upon Him for mercy; let us at least come with serious, thoughtful hearts. To join in saying the Litany is a great gift, a great privilege, a noble chance of obtaining a blessing for ourselves and for the whole Church. To say it coldly, inattentively, disrespectfully, wilfully to slight it in any way, is behaving as if God were not God, as if we were not sinners. And how then can we be forgiven or blessed?

SERMON XXXVI.

ON THE LITANY. II.

ON THE SPECIAL INVOCATION OF OUR LORD IN THE "REMEMBER NOT &c.

JOEL ii. 17.

"Let the priests, the ministers of the Lord, weep between the porch and the Altar, and let them say, Spare Thy people, O Lord, and give not Thine heritage to reproach, that the heathen should rule over them."

HAVING, in the first Invocation, or beginning of the Litany, called upon the most Holy Trinity, Three Persons, and one God, and humbled ourselves in that aweful Presence as miserable sinners, we go on to pray against sundry evils, and to ask sundry blessings of God. But first of all we turn as it were to our blessed Redeemer Jesus Christ, and put our cause into His hands: we turn to Him as to God Incarnate, God made manifest in the flesh, because we know that He can be touched with a feeling of our infirmities. Apart from Him we should not have boldness to enter into that glorious Presence. It would be far stranger than for the meanest beggar to press forward with a petition to the proudest and greatest monarch. But as it is, we may and must come, for we are invited, nay commanded to come. "Come unto Me," says the Divine Intercessor, "all ye that labour and are heavy laden, and I will give you rest." "Him that cometh to Me, I will in no wise cast out." Therefore we are bold to come to Christ, to Him our only appointed Mediator, and by Him, miserable sinners as we are, to be spared, cleansed and forgiven.

And mark how we plead with Him. The prophet instructs the ancient people, when they were saying their Litany, to cry out unto Christ and say, "Spare Thy people, O Lord, spare them, and let not Thine heritage be brought to confusion." That was his plea, the plea of the good Israelite: the plea which Moses, a thousand years before, had alleged, when interceding with God to pardon them for making the golden calf. "[a] O Lord God," saith Moses, "destroy not Thy people, nor Thine inheritance, which Thou hast redeemed through Thy greatness, which Thou hast brought forth out of Egypt with a mighty hand: Remember Thy servants, Abraham Isaac and Jacob: look not unto the stubbornness of this people, nor to their iniquity, nor to their sin . . . Yet they are Thy people and Thine inheritance, which Thou broughtest out by Thy mighty power and by Thy stretched out Arm." You see, the prophets allege to God, not any good thing which His people had ever done, but His mercy shewed unto them. They put Him in mind how He brought them out of Egypt: how He had chosen them to be His own people. So we in our Litany,

[a] Deut. ix. 26—29.

approaching our Lord and Judge. We have no good thing of our own to plead, nothing but sins and offences, of our own and our forefathers, which we beseech Him not to remember. But what we *do* plead is, His past and present mercy shewn to us. "Spare us, good Lord, spare Thy people, whom Thou hast redeemed with Thy most precious Blood." 'Spare us, not because we are good, but because we are Thy people. We are Christians, Thine own people, Thine own heritage. This was Thy special, Thy distinguishing mercy to us, to choose us freely, before the world began, to be Christians, members of Christ. Forsake not then, we beseech Thee, the work of Thine own hands. As Thou hast begun to do us good, so go on with us even to the end.'

Again, we see how the prophets make mention of what God's enemies would say, if the Israelites, His people, were quite forsaken. "Wherefore should they say among the people, Where is their God?" And Moses' word is, "Spare them, lest the Egyptians say, The Lord was not able to bring them into the land which He promised them." So we Christians pray in the psalms, "[b] Lighten mine eyes that I sleep not in death, lest mine enemy say, I have prevailed against him, for if I be cast down, they that trouble me will rejoice at it." In all these prayers, you see, we plead with God by His own glory and honour, not by any good or merit of ours.

But more especially do we Christians plead with Him by what He did and suffered for us upon the Cross. "Spare Thy people whom Thou hast redeemed with Thy most precious Blood." As if we should

[b] Ps. xiii. 3.

say, 'Thou didst sacrifice Thyself entirely for us, Body and Soul. Thou pouredst out Thy Blood without stint or measure from Thy five healing Wounds. Thou didst grudge for our salvation no pain or grief, no agony or anguish of heart: Thou didst mysteriously become poor, emptying Thyself that we might be filled with Thee. And now, we beseech Thee, let it not be all in vain, miserably as we have behaved, shamefully as we have trifled with Thy loving salvation, do Thou yet find some way of making it effectual to us.' This is the Church's prayer to our Saviour when she is on her knees before Him in humble confession. And then she goes on, one by one, to mention those evils by name against which she most earnestly desires to pray; such as sin, the crafts and assaults of the devil, God's wrath, everlasting damnation, and the rest: teaching her children to make answer from time to time, "Good Lord, deliver us."

But before we go on to consider this, there are a few more observations to be made on this first invocation to our Lord. It begins, you know, with the word Remember: "Remember not Lord, our offences, nor the offences of our forefathers." This is not said as if God could ever forget: for we know that past, present and future are all alike to Him. But it is taken from a verse in the Psalms: "[c] Remember not our old sins, but have mercy upon us, and that soon, for we are come to great misery." So also the holy Nehemiah, "[d] Remember me, O my God, for good:" three times in one chapter. And in another Psalm, "[e] Remember me, O Lord, according to

[c] Ps. lxxix. 8.   [d] Neh. xiii. 14, 22. 31.   [e] Ps. cvi. 4.

the favour that Thou bearest unto Thy people." And Moses, "Remember Abraham, Isaac and Israel Thy servants." And "Lord, remember David and all his trouble." And in the history: "God remembered Rachel:" "God remembered Abraham:" "God remembered Noah:" and so in many other places. It is not, as I said, that the all-knowing God can ever possibly forget or be ignorant: but it is His gracious will that we should address Him in such words. Even as it is His will, that in the sacrifice of the Holy Communion we should offer to Him His own appointed Memorial of the One atoning Sacrifice, offered once for all on the Cross, and continually presented to Him by our great High Priest in heaven. The Holy Communion, as the Prayer-book teaches out of our Lord's own Mouth, is a perpetual memory of our Lord's precious Death: not only as putting us in mind of it, but also as putting God in mind of it: that is to say, pleading it before Him. By the Holy Communion, we say continually, not in words but in deeds, 'Remember not, Lord, our sins, nor the sins of our forefathers, but remember Thy well-beloved Son's offering of His Sacred Body and Blood, which in spirit and mystery we now present before Thee, as He commanded: and for His sake be merciful unto us.' In short our action in celebrating that Sacrament has the same kind of meaning, but greatly more virtue, than our words when we end prayers and collects by saying, "through the merits and mediation of Jesus Christ our Lord." And thus you may understand how it pleases Almighty God to be asked to remember us for good, and not to remember our sins, although in very deed He never can forget anything.

Next I may observe that the Church instructs us here to mention not our own sins only, but the sins of those also who have gone before us. "Remember not Lord our offences, nor the offences of our forefathers." Who are our forefathers, whose offences we here beseech God not to remember? In the first place, most likely, our first parents after the flesh, Adam and Eve; who by their great offence brought sin and death into the world. We all know that many, i. e. all of us, were made sinners by that one man and woman's disobedience: *that* sin is the root and ground of all that is unpleasant and bad to us. Divine providence remembers it against us continually: therefore we do well to pray to our Lord, thus earnestly, to deliver us from it.

In another way, no doubt, we suffer for the sins of our forefathers, inasmuch as by God's just judgement, the transgressions of the parents are many times visited on the children: as we learn in the second commandment, they who have made graven images to worship them must expect to be punished in their children. Therefore it is well for us to pray as we do in the Litany, that God would graciously spare us not only the punishment due to our own sins, but also whatever may in the course of His Providence be due to us in this world for the sins of those who have gone before us: and it is very well that we should all most earnestly seek to be delivered from the sin of Adam, the root and ground of all our misery.

From our own sins, then, and from the sins of our

progenitors, and from the destruction and vengeance due to them, we beseech our Lord as it were to turn away His eyes, not to think of the sin, nor to bring the vengeance on us. And we add, "Spare us, good Lord, spare Thy people, whom Thou hast redeemed with Thy most precious Blood: and be not angry with us for ever." What is "Spare us?" Deal gently with us: let us alone; let Thine hand lie lightly upon us; lay no more upon us than Thou wilt make us able to bear. We indeed deserve the worst: but we are so weak and sinful, our transgressions have brought us so very low, that we cannot but cast ourselves at Thy feet, beseeching Thee to have mercy upon us. For Thou art in a way the God of the weak and sinful: Thou invitest to Thee the weary and heavy laden: and who so wearied, so heavy laden as they?

And we trust that Thou wilt spare them, for Thou, O Lord, hast redeemed them. "Spare Thy people whom Thou hast redeemed with Thy most precious Blood." Thou hast given us Thy very lifeblood out of Thine heart, to wash away our sins, and to be the drink of our disordered souls: and wilt Thou not in due time freely give us all things? Surely Thou wilt deny us nothing, Who hast given us Thyself, to be our God, and all in all to us. Least of all wilt Thou deny us pardon and forgiveness of the sins we truly repent of, and grace to watch against them hereafter. "Spare Thy people and be not angry with us for ever." Observe those last words. "Be not angry with us for ever." It would seem as if the Church were instructing us to make up our minds to *some* anger, *some* punishment on God's part: only may it please Him not to continue it for ever. We do not ask to be free from suffering: but we do ask, please God, that our suffering may be temporal, not eternal: that it may come to an end when we are taken out of the flesh. We say, as it were, 'Do not, O Lord, as an enemy, take real vengeance of our sins: but if Thou must be angry for them (and truly they have deserved the worst of Thine anger) yet be not angry with us for ever. Strike us here, that Thou mayest spare and bless us hereafter.'

Thus we pray continually: but do we really mean what we pray? I fear not always: perhaps not even very often. For only just consider, my brethren: What is it that really takes up most of your pains, most of your attention? What sort of things are they which really interest you, which you think of day and night: "when thou sittest in thine house, and when thou walkest by the way, when thou liest down and when thou risest up?" Are they the things of this world or the things of the world to come: the business of the soul, or of the body? Surely if we will speak the truth, the more part of us must reply to such a question as this, that the body and its concerns, the world and its cares, do in effect take up the greater part of our minds and hearts: and while we pray for heavenly things, we are but too glad to get more and more of the things of the earth. But now, God looks upon our hearts; to our secret meaning, not to our outward prayer. He sees how it is with us: and if we do not strive to mend, He will take us, may be, at our thought rather than at our word: He will give us the good things of this life which we earnestly desire, and will deny us the good things of the next; which we do not earnestly desire. God forbid that it should be so with us! but that it may not be so, that we may not lose Eternity, by gaining some little matters in time, we had need look into our hearts, our prayers and our ways, more conscientiously than we have hitherto done. We have need to consider and lay things to heart, and not let them pass away altogether like a mere dream, as if nothing were to come of them.

'Be not angry with us for ever.' Think, dear brethren, of those words. To whom are they addressed? To our own, our only Saviour: to Him Who took on Him this poor mortal life of ours, and endured it so many years, that He might lay it down for us, dying in torments. He Who loved us so dearly; can there be reason to fear that He should not only be angry with us, but angry with us for ever? Yes, indeed: there is great reason to fear it. For He came to save us, not *in* our sins, but *from* our sins: and if we will keep them, or go back to them, we must give Him up, there is no help for it. And then that loving and merciful Countenance which looked down so gently upon us when by His minister He held us in His Arms at our Baptism, will be changed into blackness and darkness and tempest; in the day when it shall be clearly revealed. It will be the Day of His Wrath, the day of the wrath of the Lamb, *His* wrath, Whose love is our only hope: and there will be no change afterwards: such as He will look upon us then, such will He continue to look on us for ever. And the Day is near: the tokens of it, to the eye of faith, are not to be doubted. It may not come in your time, but surely it is near. O then, while He gives us leave, let us one and all make haste to the place of shelter. Let us by true repentance and confession, and loving obedience, hide ourselves under His shadow, yea even in His blessed Wounds: that in us may be fulfilled the gracious word, "ᶠHis wrath endureth but the twinkling of an eye, and in His pleasure is life; heaviness may endure for a night, but joy cometh in the morning."

ᶠ Ps. xxx. 5.

SERMON XXXVII.

ON THE LITANY. III.

THE DEPRECATION.

2 CHRON. vi. 28—30.

"*Whatsoever sore or whatsoever sickness there be: what prayer or what supplication soever shall be made of any man, or of all Thy people Israel, when every one shall know his own sore and his own grief, and shall spread forth his hands in this house; then hear Thou from heaven, Thy dwelling place, and forgive.*"

SEE, my brethren, what encouragement Holy Scripture here gives us, to come into God's holy house, and tell Him our wants and our griefs in such prayers as the Church's Litany. For here are the words of the wise king Solomon, put into his heart by the Holy Spirit, when he was dedicating the temple which he had builded, and asking God's blessing on the prayers which should be there offered. God's Holy Spirit put the words in Solomon's heart, therefore they are in fact the words of God teaching us how to pray to Him; and the prayers which He teaches us to ask, we are sure He will hear, if we do not by some wickedness make ourselves unfit to be heard. What is it then which He here instructs us of, as concerning our prayers to Him? It is just this, that when any trouble, public or private, secret or open, comes upon us, the way to relief is, to come and spread forth our hands in God's house: which is just what we do, when we join in the Litanies of the Church. As we read of the good king Hezekiah, that when he had received the threatening letter from Sennacherib king of Assyria, he went up into the house of the Lord, and spread it before the Lord: so our wisest way is whensoever any serious trouble or trial comes upon us, either upon our souls our bodies, or our estates, to lay it before the Lord in humble prayer, not each one by himself alone, but in union with the prayers of all God's household the Church: and this we surely do, when we join devoutly in the Litany: whether our trouble be to ourselves alone, or whether it be such as to concern the whole Church and congregation praying with us.

If you ask, in what *part* of the Litany do we more especially "spread the letter," the account of our afflictions, before the Lord, each one for himself, and for all, and all for each one: I should say it was in those short prayers, commonly called Suffrages, to which we are now come: wherein after our two invocations, one to the Holy and Glorious Trinity, the other to our Lord and Saviour especially, we mention before Almighty God the evils from which we pray Him to deliver us: as if little children should all together cry out to their loving Father, and beseech Him to take away whatever it was that hurt them: only that this our Father is so perfect in wisdom and love, as to know exactly what each one wants; which among all the sore evils here reckoned up and prayed against is most in the mind of each one, and which he is most in danger of. And so is fulfilled in each Christian congregation the gracious word which the Holy Ghost taught king Solomon nearly three thousand years ago: Whatsoever sore, whatsoever sickness there is among us: when each one, small and great, knowing each one the plague of his own heart, his own sore and his own grief, cometh here and lifteth up holy hands, in true penitence for all wilful sin: him the Lord heareth in heaven His dwelling-place, and forgiveth and rendereth unto every man according to all his ways: for He only "[a] knoweth the hearts of the children of men." And observe, my brethren, His gracious and loving condescension. He knows how much good it does us to have the prayers one of another, therefore He appoints that all should pray with all and for all; all alike are to answer and say with one voice, 'Good Lord, deliver us:' and at the same time, because He knows also that it is generally neither good nor pleasant for men to intermeddle with their neighbour's secret joy and sorrow: (as it is written, "[b] the heart knoweth his own bitterness, and a stranger may not intermeddle with his joy"): He has guided the Church to set down the prayers in such words as shall come home to every man, yet not draw particular attention to any. It is a most sweet mixture of sympathy and reserve. And now let us shortly consider what the things are which we thus pray our Lord to deliver us from.

"From all evil and mischief, Good Lord, deliver us." This seems at first almost too much to ask for: evil, of one sort or another, is so necessarily bound

[a] 2 Chron. vi. 30.   [b] Prov. xiv. 10.

up with our portion in this world, that it sounds like presumption for any of us to pray that we may be entirely free from evil. But we *may* pray; for He has promised to take us out of this world, into a world where no evil ever was or ever can be: into the heaven of the saints and good Angels: where is no drop, no grain, no smallest atom of evil or mischief of any kind; neither the evil of sin, nor the evil of suffering: for to both these sort of things, as you know, we attribute the name of evil. We call it evil and mischief, when a person tells a lie; and we call it also evil and mischief, when he breaks a limb, or suffers any bodily pain; to both, we give the same name of evil or mischief, yet they are widely different from each other: the one is the evil of sin, the other, of suffering: against both we pray in the Litany; from both we hope to be delivered, finally and for ever, in heaven.

But more especially we pray against sin, the chief evil; that is, against the breaking of God's law: which is therefore mentioned first among evils and mischiefs, as being incomparably the most evil and mischievous of all. For it separates from God, Who otherwise can and will cure all. I would we were all better able to enter into this true lesson of the Litany, that sin, and nothing else, is the chief evil, because sin, and nothing else, separates from God. We all own it in words: when shall we begin to own it in deeds also; to behave as if it were altogether true? That we may say this prayer with due earnestness, let us consider how in the next words the Church helps us to pray against him who is the author of sin, and also against that which always accompanies sin, and against that which is the certain end of sin. The author of sin is the devil, therefore we say, "From the crafts and assaults of the devil, Good Lord, deliver us." From his crafts and assaults, his secret and open attacks: whether he come upon us as a declared enemy, as he came upon S. Stephen and the other martyrs of old, and as he came upon our Lord in the last of his three temptations, openly proposing to Him to fall down and worship the Evil one: or whether on the other hand he come craftily, as he commonly does now, transforming himself into the likeness of an angel of light. O, my brethren, beware of these crafts of the devil, beware of being led into sin under the notion of good nature, and pleasing those whom you ought to please; beware of cheating or stealing under pretence of providing for your wife and children; beware in short of doing evil that good may come.

Thus the Church teaches us to pray against the author of sin: next she teaches us to pray against that which is the constant companion of wilful sin; and that is, the wrath of Christ. "From Thy wrath, Good Lord deliver us:" i. e. from the wrath of the Lamb, from His wrath Whose love is our only hope. Well may we pray to be delivered from this, for this is putting out the last ray of our light and comfort. If Christ be angry, who shall forgive? Who shall plead our forgiveness? And yet most certain it is, that He is and ever will be angry with such as go on wilfully in their sins: and vainly do we cry out so earnestly, "From Thy wrath, Good Lord, deliver us," so long as we permit ourselves in any secret abominations, whether of the flesh or spirit.

And of this we are fearfully reminded by the last words of this petition, "From everlasting damnation, Good Lord, deliver us." Everlasting damnation: that is the end of sin; that is the consummation of the wrath of the Lamb; as those will miserably find who go on tempting that wrath. Everlasting damnation: think of that fearful word: not *my* word, brethren, but the word of Christ and His Church, the word of our loving mother in whom we have our heavenly birth: the word of our most loving Saviour, Who laid down His life for us. He it is Who has said plainly, "These shall go away into everlasting punishment:" Their "worm dieth not and their fire is not quenched." He hath said it: you cannot doubt that it is so. It is not a frightful vision, but an aweful reality. Oh, pray against it earnestly, live against it with all your might: for this is the chief evil, the evil of evils, all other evils put together. Our Lord reminds you of it continually: continually, day by day, if you are not watching and praying, you are drawing nearer and nearer to it: What if it should be your portion at last? With what horror, with what self-reproach, will you then look back upon the many warnings you have had, the many times the terrible words have rung in your ears from the Church Litany, and that you yourselves have joined in them: "From Thy wrath and from everlasting damnation, Good Lord, deliver us." Each time it was God Almighty speaking to you as a loving Father, and offering you His good Spirit, to get out of the way of damnation if you would: and each time you put it off. Alas! what will be your thoughts of this, when all thoughts will come too late?

But as yet, God be praised, it is not too late: and that it may never be so with us, we are to pray and to fight, by God's help, not only against sin in general but against the several sorts of sin: and first against blindness of heart: which is when the eyes of men's understanding are blinded, as S. Paul says, by the god of this world, so that they cannot discern the things which belong unto their peace; the light of the glorious Gospel of Christ cannot shine into their hearts. For most true it is that when men have gone on for a certain time unwilling to see the truth, they become by God's just judgement unable to see it: they are as if they had lost the very power of thinking on the true, eternal, Divine things: heaven itself, if it were thrown open to them, would not to their eyes be anything particular to look upon; the Cross of Christ with Him crucified upon It, would be no very moving spectacle. Especially blind are such persons to their own sins, the real state of their own souls: they think with that unhappy Church in the book of Revelations; 'I am rich and increased with goods, and have need of nothing; and know not that they are wretched and miserable and poor and blind and naked.' Therefore after this 'blindness of heart' the Litany mentions three things, 'pride, vain-glory and hypocrisy:' which mark surprisingly how little people know of themselves: that is to say, how blind they are in their hearts. For, to be proud, is surely a very great blindness of heart: just as being humble is nothing more nor less than seeing ourselves in our true light. The wise man asked, 'Why is earth and ashes proud?' and we may ask yet more seriously, Why is he proud, who has sinned, and is in danger of everlasting death? Again, vain-glory which comes next in our petitions, is also a very great and miserable blindness of heart: for it is seeing and minding what men think of you, and not seeing or minding what judgement the great Almighty God is passing upon you. What greater blindness can you well imagine than that? And hypocrisy, that fearful vice, which our Lord so particularly hated and denounced, *that* also comes of blindness of heart. A hypocrite is one who tries to make others think better of him than he deserves: and who also behaves to Almighty God as if he could deceive Him: and when a person goes on so, he is almost sure to deceive himself likewise: a strong delusion is sent upon him, whereby he believes all manner of lies: and especially this lie, that he is good enough to be saved, when if he were not blinded in heart, he would know for an absolute certainty, that dying as he now is, he would be lost for ever. Thus hypocrisy makes blindness of heart.

These sins which have been mentioned put us wrong in regard of ourselves and our God: the next sort of sins mentioned in the Litany relate rather to our dealings with other men: " From envy hatred and malice and all uncharitableness, good Lord, deliver us." These all come of extreme blindness of heart: for what can be blinder or more stupid than to envy another, to bear him malice or hatred, or to be uncharitable towards him? as if his prosperity could hurt us, or his misery do us good. O, if we really and truly knew beforehand but ever so little of the wretchedness of giving way to such feelings, how envy and hatred indulged make a sort of hell upon earth, even *that*, apart from the hell which is to come would cause us to pray the prayer of the Litany, 'Good Lord deliver us from all these,' with our very heart and soul.

There is more to be said about the sins and miseries against which we fight and pray in this portion of the Litany: more than can well be said now. For the present I would say one thing: God grant it may sink deep into the heart of every one of us: and it is this: if we *pray* against all these sins and miseries, we must surely *fight* against all: our prayers will else be little better than a mockery of Him to Whom we pray. You pray against blindness of heart: then you must open the eyes of your heart: you must not keep them wilfully shut against the light of God's Truth. You pray against pride: away then with all thoughts of praising yourself in your heart and fancy. You pray against vain-glory: how dare you listen to the flattering words of men? You pray against hypocrisy: beware of deceitful dealing; beware of all dissembling with God. You pray our loving Lord to deliver you from envy, hatred, malice, and all uncharitableness: take care to put down the first harsh thought; to keep silence, yea even from the first unkind half-word. Remember these your good prayers, both to guard yourselves beforehand from sin, and to examine yourselves afterwards, and call yourselves to account for it: that you may not have to remember them hereafter, to your shame and everlasting condemnation.

SERMON XXXVIII.

ON THE LITANY. IV.

2 Thess. iii. 3.

"The Lord is faithful, Who shall stablish you, and keep you from evil."

WE have seen how the Church instructs us to pray for deliverance from all evil and mischief, more especially from all sin. Now this might seem almost too bold a prayer, seeing how "[a]man is born to trouble, as the sparks fly upwards," and how he is shaped in wickedness and conceived by his mother in sin. Therefore Holy Scripture is very express in making us promises, and teaching us to pray: teaching us to pray, as in the Lord's Prayer, that we may be delivered, not from some evil, but from all: and making us promises like that in the text: "the Lord is faithful, Who shall stablish you and keep you from evil." He is faithful, He may be depended on, He cannot deceive, nor fail you, He would not have taught and encouraged you to ask Him to deliver you from all evil, if it were not His gracious purpose so to do, on your properly asking Him. Therefore the Church, both elsewhere and here in the Litany, makes bold as a loving child to ask of her Father entire deliver-

[a] Job v. 7.

ance: and having mentioned in a former petition the great inward and spiritual sins, which are the roots of all that is said and done wrongly—blindness of heart, pride, vainglory and hypocrisy, envy, hatred, and malice and all uncharitableness—she now, in the petitions on which we have been catechising to-day, prays against their outward and visible effects, whether of sin or of punishment: and first she causes us to beseech our good Lord to deliver us "from fornication and all other deadly sin." On which we are to take notice, first, that there is such a thing as deadly sin; sin so exceeding black and foul and poisonous, that even one act of it, willfully and deliberately committed, kills for the time the life of the soul, separates from God, and stops the communication of His grace: so that a person dying in such a condition would have no chance of going to heaven. This is very plain from the Scriptures: as for example, from S. John's first epistle, "[b] There is a sin unto death: .... all unrighteousness is sin, and there is a sin not unto death." And in several places of the New Testament certain kinds of sin are reckoned up in which if a man dies he is sure to be lost for ever: the works of the flesh, which they who practise shall not inherit the kingdom of God. Distinct from this worst sort of sin is that which is sometimes called venial or pardonable, because it is more easily pardoned than the former kind; it does not at once kill the soul, and separate us entirely from God; it is like sickness and not like death, but if it is encouraged it will soon become worse, and end in death: I mean what we call sins of surprise and infirmity,

[b] 1 S. John v. 16, 17.

e. g. when persons before they are quite aware give way to their anger and say unkind words: it is a sin, and needs to be repented of and forgiven, but it is not such a sin as fornication, or pride, or malice: a person dying with such a sin upon him, not having distinctly repented of it, would not, we may believe, be of course lost for ever and ever. But even of such sins we cannot be too much afraid; for besides their own badness, no one can tell exactly when they become so much worse as to bring on us the guilt of the other and more fearful sort of sin: and a man may well say to himself, 'What if my indulging in this one liberty, which seems to me not so very bad, should be in the sight of God as if I were putting a kind of seal to my past transgressions? What if it turn the scale against me, when at the last day I shall be judged according to my works? For fear then of deadly sin I will keep myself as well as I may, through Jesus Christ from lighter and pardonable sin.' That is the only safe way: that is the only true way for us, who pray to Jesus Christ continually, "from all deadly sin, good Lord deliver us."

As the Litany thus teaches us that there is such a thing as deadly sin, sin so bad, that a single deliberate act of it, is enough to kill our souls and cut us off from Christ for ever; so it teaches us at the same time that fornication is such a sin: that is, when people, not being man and wife, come together as man and wife. Whatever may be said of other sins, this surely is deadly sin. Holy Scripture teaches us so expressly, reckoning it among the works of the flesh which are not to be named among Christians:

and the Litany, as often as ever we hear it, puts us
in mind of the same; puts us in mind that fornication
is deadly sin. It is mentioned especially, rather
than any other sort of wickedness, perhaps, because
very often the temptation to it is so strong, perhaps
because too many are inclined to think lightly of it,
and pass it over easily, more especially if it be healed
(as they imagine) by after marriage. But this is
not so at all, brethren; the sin I speak of is so great,
that as our blessed Lord Himself assures us, he that
doth but allow himself to look with his eyes, and
encourage the desire of it in his heart, is, before his
God, guilty of adultery in his heart. Therefore watch:
believe the Bible and the Church: believe the great
Lord, your Creator and Redeemer, the Maker of
heaven, earth, and hell. He surely knows for whom
He prepared that aweful place of punishment: He
surely knows what sins are deadly, what, in comparison pardonable: and He plainly tells you that sinful
lust, and much more actual uncleanness, is before
Him as adultery, and requires, as adultery would,
to be healed by very deep and special repentance,
before the persons so sinning can be again fit for the
kingdom of God. What a pity it would be, should
any of those who unhappily have suffered Satan to
delude them into sins of this kind, find their mistake
too late! What a pity again, nay rather, what a fearful horror, should others coming after, be encouraged by their bad example to make light of such
things, and so they should prove a cause of sin to
the little ones of Jesus Christ. It were better for
them that a millstone were hanged about their neck,
and they drowned in the depth of the sea. My dear

brethren, **my children in Jesus Christ, this is the** great, the distressing **anxiety** of those who **have now** the care of souls. A notion is gone abroad in the **world,** that persons turning to God need not trouble themselves to repent **so very** particularly of their **past sins**: committed, it may be, many years ago: that we need not confess **such sins one by one to God**: that it is enough **if we feel to our own** satisfaction, a certain general **change of heart. Now this** is right against **the** doctrine, that **certain sins are** deadly, and **cut off the** soul from God: that **they** leave a bad **mark** upon us, which **must be done away** with before we can come to God. **It is** right against the Bible, which teaches **us** that the work of **godly sorrow** by which alone persons can approve **themselves** to be clear after wilful sin, is a long, a hard, **a manifold work.** It is right against the Prayerbook, **which every** where teaches that we must be very **particular** in confessing our sins, our **own** special sins, **one by one if we can, to God**: and in very many cases teaches also, that **we ought by all means** to confess them to him who is **over us in God's place.** Let there be no mistake in this matter, for indeed it is of the greatest importance. **We cannot be forgiven,** nor come worthily to the Holy Sacrament, without Christ's absolution: **we cannot** have Christ's absolution without **real sorrow and** distinct confession of our own **several** sins, **as** distinct **as we can** make it: confession, I say not, **to a** Priest, (it may or not be so,) but, **to Christ Himself.** In this we must exercise ourselves, as ever we hope **to be heard, in** our prayer to be delivered from fornication and other deadly sin.

c c

Next we pray against a sort of dangers, more subtle, more out of sight, and therefore more dangerous. "From all the deceits of the world, the flesh, and the devil, good Lord, deliver us." Not now from their open assaults, from temptation to gross sin, such as fornication: but from their crafts and deceits, the thousand hidden ways in which they steal into our hearts and imaginations, and turn us away from the Truth before we are aware. As for instance, the world says, you must take this or that liberty, since every one else takes it: you must not set up to be so much better than other people, else you will never be able to do them any good. The flesh says, you have denied yourself enough: now is the time to enjoy yourself: you will be forgiven, though you be a little out of order. The devil whispers, 'Another person might be wrong in doing this: but yours is a special case: you have done so many things well, that God will not be angry with you for this one transgression.' These are the deceits of our enemies: from which if we pray to be delivered, we must in all reason watch against them. O, indeed we must watch, and that perseveringly, for these our three enemies are ever at hand, they are ever busy and awake, and we can have no security, except in hiding ourselves under His wings, and asking Him daily and hourly, 'Lord, what wilt Thou have me to do?'

From these prayers against sin, the Church leads us on next to pray against the temporal punishments of sin, such as lightning and tempest; plague, pestilence and famine; battle and murder, and sudden death. Some of these calamities, you perceive come suddenly on man, and as it were by strokes, as lightning and tempest: some are wasting and lingering, as plague, pestilence and famine: and again some of them are brought on man by his fellow men, such as battle and murder, others as sudden death are by the immediate visitation of the Almighty. But all of them either come directly from our good God and Father, or are at least allowed and overruled by Him for the punishment of transgressors and for the warning of those who need to be warned: and so we pray against them all: we should be worse than heathens if we did not so pray; to Him Who holds them all in His Hand, even to our Lord Jesus Christ, to Whom is given, as He Himself said, "all power in heaven and in earth." Let it be the comfort of those who have seen their friends fall or who fear to fall themselves, under any of these visitations, that none of them can possibly happen: not a sparrow can fall to the ground: without the consent of this our tender Father, Who will lay no more on us than He will make us able to bear: and let those who pray not to die suddenly take care to live so that no death may be quite sudden to them: but that when their Lord shall come and knock (who can tell how soon?) they may open to Him immediately.

But there are worse evils than plague, pestilence or famine, or any of the rest which can only kill the body: there are evils of the Church, spiritual enough in their effect to destroy thousands both of souls and bodies in hell: storms and tumults which have their beginning, not in God's outward and visible world, but in the restless and unquiet hearts of men. Against these, and their sad ending, we supplicate our Lord once more. "From all sedition, privy conspiracy, and rebellion; from all false doctrine, heresy and schism; from hardness of heart, and contempt of Thy Word and commandment, Good Lord deliver us." Here we see very exactly reckoned up the chief disorders in society, as before in the air and elements. In the State we pray to be delivered from sedition, privy conspiracy and rebellion: in the Church from false doctrine, heresy and schism. Three bad things in the State, and three bad things in the Church, in either case going on from bad to worse. In the State sedition, privy conspiracy and rebellion: sedition, that is, when people allow themselves to dishonour and disobey the king, and those who are in authority under him; privy conspiracy, when they band themselves secretly together, to do something against the law by fraud or by force: rebellion, when they actually lift up their hands against the Lord's anointed, the appointed Governour of the land. And nearly as these sins are in the State, so are false doctrine, heresy, and schism, in the Church. When all come together as too often happens, it is indeed utter confusion. But there are one or two things here, of which I am desirous that we should none of us be utterly ignorant: I mean about false doctrine, heresy and schism: whereof false doctrine in the Church is like sedition in the state: it infects people, poisons their talk, puts them altogether wrong. And it becomes heresy, when it contradicts the Creed: and the person who holds it is a heretic when he goes on obstinately holding it, after the judgement of the Church has been sufficiently clear against it. And schism, which comes after, is separation from the Apostles' fellowship, as the other was from the Apostles' doctrine. Schism, or cutting off, for so the word means, is when a person cuts himself off from the body that is in communion with the Apostles, i. e. with their successors, the bishops of the Church. How grievous a sin this is, we may judge by its being just contrary to our Lord's last and very earnest prayer just after consecrating the first Eucharist. *He* prayed over and over that we might all be one: but one who goes into schism, one who leaves the Church and chooses a new place for himself, does all he can to keep the Church from uniting: he is therefore working (though he little thinks it) exactly contrary to the Son of God. This is what we beseech God to deliver us from, when we mention false doctrine, heresy and schism: and believe me, dear brethren, the only safe way for us of this country to receive the blessing we pray for, is to keep faithful, whatever difficulties occur, to our old Prayer-book, to our old Apostolic ministry. That is the way whereby the first Church, the Church of Jerusalem, continued and grew in Christ: God grant it may be our way, and that of all near and dear to us, and of all committed to our charge.

For besides being the right way in itself, it is the way given us, in these trying times, to get over that last and worst evil, hardness of heart, and contempt of God's word and commandment. *That* is the lowest deep of sin in this world, and will lead, we may be sure, to the lowest deep of misery in the other world. "Hardness of heart," when the soul wilfully shuts itself up against the voice of God, and the gentle teaching of His Spirit: when it makes itself like the flinty rock, into which the rain of heaven cannot at all sink or penetrate. How can such an one ever be cured, who rejects the only remedy? And then he makes himself too, more and more guilty, for he goes on not in ignorance but in contempt of God's word and commandment. He absolutely scorns and despises the known will of his God and Saviour. Alas! how many are there who do so! how many who are in a way to do so! for every one, brethren, who indulges himself in anything which he knows to be wrong, is surely in the way to this fatal hardness of heart: and as we are continually on the edge of the most fearful *bodily* evils, which are mentioned in the Litany, lightning and tempest, plague, pestilence and famine, it is but a hair's breadth, for aught we know, between us and the worst of these, and not our wisdom, but God's mercy, keeps them off from us: so is it most alarming to think, how near we have often come, how near we may be now, to these more grievous spiritual evils—rebellion against those who are set over us in the state: false doctrine, heresy, schism in the Church: hardness of heart, and contempt of God's word and commandment. Good Lord deliver us from these things, and in Thy tender mercy pardon us for having so long and often trifled with them: through Jesus Christ our Lord. Amen.

SERMON XXXIX.

ON THE LITANY..V.

HEB. ii. 14, 15.

"*Forasmuch then as the children are partakers of flesh and blood, He also Himself likewise took part of the same: that through death He might destroy him that had the power of death, i. e. the devil; and deliver them who through fear of death were all their lifetime subject to bondage.*"

In these words the Apostle sets before us, first, the fact of our Lord's Incarnation, and then the unspeakable benefit freely bestowed upon us thereby.

God the Son, the Second Person in the Holy, Blessed, and Glorious Trinity, made Himself Man, true Man, for us. Forasmuch as the children are partakers of flesh and blood, He also Himself likewise took part of the same. Here is the fact of the Incarnation; next follows the account of the deep, eternal blessings which He by becoming Incarnate, has provided for us. The Son of God, by being made Man, and by what He did and suffered as Man, delivered us both from the power and the punishment of sin. Through His Death, which He could not have borne but as Man, He destroyed him that had the power of death, i. e. the devil. He overcame him, and thereby freed us from his power, that is, from the *power* of sin. He also delivered us from the *punishment* of sin, i. e. from the death and the fear of it, and from the sad bondage of spirit, the weary and heavy heart, from which they never can be free who know that they must die, and have no hope after death. Thus the Apostle describes the Incarnation and Death of Christ as delivering us from both the power and punishment of sin: as being to us indeed all that we pray for in those earnest petitions in the Litany which we have hitherto been considering. For when we said, "From sin, from all blindness of heart, from pride, vain-glory and hypocrisy, from envy, hatred, and malice, and all uncharitableness; from all sedition, privy conspiracy and rebellion, from all false doctrine, heresy and schism, from hardness of heart, and contempt of God's word and commandment: Good Lord deliver us:" we were praying the Lord to set us free from the power of sin. And when we said, "From all evil and mischief, from the crafts and assaults of the devil, from Thy wrath and from everlasting damnation; from lightning and tempest, from plague, pestilence, and famine, from battle and murder and from sudden death, Good Lord, deliver us," then we were asking for deliverance from the *punishment* of sin, temporal and eternal.

And now observe, brethren, on what we are taught to rely, as our only deliverance both from sin and from the misery which sin brings after it. Both by

S. Paul here in the Epistle to the Hebrews, and by the Church in her solemn Litany, we are taught to rely, solely and entirely, on the Incarnation of the Son of God, and the chain of mercies whereof that was the first beginning. S. Paul says, He "took part of flesh and blood, that through death He might destroy the devil, and deliver them that were in bondage." The Litany says, 'From all these evils: from both the power and the punishment of sin: do Thou Good Lord, deliver us, by the mystery of Thy Holy Incarnation, by Thy Holy Nativity and Circumcision, by Thy Baptism, Fasting and Temptation, by Thine Agony and Bloody Sweat, by Thy Cross and Passion, by Thy precious Death and Burial, by Thy glorious Resurrection and Ascension, and by the coming of the Holy Ghost." Are they not most blessed and comfortable, as well as very noble and heart-cheering words? a true golden chain let down from heaven to earth, yea to the very lowest places and darkest corners of the earth, to draw lost and undone sinners up to the very house of God? And observe, the first link in that chain, that on which all the rest depend, that without which heaven and earth could not really be bound together, is the Incarnation of God the Son. "By the mystery of Thy holy Incarnation, good Lord, deliver us." As if we should say, 'We desire, O Lord, to put Thee in mind of all those unspeakable and wonderful mercies, which had their beginning when Thou, the Only-Begotten Son, didst come down to do Thy Father's Will by taking to Thyself a Body and Soul like ours; a true Body formed from her body who was truly one of the seed of Adam: a true Soul breathed into that Body, and like the soul of Adam in all things only without sin. We beseech Thee, for this Thy great mercy's sake, deliver us both from sin and punishment. Remember Thy gracious beginnings towards us, and let them not prove vain and fruitless at last.' Then in like manner we go on to remind our good Lord of all that He did besides, and is doing, as our Mediator. "By Thy Holy Nativity;" as if we should say, 'Remember how in great humility Thou didst vouchsafe to be born of that poor and humble maiden; remember the stable at Bethlehem, the manger and the swaddling bands: how low, how very low, Thou didst stoop from Thy Throne in heaven; and for Thy lowliness' sake deliver us.' "By Thy Circumcision;" i. e. Remember the first bitter taste of pain endured for our sins: let not those precious drops of Thy holy and life-giving Blood be lost, " by Thy Circumcision :" good Lord deliver us. "By Thy Baptism;" 'remember how at thirty years old Thou didst begin to shew Thyself to Thy people, how Thou didst come to be washed in water by Thy servant, as if Thou hadst been a sinner, Who art purer than the Angels: "By Thy Baptism, good Lord deliver us."' "By Thy fasting;" ' remember the sad and lonely hours, which Thou didst spend in the wilderness, the forty days hunger and thirst which Thou didst endure; and for their sake vouchsafe to look compassionately upon us, here in our helpless condition, for we are most helpless if left to ourselves: "By Thy fasting, good Lord deliver us."'

"By Thy temptation :" 'Thou seest how hard we are beset, how our great adversary walketh about, seeking every moment to devour us: What fatal advantage he finds against us in the evil example of others and in our own frail hearts: O leave us not to him, nor to the world, nor to ourselves; for Thine own sufferings' sake when Thou didst vouchsafe to be in all points tempted as we are, succour us when we are tempted: " By Thy temptation, Good Lord, deliver us."'

"By Thine Agony and bloody Sweat." Remember how Thou didst withdraw Thyself from Thy disciples: how Thou didst kneel upon the cold hard ground: how Thou didst fall flat upon Thy face, and pray earnestly, again and again: how Thy divine Soul was as it were torn in pieces, willing at the same moment and not willing to receive the bitter cup: how in the agony and struggle of that prayer Thy Sweat was as it were great drops of blood falling down to the ground: O Lord, Remember all this for the good of us Thy unworthy servants and of those for whom we pray: and suffer not Thy unspeakable pangs to be void and fruitless in our behalf by reason of our many and most inexcusable transgressions. " By Thine Agony and bloody Sweat, Good Lord, deliver us."

"By Thy Cross and Passion." As in all our prayers and addresses to the Father of all we plead the Sufferings and Death of the Son as our only available Sacrifice and sin-offering, so here we plead with the Son Himself by the remembrance of the same Sacrifice: as if a man should say to his friend who had done and suffered great things for him, 'Remember thine old loving-kindness, and help me once more, unworthy as I am, else all that former friendship will fall to the ground and be as if it had never been.

Thus do we Christians plead with the Saviour by His Cross, and because He has redeemed us, we beseech Him to spare us; or as Moses pleaded with God for the Israelites when he had brought them out of Egypt, that He should not cast them off, because it would be a triumph to His enemies the Egyptians and Canaanites, so we cry out, "Lest the enemy say, I have prevailed against him," lest Thy Blood be counted an unholy thing, "By Thy Cross and Passion, Good Lord, deliver us."

Then we plead with Him by His precious Death and Burial: because we are going to ask His mercy in our own death especially: as if we should say, 'Thou knowest what death is: none of us who are living know; it is a mystery alike to the child and to the aged, to the wise man and the fool: but Thou knowest by actual suffering as we shall one day know: and that suffering so endured for us, that it was as it were all the deaths of us sinners in one. Remember those better pangs we beseech Thee, and because of them have mercy upon us in the dreadful hour of death to which we are doomed: help us to prepare for it and support us when we come to it: "By Thy precious Death and Burial, Good Lord, deliver us." We put Him in mind of His Burial as well as of His Death, because that too was part of His humiliation: and even because He once lay in the grave, we pray Him to watch over us when we shall be laid in our graves, and to keep our bodies safe against the Day of resurrection: "By Thy Burial, Good Lord, deliver us."

And with that we pass from His sufferings to His triumph, from His humiliation to His glory: and we plead with Him by His glorious Resurrection and Ascension: as who should say, 'The Lord hath delivered Thee, the pangs of Thy death have been loosed, Thou Who art the Head hast been lifted up far above all heavens: now then it is meet that Thou draw up Thy members after Thee. Thou sittest at the Right Hand of God in the glory of the Father: We believe that Thou shalt come to be our Judge: We therefore pray Thee, help Thy servants whom Thou hast redeemed with Thy precious Blood;' "By Thy glorious Resurrection and Ascension, Good Lord, deliver us."

And finally we plead with our Lord by that which is the crown of all His mercies to man, even the sending down His Holy Spirit. I call it the crown of all His mercies, because it is that by which He applies all, and brings them all, as it were, home to us. "By the coming of the Holy Ghost, Good Lord, deliver us:" i. e. seeing that Thou didst vouchsafe according to Thy promise to send to Thy faithful people after Thy departure Thine own Co-equal Spirit to be their Comforter, and to give us in Holy Baptism our portion of the same Spirit; remember this Thy mercy most especially in our behalf, and let it not be lost upon us: for Thine own sake continue it to us O Lord and suffer us not to cast it away: let us not sin against the Holy Spirit. 'By His coming, His gracious coming to the whole Church at Pentecost, His coming to each one of us in His Holy Sacraments, again we pray, Good Lord, deliver us.'

There is yet another meaning, another thought, which runs as a thread through all this part of the Litany: viz. that when we say to our Lord, '*By* the mystery of Thy Holy Incarnation, *By* Thine Agony and Bloody Sweat:' and all those other petitions: we mean to pray that each one of the great mysterious things which He did and suffered for us may do its proper work, and tell towards bringing about the salvation of us sinners, as He graciously designed. For so it is, brethren, that in all that course of wonders, from His Conception in His Mother's womb to His sending down the Comforter on His Apostles, He had each one of us in mind: we, even you and I, and every one here present, were so much in His mind, as if there had been no one besides to be saved or lost. Here then we pray for ourselves and for one another, that what He then did and suffered for us may not be frustrated by our manifold faults. For thus it is: Before the world began, He knew and purposed in His Divine Wisdom that such and such persons should be: that they, by their own sins and the sins of their forefathers being in danger of eternal death, He, in His own good time would come down from heaven for their salvation, and would be Incarnate by the Holy Ghost of the Virgin Mary, and would be made Man, and would suffer death for them, and would rise again, and ascend into heaven, and send down the Holy Ghost. And in all this chain of mercies, observe, the first link is the Incarnation, i. e. His being made Man. He could not die and suffer for us, unless He had a Body and Soul like ours: for death is the parting of body and soul: He could not be a perfect Priest and Sacrifice, unless He were in all things made like unto His brethren, only without sin. His Burial and Rising again, and Ascending into heaven, were all in the

Body, and so, in some way, was His sitting at the Right Hand of God. And the very purpose of His sending the Holy Ghost was to make us sacramentally partakers of His spiritual Body, that so we might be joined to His mystical Body, the Church. So that even according to our weak understanding, all depends on the true and real Incarnation of the Son of God. *That* is the Foundation: every thing depends upon it. *That* is the one Truth, by which we are to judge and try all other doctrines that are preached to us. "ᵃ Every spirit that confesseth that Jesus Christ is come in the flesh is of God: and every spirit that confesseth not that Jesus Christ is come in the flesh is not of God: and this is that spirit of Anti-christ, whereof ye have heard that it should come, and even now already is it in the world."

But, my dear brethren, we must not go away, without some serious thought of the various times in which the Church teaches us to call for the help of this our Incarnate Saviour. 'In all time of our tribulation, in all time of our wealth;' tribulation, i. e. trouble and sorrow; and wealth, i. e. (here) prosperity and success, take in between them all possible conditions, all possible events in the world: but perhaps the prayer is more especially meant to ask the aid of God Incarnate, i. e. of our Lord Jesus Christ, in times of more than usual distress, and also in times of more than usual joy. The first of these we understand very well: it is the most obvious of all things, it is what all but unbelievers practise, to call upon the Lord in time of trouble:

ᵃ 1 S. John iv. 2, 3.

but why should we so especially cry out, "Good Lord deliver us," in times of wealth and enjoyment, and when all seems going well with us? Our Lord Himself will presently help us to an answer. "[b] Woe unto you that are rich, for ye have received your consolation:" and "it is easier for a camel to go through a needle's eye, than for a rich man to enter into the kingdom of God." Because the snares of Satan are so very crafty and the temptations of the world so very alluring, when a man by his wealth has power in a great measure to please himself. Let us pray, then, brethren, with all our might, "In all time of our wealth, Good Lord, deliver us:" and as we pray, so let us watch: whenever God sends any special joy or blessing, yea even if it be spiritual joy and comfort, let us watch and stand on our guard, that neither we in our frailty, nor the enemy in his malice, pervert the good gift into an occasion of offending. Let us ever pray and strive that our satisfactions and prosperities may have in them a touch of what is humiliating, and chastening: even as our Redeemer won His victory for us no other way but by His Cross and Passion.

Yet once more: we pray also, and it is the last prayer in this part of the Litany, that our Lord would deliver us from all the evils which have been mentioned in the hour of death more especially, and in the day of judgement. For we know not whether or no our time to come will be a time of wealth or of tribulation: but whichever it be, we know for certain that it will end in death and judgement: and that in death and judgement there can be no hope, no

[b] S. Luke vi. 24.

rest, no comfort, no help, but only in Christ our Lord: Who will surely be there, if not to deliver, to condemn us. O then how can we help praying as we do here in the Litany? how can we help calling night and day on our gracious God, Incarnate to be our Saviour, and with all our might beseeching Him to own us on that great and dreadful Day. Be sure, He loves to be so prayed to: He made Himself Bone of our bone and Flesh of our flesh, He sacrificed Himself for us, He gives Himself to us in His Sacraments, that we may pray to Him in earnest. Do so, my brethren, pray to Him and live to Him, in earnest: and be sure He will not forsake His own work. The mystery of His holy Incarnation, which is your only hope now, will be your stay in death and judgement, and after judgement will prove to you an exceeding and eternal weight of glory.

SERMON XL.

ON THE LITANY. VI.

THE INTERCESSIONS.

1 Tim. ii. 1, 2.

"I exhort therefore, that first of all, supplications, prayers, intercessions, and giving of thanks, be made for all men: for kings, and for all that are in authority; that we may lead a quiet and peaceable life in all godliness and honesty."

We have now finished that part of the Litany, in which the Church calls upon her Lord to deliver us from all evils, both of this world and of the next: reminding Him at the same time of His great unspeakable mercies, from His Incarnation to His sending down the Holy Ghost. And now we go on to pray and intercede with Him to bestow upon us all good. The first petition being that He would rule and govern His holy Church universal in the right way: the last, that He would "give us true repentance, forgive us all our sins, negligences, and ignorances, and endue us with the grace of the Holy Spirit, to amend our lives according to His holy Word." And after each petition the congregation are to make answer as you know, "We beseech Thee to hear us, good Lord." There are twenty-two short prayers of this kind, and when we consider them, we shall find I think, that the first ten are petitions for public blessings, blessings which we need as belonging to the kingdom or people in which God has cast our lot: and in the other twelve we ask Him for things which we or others need each one for himself. They are for the most part prayers of intercession, that is to say, we pray in them for other people as much or more than for ourselves. And this is a great part of Christian charity: to speak a good word for one another, as often and as earnestly as we can, to the everlasting Father, in the Name of our Lord; or, as in the Litany, to our gracious Lord Himself. Even as He by His Apostle ordains in the text. For in those verses which I read to you for the text, S. Paul is giving directions to Timothy, whom he had ordained to be a Bishop, how he should order the public prayers of the Church. And he exhorts, first of all, that prayers and thanksgivings be made for Christians to use in common, not each one for himself only, nor in their families only, but in the Church and congregation, when we meet to offer to God His own memorial Sacrifice of His Son's Body and Blood. At such times, S. Paul directs that prayers should be made for all men, especially for kings and all who are in authority. Accordingly we find that the first good thing which we beseech God in the Litany to grant us, after we have prayed for deliverance from all evil things, is His ruling and governing the Church in the right way. And observe, we say the Church universal: the whole body of Christians everywhere. They are His Body, having His Spirit breathed into them: even as at the beginning He breathed into Adam's nostrils the breath of life: and He hath promised the same Spirit to guide them into all truth: so that we are sure that the holy Church Universal, i.e. the Church of all times and all nations, will not err, will not go wrong; as it is written, "[a]My Spirit which I have given thee, and My words which I have put into thy mouth, shall not depart out of thy mouth, nor out of the mouth of thy seed, nor out of the mouth of thy seed's seed, saith the Lord, from henceforth even for ever." A particular nation, or a particular generation of the Church, may perhaps err, and that grievously, but not the whole Church from the Apostles until now: and therefore we are sure that the Creeds are all right, and also all the chief parts of the Prayer-book: because they are what has been taught and practised, as the true meaning of the Bible, in the whole Church from the Apostles until now. Well then, in this first intercession of the Litany we do as it were put our Lord in mind of His gracious and bountiful promises to this His holy Church, and beseech Him that He would never suffer it in any generation to fall away from the faith and practice of the saints; and especially not in our generation, nor for our sins, as we have too much reason to fear. We beseech Him as sinners: not for our own righteousness, but for His manifold and great mercies: and unworthy as we are, He permits us to take comfort in the great things which He has done for other generations of sinners within His Church. Ten thousand times, we may well fear, have both our fathers and we forfeited all

[a] Isa. lix. 21.

right to this His merciful protection: but He "[b] hath delivered us from so great a death, and doth deliver; and we trust in Him that He will also yet deliver us:" but He expects that we should all help together with our prayers. Pray then, brethren, pray more and more earnestly, for the Church of God, now in her time of trial. She is always in warfare, but never more so than now. Pray night and morning for the whole Body of Christ, your brethren in every Christian land far and near: pray humbly, pray earnestly, pray with a heart set against sin, and your prayer will return into your own bosom; whether you see any fruit of it in the conversion and improvement of the world or no, the God of love and peace, will surely bless it to the improvement of your own heart in peace and love.

And for the same kind of reason which would make you pray very devoutly for the whole Church, you will be serious and devout also in the following petitions of the Litany, in which we proceed, according to the Apostle's direction, to make intercession for our Sovereign and for all who are in authority. You may easily understand why the Church prays so often for the king or queen of the land, remembering them in all her solemn services. The Sovereign is over us in the place of God, and has to bear the burden of the whole state: he is the person of most consequence, the well being of the nation chiefly depends upon him: he is also in a place of great danger and temptation, and we are too apt through the stubbornness and wilfulness of our nature, to forget our duty to him in one respect or another. All these

[b] 2 Cor. i. 10.

are reasons for our often and cheerfully remembering the king or queen in our prayers. S. Paul and the first Christians never omitted to pray for the Roman Emperor, though he was always a heathen, and very often a cruel tyrant: let us all try at least to be in earnest when we pray for our Christian queen, for indeed her place is as hard as it is high, and she needs all the help her loving subjects can obtain for her from the King of kings. Who would not pray with all his heart that she may be kept and strengthened in God's true worship, i.e. the faith and practice of the Prayer-book to which she is so many ways pledged, but in which whoever is earnest, and most especially in such a high place, must expect to find many hindrances? Who would not pray that she may be kept in righteousness and holiness of life, so hard to be practised by the rich and great ones of the earth? Who would not pray that her heart may be ordered in the faith, fear, and love of God? that she may evermore have affiance and trust, not in her great and rich dominions, but in Him? that she may ever seek, not any thing in this world, but always His honour and glory? Who would not pray that the Allmerciful would continue to be as He has hitherto proved in a remarkable manner, her defender and keeper, giving her the victory over all her enemies, and especially over all those evil men and evil spirits, who are her worst enemies, because they are also the enemies of God and His Church? And as we pray for her, so in dutifulness we pray for those who are nearest to her, as being in many respects partakers of her burthen, and in their example, of great consequence to us.

After interceding for our chief governour in the state, we proceed to mention our spiritual fathers and governours the Bishops, Priests, and Deacons; those to whom God has given His Spirit to be over us in holy things. We beseech Him to illuminate them with true knowledge and understanding of His Word, that is of the Bible according to its real meaning, taught to the Church from the beginning. Take notice of this, brethren: we pray to be taught, not simply the Bible, but the true meaning of the Bible. And another thing: you pray that we may teach it you, not by word only but by example, not only by preaching but by living. For if we say and do not; if we lay heavy burthens on you, and ourselves touch not the burthens with one of our fingers; if we shew others the way of goodness, ourselves going on in impurity and falseness of heart: who can express the greatness of our misery? Of your charity then pray for us, that we may be saved from this worst and most shameful of all miscarriages: that we may not be found at last such as Judas Iscariot: cast away ourselves, after preaching to others. Pray for us, that we may preach faithfully, and that as we may preach, so we may live: that it may not be said to us at the Day of Judgement, "out of thine own mouth will I judge thee, thou wicked servant." And as we pray for our queen by name, so it may seem natural that in our hearts, even though not in our lips, we should name our own bishop and the priest or other minister who has the care of our souls. May we not hope that many do so both here in the Litany, and at home when you are praying for those whom Christ would have you pray for? Certainly, in such measure as the ministers of Christ are in earnest, it will be a real comfort to them in their anxious duties to know that you, the sheep of Christ, pray earnestly and particularly for them. It ought to help us very much in our duties towards one another, our being in the habit of praying one for another.

After the Clergy we pray for the nobility, and all the counsellors of the Sovereign, that God would endue them with grace, wisdom and understanding: and then for the magistrates, that they may have grace to execute justice on criminals, and maintain truth in disputes and lawsuits. Thus we call down the blessing of Him Who is the perfection of wisdom and justice, both on those who advise the king or queen what to do, what laws to make: and on those whose duty it is to enforce and fulfil the law after it is made. We pray for them, and of course it is our duty to do nothing which may hinder them in their good work; to judge them charitably, and speak respectfully of them.

The prayers for all sorts of governours being finished, a petition for the Christian people comes next in order: 'That it may please Thee to bless and keep all Thy people.' *Thy people:* i. e. Christ's people, especially those who belong to the particular congregation which is saying the Litany: and here again each person will naturally and rightly remember his own special kindred, friends and neighbours: those for whom he is bound to pray.

The last petition on which I shall say anything to-day, is that in which the Church teaches us to remember other nations besides our own, and to pray that God would give them unity, peace and concord.

He is the God of peace: **He came to be our Peace:** the Angels at His coming sang 'Peace on earth:' yet it is a sad truth, that not only the heathens and unbelievers, who refuse in all things to hearken to His voice, but **Christian** nations, made **up of** members of **Christ,** have been, some or other of them, almost always at war with one another: and what is still a deeper ground of sadness, Christian Churches are divided one from another. When the Church first begun, it was not **only one Church** all over the world, but it was plainly seen to be one Church, in that everywhere they received Christians coming from another country into Communion: but now there are sad divisions: if we go across the sea we find whole nations of Christians, not willing to communicate with us, nor to receive us into their Communion. It need not disturb any one, for it is only what our Saviour prophesied: but it is very sad, and very hurtful, and very contrary to His Will, being in fact altogether occasioned by the manifold sins of Christians: and therefore we do well to pray with all earnestness that this great evil may be remedied: that there may not only be peace among Christian nations, but unity also and concord,—visible unity and concord—among Christian Churches. It is one of our most solemn prayers, both here in the Litany and afterwards in the Communion office: as our Lord Himself offered it up the night before His Death along with His first Sacrifice of Communion: "I pray that they all may be one, as We are." When we think of that prayer, brethren, how can we help offering up with all our hearts, the petition for unity and concord, seeing that the wish for it was so very near the Heart of our pierced and dying Lord? If we at all love Him, if we at all care for Him, let us sincerely watch ourselves, that we do nothing, say nothing, if possible think nothing, which may tend to divide and scatter the Church: as for instance, if a preacher not of the Church should come here, or if any of you should be called by God's providence to live in a place where you were tempted to attend such preaching, it is your plain duty to know no such thing as doubt or unbelief in the matter, but to decline all such preaching as contrary to His Will.

In this respect, as in respect of the other petitions which have been considered to-day, the poorest, the humblest, the most ignorant, may do great things if he will. He may say to himself '*I* do great things! *I* who am so weak, so simple?' 'Yes,' Christ says to him, '*You* may, if you will, be of great service to the king, the bishops, the nobles, to the divided Church, if you will but pray earnestly and worthily.' The poor widow, the lonely orphan, praying patiently may do great things for the Church. Remember Cornelius and how his private prayer was answered. God is the same God as He was then. He will hear you as He did Cornelius, if you try to be like Cornelius. Your quiet prayer and self-denial in secret may go farther than you imagine to restore that greatest blessing, the unity and concord of the Church.

SERMON XLI.

ON THE LITANY. VII.

THE PRIVATE INTERCESSIONS.

HEB. xiii. 18.

"Pray for us: for we trust we have a good conscience, in all things willing to live honestly."

AFTER our intercessions for public persons, our mother the Church helps us to pray for private and individual Christians, i. e. for ourselves and for one another and for those who need to be prayed for all over the world, according to their several circumstances and wants. I say, the Church our mother thus helps us to pray: for this is the way in which I should like that we should all use ourselves to look at the Prayer-book, viz: as though we were little children kneeling at our mother's knees to learn how to pray, and she was teaching us, as of course all good and religious mothers do teach their children. When we are willing simply to learn of her, and to pray in such words, and in such a spirit, as she approves, then we are in the right way of prayer, then we are sure of not going away from our prayers without a blessing. And now in the particular part of the Litany we are come to, the Church in her wisdom and charity instructs us, to offer up our prayers for the souls and bodies of our brethren, as well as our own, according as every man hath need. We may understand it as if the whole congregation of Christ's flock called on us in the words used by the Apostle in the text: "Pray for us: for we trust we have a good conscience, in all things willing to live honestly." We pray for all, but especially for those who are of the household of Faith; those who have a sort of good meaning: who have not quite given themselves up to hardness of heart and contempt of God's Word and commandment. They wish to live honestly in all things, and we pray for them that they may be helped to do so.

And the first thing we ask is, that they and we, and each one of us, may walk in the fear and obedience of Christ. "That it may please Thee to give us a heart to love and dread Thee, and diligently to live after Thy commandments." Not only to love, but also to dread and fear Him: not only to dread but also to love Him. And that because He is our Father, and a dutiful child both honours and respects his father, i. e. has a religious fear and dread of doing any thing which may displease him: and also loves him very dearly, and therefore is most earnest in doing all things to please him: according to the end of this petition. Where there is true love and fear, there is also the living diligently after His commandments: after *all* of them; dutiful children do not pick and choose which of their Father's sayings they will mind and which they will not mind, but they live diligently after them all. And this we ask for every one alike, for to every one it is alike needful. It is absolutely necessary: no man can be saved without it. I mean, it is absolutely necessary that we should be so far turned to God, as to have a heart, i. e. a mind and purpose: not merely an unsteady wish, coming and going, and blown about by every wind of temptation, but a real, settled, mind and purpose, to love and fear God, and live by His law, in all things. This, I suppose, is what our Saviour meant, when He said to that young man, "If thou wilt enter into life, keep the commandments:" that it should at least be the rule of his life to do so, and that if ever he turned from it, it should be by infirmity, not of set and deliberate purpose. And then, as our Lord went on and added what may be called Counsels to necessary commands; saying first by way of command, "If thou wilt enter into life, keep the commandments," and afterwards by way of counsel, "If thou wilt be perfect, sell all that thou hast, and give to the poor;" so the Church after praying for a heart to love and fear and obey God, goes on and prays for increase of grace: that we may abound more and more, not only doing those things which not to do would be deadly sin, but from day to day hearing God's Word, and receiving it with pure affection, and bringing forth the fruits of the Spirit. See, brethren, what you pledge yourselves to when in answer to this petition you say, 'We beseech Thee to hear us, Good Lord.' You do in effect promise to hear God's Word meekly: i. e. with a sweet, affectionate, teachable mind: not fretting nor being angry when you feel yourselves reproved by it: like David and not like Pharaoh or Jeroboam. You promise to receive it with pure affection: i. e. with a single and simple purpose to please Him and not yourselves. You promise to bring forth the fruits of the Spirit, i. e. really to do, on occasion, the things which God's Word tells you that you ought to do. I say, you *promise* all this: for in praying for grace to do it, you surely pledge yourself to do what in you lies towards it: just as if you asked for seed to sow a field, the person giving you the seed would understand that you promised to sow it. Take care then, you who come here and say the Litany, that you listen to God's Word, that you let it sink into your hearts, above all, that you obey it in your lives: else you condemn yourselves, every time you say this petition.

After this praying for all Christians, first that they may be good, then that they may go on better and better, we proceed to pray for different sorts of persons, who more particularly need our prayers, and first, for all such as have erred and are deceived, that they may be led into the way of truth. This is what the Church would have us do with regard to all who are in error, she would have us pray for them, even as we pray for ourselves. And great need there is that we should do so: more and more need, as the world grows older and older, and divisions and heresies grow alas! more common among Christians. We in our blindness are too apt to dislike those who differ from us, but the Church's way is to teach us to pray for them; and in doing so we pray for ourselves also, in whatever respect we ourselves are deceived, and in error about the things of

God: for of course we cannot suppose that *we* are *exactly* right in every thing, though we trust that by His mercy we are not in fatal error. Well, whatever our errors and mistakes, as concerning holy things, may be, we here pray against them: humbly claiming the gracious promise of our Lord to all His people, " when He, the Spirit of truth, shall come, He will guide you into all truth."

And next, the Church will have us remember the different spiritual conditions of our brethren that are in the world: all tempted, all in danger, all by nature children of wrath, and carrying about with them the seeds at least and deadly infection of original sin; but in very different stages of the way towards heaven: some remaining in that happy state to which they were admitted by holy Baptism: keeping their first love, their garments yet pure and undefiled: and concerning these we pray our good Lord, that it may please Him to 'strengthen such as do stand.' For as we need His special grace to be converted and regenerated at first, so we need it no less for our continuance but for one hour in the grace of our regeneration and union with Christ. He is not only our Creator but our Preserver. Perseverance, the crown of all Christian graces, must come from Him: and who that knows the misery of backsliding and falling away will not pray with all his heart to be kept firm and constant, both himself and all whom he prays for? Or if any be shaken and unsettled, will he not in charity pray for them too, saying as the Church next teaches, 'That it may please Thee to comfort and help the weak hearted?' Surely, whether it be in matters of faith or of practice, there is nothing more miserable, there are few things more likely to give occasion to the crafts and assaults of the devil, than to be put in doubt, to be hesitating and perplexed about things which one had seemed to one's self clearly to know. It was indeed the Evil one's first step in tempting Eve: "*Hath* God said?" he wanted to make her *doubt*, whether God had forbidden that particular fruit to them, or no. And there is another hesitation and weakness of heart, even worse than this of doubt: i. e. when persons knowing their duty for certain, have not the heart, the courage, the spirit, to do it. Pilate for instance was weak-hearted when he gave up our Lord in order to content the people: and Saul was very weak-hearted, when for the same reason he spared the choice of the Amalekites. We have great need to ask God for comfort and help against *this* weakness of heart, which would lead us every day to give up our plainest duties, and in the end to throw away our souls, out of mere cowardice —fear of pain or ridicule.

Next, as it is more miserable to sink down than merely to tremble, we say, 'That it may please Thee to raise up them that fall,' them that fall into sin, be the sin ever so great and deadly. Here, as in all these petitions, we shall naturally each one of us remember those persons for whom we are especially bound to pray, those among our own acquaintance or kindred, or with whom we are any way entrusted, who are unhappily living in any serious sin. They cannot be named aloud to be prayed for, as the afflicted sometimes are. It is therefore the more necessary that we should of our own accord call them to mind: that we should **beseech God** to grant them in particular the benefit of the prayers of the Universal Church. We must pray for them the rather, on account of their never praying for themselves. And who knows what good it might do them: how many poor lost souls might be won back from Satan, if sincere persons would only be thoughtful and constant in praying for them that fall?

Suppose then these three sorts prayed for: the fallen, the wavering and such as do stand, and God to hear our prayers for each: you see that the next petition would at once be fulfilled. Satan would be beaten or bruised under our feet, and as often as he tried to raise himself up, he would be thrust down again as by the strong spear of an Angel: till at length all God's faithful servants would be taken for ever out of Satan's reach: out of temptation and danger; out of this world.

From spiritual and invisible troubles we pass to the earthly and temporal miseries by which God tries us, and we mention one by one the classes of persons, whom we suppose to be most helpless, most in need of God's very special care, because there is no one on earth who knows how to help them. In general, all in danger, necessity, tribulation: In particular, all travelling by land or by water: and among these we shall ever do well to remember those who are gone out, as zealous preachers and missionaries, to make known the Gospel in the four corners of the earth. Again we pray for all women labouring of child: for such an one, too, is both in great pain and peril and also very much hindered from regular services and devotions of her own. For the same reasons we make mention of sick persons and young children: the more *their own* prayers are hindered, the more active must be *our* intercession. Think too of the many casualties to which young children are especially exposed: so that the two first years after birth are beyond comparison the most dangerous and difficult years for a person to get through: and join with all your heart in the touching prayer for those little ones: which before now, I doubt not, has been many a broken-hearted parent's comfort. And be not inattentive to the next clause, which mentions all prisoners and captives: considering what a rest and relief it would be to you, were you yourself in prison and captivity, to know that the whole Church of God and especially your friends and relations at home, were calling upon the great Deliverer for you: after the pattern of that first Church which when Peter was kept in prison, made prayer unto God for him, and that without ceasing.

As for the next petition, for 'the fatherless children and widows, and for those that are desolate and oppressed,' I need not say much of it: it tells its own meaning plainly, and who can doubt that it is a petition most acceptable to Him Who proclaims Himself a Father of the fatherless and an Avenger of the cause of the widows? And observe that it adds, 'all that are desolate and oppressed:' all that are forlorn in heart and circumstances, though they be not exactly fatherless children or widows. O what tender, considerate love is here: what support for the sufferer, what deep reproof for the oppressor! Who would not love that holy Church, and pray for her in her wrongs, when she is oppressed by ungodly and undutiful men; she who pleads thus earnestly for all that are oppressed before her God?

In the next sentence she spreads her wings as it were, to gather under them this whole world of sinners: beseeching the God of all to have mercy upon all. And in the next after, she causes us to pray—let us take care that we pray in earnest: for those whom men would be least inclined to mention in their prayers, were God Almighty to leave them to themselves; i. e. for 'our enemies, persecutors and slanderers.' These two petitions between them are as wide as Christian charity, shewing that nobody can be so far from us, nor yet so much our enemy, as that we ought not to love them and pray for them, and if we can, do them good: even as our Lord died for all, and in dying prayed especially for His murderers. They shew also, as He in that prayer, that we should never despair of anyone.

After all these intercessions for others and prayers for spiritual good, comes in one short prayer for the things needful to our temporal and earthly life. 'That it may please Thee to give and preserve to our use the kindly fruits of the earth, so as in due time we may enjoy them.' Whereby we are taught the same lesson as in the Lord's prayer: 'Give us this day our daily bread:' which words not coming in till we are half way through the prayer, shew us that we are not to make so very much of the good things of this world, in comparison of the better things of heaven. At the same time we are instructed to depend not on our own skill and industry but on the blessing of our Creator both for the growth and preservation of the fruits of the earth, and for our enjoyment of them.

But what is this which comes in at the end of all? 'That it may please Thee to give us true repentance:' as much as to say, 'We have made bold to ask of Thee all these things, but too well do we know how unworthy we are to ask Thee for anything at all.' When we have done our prayers, we have need to begin again with a prayer that we may pray better: and we have much cause to repent of our very repentance. But Thou O Lord have mercy upon us and accept of our most imperfect services; and grant that all our life hereafter may be an exercise of true repentance, Thou forgiving us and we amending our lives. Forgive us what we have done ignorantly, what we have left undone negligently, and especially forgive us our known and wilful sins: and grant that the time to come may be really better, far better than the time past. May Thy Word and Will be henceforth the rule of our lives: and for the rest, 'Thy Will be done.'

And so end the petitions and intercessions of our solemn Litany. We have used it, some of us regularly for many years. God forgive us that we are not very much more improved and bettered by it than we now are. God give His grace to those who are to come after, and to ourselves in future years, that the fruit of our prayers may appear in our lives, and that both our lives and our prayers may prepare us for a blessing hereafter, through Jesus Christ our Lord.

SERMON XLII.

ON THE LITANY. VIII.

THE SUFFRAGES.

Heb. vii. 25.

"He is able to save them to the uttermost that come unto God by Him, seeing He ever liveth to make intercession for them."

Yes, my brethren: "even to the uttermost." There is no evil from which we may not hope to be delivered, there is no degree of joy and mercy, at which we may not hope to arrive, by the mercy of Him on Whom we call in the Litany: Him Who redeemed us with His precious Blood, Who gave Himself for us, once for all, on the Cross, and is daily giving Himself to us in His holy Sacraments. On Him we must call, to keep us safe in ordinary times; to Him we must cry aloud, and run for shelter, when the worst comes to the worst: in all the storms and tempests, and sore trials and troubles, which are sure to come upon us all, more or less, sooner or later.

The Litany, and especially this latter portion of it, to which we are now come, seems especially intended to help us in the worst of times, and most especially of all, perhaps, when the times are bad in respect of God's Holy Church: as we shall see by examining the words of it more particularly.

The point in the Litany at which we began this afternoon in our catechizing, was the end of what are called the Suffrages, or special petitions, the last 'we beseech Thee to hear us, good Lord.' Having in those special petitions besought our Lord to hear us concerning all the sorts of blessings, spiritual and temporal, which we may hope for at His merciful hands, and also for all the persons on whose behalf we are bound to pray: having prayed for each severally: we now proceed to gather up all in certain short addresses and calls on our Blessed Lord, in some respects not unlike the cries of an infant to its parent, cries not expressed in words, yet truly signifying the wants and distresses of the child, and so understood by the parent. Not unlike to these in some respects are the short ejaculations, "Son of God, we beseech Thee to hear us;" and the others which follow it, wherein both Priest and people take part. Rightly used, those short prayers are a kind of darts kindled by adoring love, and sure not to miss their aim; sure to reach the heart of Him to Whom they are directed, if we do but direct them towards Him in spirit and in truth: if we do but say the words sincerely, earnestly, humbly. The time is very short, which we have for so lifting up our hearts: 'Son of God, we beseech Thee to hear us;' and 'O Christ, hear us,' take up but a moment in uttering: but who knows how great things may be done in that moment, if we really endeavour to throw our whole heart and soul into the words so uttered? To be born, to die, to rise again; to be baptized, confirmed, ordained, to receive Holy Communion, are things done each in a moment, or a very few moments: but how infinitely important are they to be well or ill done: and so it may be, that if Christians would really join, with serious, clean, and prepared hearts, in such brief prayers as these, blessings beyond thought would be won in a few moments, which are now lost, perhaps for ever, for want of such diligence in prayer. You might think perhaps that these prayers must be easy to offer, because the words are so short, few and plain; but do you find it so yourselves, my brethren? Is it, or is it not, easy for you to say *with all your hearts*, 'Son of God, we beseech Thee to hear us,' or 'O Christ, hear us?' No, it is not easy, nor common for persons to pray these prayers in earnest, for it is both a hard and an unusual thing for any of us truly and really to feel with all our hearts that we are speaking to the Son of God, to Jesus Christ, really present, really close to us, really hearing and listening to what we say, really seeing and marking which way our thoughts are turned: it is a hard and rare thing to feel this, and to call upon Him accordingly, with all our heart soul and strength, as a drowning man would call for aid to a friend standing on the shore; as S. Peter called to Jesus when he found himself beginning to sink; as an infant in distress calls on its mother or its nurse. Depend upon it, by the time you are got to be quite in earnest in these calls to Christ in the Litany, you will have made, by God's mercy, no small step in the spiritual life. But now let us see what the titles are, whereby the Church teaches us to address our Saviour in these our child-like outcries to Him. The first is Son of

God: before, in the Litany, it had been God the Son, and Good Lord: now it is Son of God: as though we should say, 'we call upon Thee, as on that Man, Who is also God, the Only-begotten of the Father: hear us and plead for us with Thy Father.' Again the priest teaching us to call Him, as S. John the Baptist did long ago, 'The Lamb of God that takest away the sins of the world,' we answer first, 'Have mercy upon us,' and then 'Grant us Thy peace:' meaning that both from Him and through Him only can we have either mercy for past sins or the peace of the Lord to help us on our heavenly way: and not only meaning and believing that it is so, but earnestly speaking to Christ as present, and praying Him that so it may be with us. How many of us, my brethren, who joined in the Litany this morning, did at these words really in his heart ask Christ for pardon and peace?

But observe what follows next. The Church, under the shadow as it were of our Lord's protecting wings, leads us to the very throne of the Most High God, and instructs us how to bring our cause before Him. All the Three Persons are called upon in order: the Incarnate Son presents us in a manner to the Holy Blessed and Glorious Trinity. Thus once again are we solemnly taught that He is our only Mediator and Advocate: there is no approaching God but through Christ. But being introduced by His gracious favour, we go on and say to the Father the prayer which Christ Himself taught us. We say the Lord's prayer: *that* of course is a necessary part of every Christian Litany: and we say it, here perhaps most especially, in our Saviour's sense and not in our own. Consider a little while what this comes to. It is likely that in using any good prayer we who do but use it would fall far short of the meaning of him who composed the prayer. We might think much and cleverly, but we should not think exactly as he did. How much more, when we reflect Who was the real Author of this prayer: even the Most High God, the Searcher of hearts, Who only knoweth what is in man. Therefore it is well that on joining here in the Lord's prayer we should strive to remember that it is Christ praying for us, not so much we praying for ourselves: and accordingly throughout the prayer we may submit ourselves to Him and to the Father in this way: 'Our Father which art in heaven; high over us as heaven over earth, and in wisdom and love infinitely more in regard to us than the dearest of earthly parents to his offspring: Hallowed be Thy Name; we know not how, but in such ways as Thou knowest to be best: Thy kingdom come; though we be brought very low: Thy will be done; though on earth it be most contrary to ours: Give us this day our daily bread; give us what is meet for us, though it be the bread of tears: Forgive us, especially those sins which we ought to have remembered and did not; as we forgive and pray for those who unknown to us may have transgressed against us: Lead us not into temptation; rather deny, if need be, the thing that we most desire: but deliver us from evil, especially from that evil, which we may be ignorantly wishing and praying for.'

Thus having called on our Lord in His own prayer, and tried to do so, as near as might be, in His own mind, we go on to the special point whatever it be which especially troubles ourselves or the whole Church at the particular time when we offer the Litany: for the collects and short verses and answers which follow do undoubtedly suppose that we are in a time of trouble, though the words spoken do not express any particular kind of trouble. But first we prepare ourselves for such earnest application to our Lord by acknowledging ourselves unworthy in a strain from the holy Psalmist: 'O Lord, deal not with us after our sins. Neither reward us according to our iniquities.' As much as to say that we know we have deserved both to be rejected while we pray, and to find no fruit of our prayers afterwards: but we trust in that mercy which taught God's ancient people, however backsliding, to say and sing in their psalms, 'Thou hast not dealt with us after our sins, nor rewarded us according to our wickednesses; for our sins have reached up to heaven, but Thou, by our gracious Redeemer hast set them as far from us as heaven from earth: and our wickednesses are a sore burden, but Thou hast taken on Thee both them and the far greater burden of Thine own Cross:' and so we, even such as we, are bold to say to one another, 'Let us pray:' and to plead with our Lord in that affecting prayer, which begins, 'O God, merciful Father.' Observe, brethren, the course of that prayer. The address, or usual acknowledgment rendered to God at the beginning, is, 'O God, merciful Father, Who despisest not the sighing of the contrite heart nor the desire of such as be sorrowful:' as much as to say, 'We venture to come before Thee, knowing that Thou never scornest those in distress, and we are sure that we are in distress: and knowing also that Thou never turnest a deaf ear to the lowest sigh which can be breathed from a contrite heart, and though we dare not call ourselves contrite, yet we hope that we are trying to be so:' and in that hope we proceed to offer up to Him two petitions: first, that He would be with us in our prayers in the present trouble whatever it be: 'Mercifully assist our prayers that we make before Thee in all our troubles and adversities, whensoever they oppress us;' as much as to say, 'We do not ask to be free from troubles and adversities; we know what we deserve, and what we must expect: we do not even ask that those troubles may never oppress us; that our hearts may never sink under them; that they may never seem like a sore burden, too heavy for us to bear: to all this we make up our minds, for all this Thy saints have borne, and do bear, and what are we, that we should think to be better off than they? but what we do humbly and earnestly ask is, that Thou wouldest be with us in such sore troubles and trials, both inward and outward, to teach us how to pray, and to help us while we are praying.'

So much we ask, in respect of all evils in general: and then we go on to speak of one class of evils in particular; those evils, namely, which the craft and subtlety of the devil or man worketh against us. You see by the Church's instructing us so to pray that she takes it as a thing not to be doubted, that we as Christians must expect to have evil at all times being wrought against us, not only by the devil, but also by man, and that in a crafty and subtle way. Not of course that each one of us without exception has personal enemies, fellow-creatures who hate him and are plotting to do him mischief: for I trust that *that* is a rare thing, although in our complaining and ill-tempered ways we are apt not seldom to imagine it: but as we all have one crafty and subtle enemy, the devil, who is never tired of contriving how to ruin us, so a great portion of the world being blinded by him, and led captive at his will, is really engaged in harming us by subtle ways, even though it bear no particular malice against us: e.g. people who do not like strictness and self-denial will always be sharp and subtle in devising ways to put those out of countenance who in earnest try to follow Christ as well as they can. They will scorn and teaze a man for being exact and particular in his duties: and this in a small way is an instance of the warfare which is always going on, on a large scale, between the world and the Church: every where and in all times there will always be two kingdoms and two parties, the Church and the world, believers and unbelievers; and as it was in S. Paul's time, even so it is now: "he that is born after the flesh" will manage, craftily if he cannot openly, to "persecute him who is born after the Spirit." This is the condition which the Litany supposes us to be in. Persecution, crafty and subtle, our state; contrition and godly sorrow, our mind; and thankfulness to God in His holy Church, our end. For thus we go on to pray, 'graciously hear us that those evils, which the craft and subtlety of the devil or man worketh against us, be brought to nought, and by the providence of Thy goodness they may be dispersed:'

i. e. that in Thine own good time Thou wouldest scatter and frustrate whatever the world or the devil in their deepest and most cunning ways may contrive against us: as it is in the Psalm, "ᵃ Let God arise and let His enemies be scattered; Like as the smoke vanisheth so shalt Thou drive them away, and like as wax melteth at the fire, so let the ungodly perish at the Presence of God: but let the righteous be glad and rejoice before God, let them also be merry and joyful": which at latest will be in the hour of our death, if we are faithful: and therefore those verses are often used in the Church by the deathbed of a penitent Christian. But in the mean time we have need of patience: we must not expect our deliverance all at once: as the Church signifies where she says, 'By the providence of Thy goodness, they may be dispersed:' for providence looks far onwards, and when we here speak of it, we naturally think of tarrying and waiting patiently. In the meantime our request is, not that there may be no persecutions, but that we may be such true servants of God, that no persecutions may hurt us: i. e. that none may hurt us indeed, or for ever: that none may hurt our souls, nor turn us out of the Church, nor hinder us from giving thanks to God evermore as part of that holy and happy company: 'That we Thy servants, being hurt by no persecutions, may evermore give thanks unto Thee in Thy holy Church.'

This is the prayer, and instead of the usual Amen, the Church directs the congregation to answer, "O, Lord arise, help us and deliver us for Thy Name's sake." This circumstance, being so unusual, marks

ᵃ Ps. lxviii. 1—3.

the depth of the Church's distress: she takes up a word from holy David, and Daniel, and from the other Prophets, for they often plead with God by His great Name: taking the hint as it seems from Moses, who making intercession for Israel saith, "[b] What wilt Thou do unto Thy great Name?" so here we cry out with one voice, 'O Lord, arise, help us and deliver us for Thy Name's sake.' God's Name may be pleaded in behalf of Christians even more than in behalf of Israel, for never were the Israelites made partakers of His Name in the mysterious way in which we Christians are in the Sacrament of Holy Baptism, when we are made one with Him, "[c] partakers of the Divine Nature." And when we say for Thy Name's sake, we put Him in mind both of what He is in Himself, and of what He has made Himself, if so be He will be merciful. Then the priest following as it were the note which the congregation has sounded for him, utters a voice from the book of Psalms, "[d] O God, we have heard with our ears, and our fathers have declared unto us, the noble works which Thou didst in their days, and in the old time before them." It is the first verse of that Psalm which more exactly perhaps than any other seems as we read or hear it to prophesy the present broken and decayed state of God's Church: and very comfortable it is to be allowed, as our fathers were, to put God in mind of His noble deeds and miracles of mercy wrought of old time and declared unto us by our fathers, both in their days and in the ages long before them: one generation handing on to another the lamp of Truth and the watchword of Hope. And

[b] Josh. vii. 9.   [c] 2 S. Pet. i. 4.   [d] Ps. xliv. 1.

then once more the congregation pleads with Him by His own honour and glory; 'O Lord, arise, help us, and deliver us for Thine honour:' as though we should say, 'Deliver us, for else the enemy will say, He could not, or would not be their God, and so I have prevailed against them.' After which both priest and people join in the hymn of glory, praising Him devoutly in the midst of their cries or distress saying the Gloria Patri on their knees, like holy Job when he cried out, "Though He slay me, yet will I put my trust in Him."

So be it, O Lord, with us always, in all our afflictions, in all that we have to bear, whether each one for himself, or together as members of Thy Church. As the clouds gather, as the distress increases, may we still more earnestly give Thee glory, humbling ourselves under Thy mighty hand, and casting all our care upon Thee; and we shall soon find how truly Thou carest for us.

SERMON XLIII.

ON THE LITANY. IX.

CONCLUSION.

Psalm xxxiii. 22.

"*Let Thy merciful kindness, O Lord, be upon us, like as we do put our trust in Thee.*"

We left off last week at that part of the Litany, where in the very midst of her deepest complaint and misery, the Holy Church breaks out into a hymn of glory to God: saying the Gloria Patri on her knees. In the midst, I say, of her complaint and misery: for just before she had been pleading with her God and Lord by the remembrance of His noble works of old time: 'Arise and help us, and deliver us for Thy Name's sake; Arise and help us, and deliver us for Thine honour.' Then comes the Gloria Patri, and immediately after it, all is again in the tone of sadness and alarm: 'From our enemies defend us, O Christ; graciously look upon our afflictions.' Do you not see how exactly it answers to the faithful and loving words of the most patient of men; holy Job: how even in darkness and the shadow of death; when all seemed not only most painful, but also hardest and most unaccountable, even then he holds fast by the Saviour Who seemed to have deserted him? As that poor woman came behind our Lord, and touched the hem of His garment, not counting herself worthy to see His face: as the other, the blessed woman of Canaan still continued calling upon Him, though He turned away and hid His face from her, yea even though He made as if He was scorning her; so the holy Job, true type of the Man of sorrows, had made up his mind never to cease trusting in God: though his misery go on from want to desolation and from desolation to sickness, and from sickness to reproach, and from reproach to persecution, and from persecution to death, he will not cease trusting in the Lord[a]: he will adore the hand that lays the stripes upon him. Is not this just like the holy Church our mother in this part of the Litany? It is not that she does not feel her distress, and feel it too very bitterly; she knows what it is to be persecuted and oppressed, to have the craft and subtlety of the devil and man working against her; she is not dead and insensible to all this; rather the iron enters into her very soul, and she pleads most earnestly with her God and Father, by all His past mercies, to deliver her. But in all her complaint, in all her earnest supplication, she is childlike and confiding, she clings to Him Who is chastening her, and therefore (for I will repeat it once more, wishing that we all take notice of it) she gives glory to the Lord on her knees; or rather when

[a] Job xiii. 15.

she is lying prostrate before Him, humbled to the dust by her sins and the sins of her forefathers. Though He slay her, yet will she put her trust in Him: nevertheless, she still feels that He is slaying her, and renews accordingly her loud and bitter cry, in the short verses and answers which immediately follow. In the first of these we make mention of our enemies, in the second of our afflictions, in the third of our sorrows, and in the fourth of our sins. 'From our enemies defend us, O Christ,' i. e. especially, the enemies of our souls, the evil spirits and evil men, who sometimes knowing what they do, sometimes from ignorance, and not caring what comes of their conduct, are but too busy in helping us along the broad way. Then we put Him in mind of our afflictions: we plead with Him, as persons asking charity commonly plead, by simply telling Him how very miserable we are; how very much we long to have but a look from Him: we urge Him to look upon us as the Psalmist said: pleading not any good thing in ourselves, but only our great load of troubles: "graciously look upon our afflictions." In this, as almost always, we follow the Psalmist's pattern: "[b] Look upon my adversity, and forgive me all my sin."

Next, from outward afflictions we go on to inward sorrows: for such I take to be the difference of the two clauses, 'Graciously look upon our afflictions,' and 'Pitifully behold the sorrows of our hearts.' We pray our only and most loving Father, the Creator of our souls and minds and hearts as well as of our bodies, not only to spare these our weak and frail

[b] Ps. xxv. 17.

bodies, but to have compassion also on the wayward and infirm, the fallen and sinful spirits, which dwell in these bodies, and suffer so grievously with them: which also have so many trials and passions of their own, so many fears, griefs, regrets, suspicions, jealousies, discontents: arising indeed often from mere fancy, mere dreams of disordered imagination, but in the misery they cause not at all unreal nor fanciful: the deepest of sorrows to those who feel them, though in themselves the merest dreams. Concerning all these as well as all afflictions from without, the Church here instructs us to pray that our Lord would pitifully behold them, and we cannot have the smallest doubt that He will do so, since He hath Himself taught us by His Holy Spirit that He can be touched with a feeling of all our innocent infirmities. Nay more, my brethren, we are permitted in a way to plead our very sins before God as a kind of reason why He should forgive us: for our sins that are past do beyond all things shew how very helpless we are, since of ourselves we cannot clear our consciences of any part of any one of them: there are the stains, there is the guilt, and there it must abide for ever, if He take not pity upon us. Therefore, as I said, our very sins may be mentioned in our prayers as a reason why He should pity us: as we find over and over in the Psalms: "[c] Innumerable troubles are come about me: my sins have taken such hold upon me that I am not able to look up: yea, they are more in number than the hairs of my head, and my heart hath failed me." What follows? Am I therefore to leave off prayer? Is there no hope?

[c] Ps. xl. 12.

Is all lost? Nay, in the very next verse we read, "O Lord, let it be Thy pleasure to deliver me, make haste, O Lord, to help me." So in these earnest breathings, these quick dartings of prayer, which we find in this portion of the Litany: having mentioned our enemies, our afflictions and sorrows, we go on to mention our sins: 'Mercifully forgive the sins of Thy people:' of Thy people, brethren, observe *that:* for it makes a very great difference. The sins of God's people are as much worse than the same sins in others who are not God's people, as their helps and privileges and graces are greater, as the Truth Itself hath told us: "[d] Unto whom men have committed much, of him they will ask the more." Therefore it is a great thing indeed, for the people of God to ask for *their* sins to be forgiven, and we could hardly have ventured to do so, had He not so mercifully encouraged us. I wish we thought more of this than we are apt to do. We have heard so much of His pardoning love from our very cradles upward, that there is too much fear of our saying this petition and others like it with a sort of unconcern, as if what we were asking for was an ordinary thing, a matter of course. O let us endeavour to cure ourselves of this, for indeed it is a great and a very dangerous mistake. Our wilful sins, inasmuch as they are the sins of God's people, cannot be ordinary things, matters of course, nor is it an ordinary mercy for Him to forgive them, but a very miracle of grace. Unless we pray very earnestly to have them forgiven; pray with somewhat of a true feeling what a great thing we are praying for: we shall not feel half the fear which we ought

[d] S. Luke xii. 48.

of falling into the same sins or worse again. The tempter will have a great advantage over us.

And there is another thought, which may sometimes well come into a Christian's mind, when he prays this short prayer, 'Mercifully forgive the sins of Thy people.' It is this: that not only particular persons, men and women are continually sinning and needing forgiveness, but the whole Church also and the people of God, and much more a particular portion of it, such as the Church of England or the Church of Rome, may fall into sin, and bring God's anger upon it: as we read in Solomon's prayer at the Dedication of the temple, all the way through mention is made of the sins of God's people Israel, and God is asked to forgive them, as well as to forgive the several sins of the men and women of whom that people is made up. Now, without undutifully judging of our mother the Church: since it is made up of men, and there is no man that sinneth not; we may well believe that the Church also has its sins; for which we may and ought to pray to God to forgive it: and it is well that this should sometimes come into our mind, when we beseech Him to forgive the sins of His people. As a man's parents may and do sin, without ceasing to be his parents, so the Church to which he belongs, or the whole Church of his time may sin, without ceasing to be a Church: and as it is his duty to ask forgiveness for his parents' sins, so also for the Church's sins, whether he knows of any special sin or not. Who can doubt that the Laodicean Christians in S. John's time were bound to pray that God would mercifully forgive the sin of lukewarmness, which Christ Himself declared to be their

Church's sin, saying, "ᵉBecause thou art lukewarm, and neither cold nor hot, I will spue thee out of My mouth?" It is not impossible, surely, that the Church of England in our time, or any particular portion of it, may be in the same sin, and in danger of the same dreadful sentence. O then how earnestly ought we to pray that He would pardon and amend this great sin of lukewarmness, not in ourselves only, but in our whole Church and nation! that in His tender love He would rebuke and chasten us, if so be we would be zealous and repent!

Having thus mentioned before God our enemies, our afflictions, our sorrows, and our sins, we dart another short petition upwards, like a sort of Amen, to confirm and recommend all our other petitions: 'Favourably, with mercy hear our prayers;' favourably, for we know too well how much favour they need, how poor and unworthy they are in themselves: with mercy, forgiving the many sins and negligences of which even in these very prayers, since we knelt down, we know ourselves to be guilty.

And this great indulgence we are the more hopeful to ask, because, as the next short petition expresses, He permits us to call Him Son of David: "O Son of David, have mercy upon us:" words taken as you know from the lips of the blind men who sat by the wayside as our Lord was journeying near Jericho: and well used by us sinners in our Litany, because of David's being both a great king over God's people, and in one instance a great sinner; and the Litany as we have seen is especially put up for God's people,

---

ᵉ Rev. iii. 16.

and most especially asks to have their sins forgiven and cured. By allowing us thus to call Him Son of David, He gives us a token that He never can forget His Church, nor ever fail in most tender mercy towards any returning penitent.

Then we acknowledge to Him that we need His mercy not now only, but at all times; we take Him to be our God for ever and ever: for such is the meaning of the next short prayer, "Both now and ever, vouchsafe to hear us, O Christ." As much as to say, "'Whom have we in heaven but Thee? and there is none upon earth that we desire in comparison of Thee. My flesh and my heart faileth, but God is the strength of my heart and my portion for ever." Well will it be with us when we can pray this prayer in earnest.

Once again we call Him Christ and our Lord Christ, and beseech Him graciously to hear us: like eager petitioners who will not be put off, 'Graciously hear us O Christ, graciously hear us O Lord Christ.' And then, before passing into the form of collect again, as we do in the end of the Litany, we profess to Him in a few of His own perfect words both what we desire of Him, and in what mind we express our desire. "Let Thy merciful kindness, O Lord, be upon us: like as we do put our trust in Thee." That is the verse which the Church has taken from the end of the thirty-third Psalm, and transplanted it as it were to be the last of her short petitions in the Litany: whereby she teaches us out of the mouth of God this very serious truth, that free as His mercy

---

ᶠ Ps. lxxiii. 25, 26.

is, it yet in some mysterious way is made to depend on our trust in Him: so that we may only venture to ask for it in proportion as we trust in Him: even as in the Lord's prayer we are instructed by Himself to ask for our own pardon only in such measure as we are willing to pardon others. Thus our Father would bind us to our duty by our prayers. We seek for so much mercy from our Lord, as we bring to our prayers of dutiful trust in Him. Alas for the repining, dissatisfied spirits, who come to their prayers with downcast, dismal hearts, because their worldly affairs do not go on exactly to their wish! and alas (no less) for the prosperous and thriving, if they allow their prosperity and hopefulness to carry them away from Him Who is their only sure hope: if while they say with their lips these lowly words of the Church, they are in their hearts depending on their own skill, their own wealth or good luck! Sad or joyous, they are alike wrong, because their hearts are alike set upon this world.

You know how in the Collect which follows, the substance of the whole Litany is gathered, after the manner of collects, into a few words. "We humbly beseech Thee, O Father, mercifully to look upon our infirmities; and for the glory of Thy Name turn from us all those evils that we most righteously have deserved." See what real lowliness we are practising, when we try to enter into the mind of such a prayer as this: how deeply sensible we must be, not of infirmities only but of ill-deserts, and observe what follows; "For the glory of Thy Name turn from us all those evils that we most righteously

have deserved; and **grant, that in all our troubles
we may** put our whole **trust and confidence in Thy
mercy, and evermore serve Thee in holiness and
pureness of living, to Thy honour and glory."** We
do not pray for deliverance so much, as for perfect
trust in Him, and for a holy and pure life. Troubles
and adversities, we take for granted, must be our
portion, only we beseech Him that they may not
separate us from Him, nor take away our power of
serving Him: but whether that service shall be in
doing or in suffering we leave to Him.

After this, as you know, come in the occasional
collects: for the parliament, the Ember weeks, and
others. These I will not now notice: but there is
one prayer which always comes in here, the General
Thanksgiving: added to our Litany after the Church's
sufferings in the time of the great rebellion, and
written by a holy Bishop, who had been a sufferer
in those bad times, Bishop Sanderson. You who
come here constantly know this thanksgiving well:
will you try and remember one or two things, quite
necessary to the right use of it? The first, that as
it is a *general* thanksgiving, for all our brethren as
well as for ourselves, no envious, grudging heart
ought to dare to use it. The second, that whereas
we often mention the names of persons for whom we
offer thanks, there is need of care, as there is when
we pray for persons by name: that we really care
for those persons, that we really join with the Church
in what she says of them: that they should not be
to us names merely said over by rote. Thirdly, you
know that in this thanksgiving we profess to be

grateful above all for the redemption of the world by our Lord Jesus Christ, for the means of grace and for the hope of glory. Evidently we cannot say this truly, unless we are really trying to care more for heaven than for anything else: there must be the right hope, the hope of glory: the right means, the means of grace, that is, the holy Sacraments with all helps to the due receiving of them, and the right foundation for both, i. e. the God-Man offering Himself on the Cross. See how much this one portion of the holy service requires of us: and besides if we have joined in it truly, we of course go out of Church as persons going from a solemn sacrifice of thanksgiving: still as we go, and whatever we go to, offering up ourselves our souls and bodies to serve Him thankfully in holiness and righteousness.

Then comes the prayer of the holy father, S. Chrysostom: where we plead our Lord's ancient promise to two or three gathered in His Name, and His present providential mercy to us in allowing us to be so gathered: and see what entire trust and childlike faith the Church supposes in us, putting this prayer into our mouths: for in it we absolutely leave all other things to God; only two things there are, which He has promised, and which He encourages us to claim: and we may claim them the more hopefully, the more entirely we trust Him with every thing else that we care for: knowledge of His truth here, and life everlasting in the world to come.

And so the Church dismisses us with the benediction of S. Paul, "The grace of our Lord Jesus Christ, and the love of God, and the fellowship of the Holy Ghost, be with us all evermore," which is specially suited to the Litany, because it mentions the grace of our Lord *first*: the two other portions of the blessing, the love of the Father, and the Communion of the Spirit, being purchased entirely for us by Christ. Now this is just the order of the Litany: in which as you heard, the special petitions are all made to Christ the great Intercessor, to be by Him presented to the Father, and made fruitful to us through the Spirit.

So you see our Litany at its end gathers in one three voices, of very holy persons, Bishop Sanderson, S. Chrysostom and S. Paul: a beautiful example of the Communion of Saints. May God in His mercy cause us to pray with them now, that with them we may thank Him for ever. And may He ever bless our use of the Litany, and make it a real help to us in these sorrowful times.

Amen
Lord Jesus

www.ingramcontent.com/pod-product-compliance
Lightning Source LLC
Chambersburg PA
CBHW032002300426
44117CB00008B/866